D0329144

LEWIS EGERTON SMOOT MEM'L. LIB
KING GEORGE, VA. 22485

*EVERYMAN, I will go with thee,*
*and be thy guide,*
*In thy most need to go by thy side*

LEWIS EGERTON SMOOT MEM'L LIB
KING GEORGE, VA. 22485

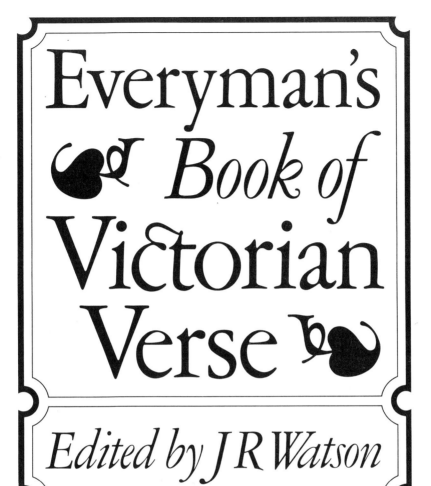

# Everyman's & Book of Victorian Verse

## Edited by J R Watson

LEWIS EGERTON SMOOT MEM'L LIB
KING GEORGE, VA. 22485

**J. M. Dent & Sons Ltd**
London, Melbourne and Toronto

First published 1982
Introduction, selection and notes © J. M. Dent & Sons Ltd, 1982

All rights reserved. No part of this publication may be reproduced,
stored in a retrieval system, or transmitted, in any form or by any
means, electronic, mechanical, photocopying, recording or otherwise,
without the prior permission of J. M. Dent & Sons Ltd

This book is set in 10/11½ point VIP Bembo by
D. P. Media Limited, Hitchin, Hertfordshire

Printed in Great Britain by
Richard Clay Ltd, Bungay, Suffolk, for
J. M. Dent & Sons Ltd,
Aldine House, 33 Welbeck Street, London W1M 8LX


British Library Cataloguing in Publication Data

Everyman's Book of Victorian verse.
  1. English poetry – 19th century
  I. Watson, J. R.
  821'.8      PR1221

ISBN 0-460-04453-2

# Contents

———————————— *Mid-Victorian (1851–1867)* ————————————

_____ *Fin de Siècle (1885–1901)* _____

# Introduction

In this anthology I have tried to select the most interesting poems written during the reign of Queen Victoria, giving space to the lesser poets as well as the greater ones, and attempting to show something of the dense, plankton-like activity of the age in poetry. A book of this size can do so only imperfectly: Alfred H. Miles, in his splendid *The Poets and the Poetry of the Century* (to which, like all students of Victorian poetry, I am greatly indebted) took ten volumes, although he included pre-Victorian poets as well. In the present volume I have tried to show something, as Miles did, of the amazing variety and heterogeneous character of Victorian verse; remembering always that he was working in the 1890s and I in the 1980s.

The time-difference is important, for any present-day reader of Victorian poetry is deeply conscious of the events which separate us from the nineteenth century. Something fundamental in a country's identity disappeared during the Great War, in the mud of Flanders or the undulating fields of the Somme; it was as though no one beforehand could have conceived of those particular horrors, just as no one before the Second World War could have imagined the vicious and systematic inhumanity of the concentration camps, the bombing of Dresden, or the dropping of the atomic bomb. Such great happenings change the face of the world: 'Never', as Philip Larkin has written, 'Never such innocence again.' He was referring to 1914, but the same could be true of 1945, or 1956, or 1968. Each of those years takes us perceptibly further from the world of imperial splendour and Gladstonian Liberalism, and from the artistic stabilities which were taken for granted in the nineteenth century. Dada, as one critic has reminded us, was born out of the 'bankruptcy of nineteenth-century rationalism and of the bourgeois culture it had animated'[1] and a swift look at any of the arts will serve to emphasize the distance which has been travelled in the last ninety years. The assumptions of Alfred H. Miles are not those of the readers of today, and any compiler of a new Victorian anthology will, I think, find this an advantage for two reasons. The first is that he can see which poems have retained their life and energy across these shaking events; the second is that he can come to terms with, and even make use of, the critical revolution of Eliot, Richards and Leavis. Their special service to English criticism was to draw attention to the strength of the line of wit, the well-constructed poem which combined thought and feeling; this was seen to be superior to the poetry in which thought and feeling were separated, as Eliot thought, in a 'dissociation of sensibility': 'Tennyson and Browning are poets, and they think; but they do not feel their thought as immediately as the odour of a rose.'[2] In this way, Eliot rewrote the history of English poetry in a few brilliant pages, in his essay on the Metaphysical Poets of 1921: no longer were the Metaphysicals seen as oddities in the great tradition of English lyric poetry 'from Chaucer to Arnold' (the subtitle of an agreeable Oxford anthology, *Fifteen Poets*, which contained Cowper and not Donne, and which was reprinted many times). When Eliot had finished it became clear that the Metaphysical Poets were central to the tradition, and that it was the Victorians who were the odd ones out: they lacked the 'direct sensuous apprehension of thought, or a recreation of thought into feeling, which is exactly what we find in Donne'.[3] Eliot's insight was joined by I. A. Richards's exposure of feeble emotional reading in *Practical Criticism*, and by F. R. Leavis's preference for Hopkins in *New Bearings in English Poetry*; all conspired to relegate traditional Victorian poetry to a position from which it has never recovered, in spite of the enormous scholarly and critical activity during the last thirty years. In their pursuit of this activity, the scholars and critics have, it often seems, settled for a peaceful co-existence with the situation as it is; they have tended to work within the limits of the Victorian reputation rather than to examine the validity of those limits.

There are some exceptions to this, but Victorian poetry badly needs some Pevsner or Betjeman to speak for it. Their work on Victorian buildings makes a striking parallel with what needs to be done: suddenly we can see the vitality of Italianate banks, Gothic town halls, and Grecian railway stations. Their solidity and character, their occasional flamboyance and ingenuity, make them an essential part of our urban heritage. We have come to see them for what they are, expressions of a commercial and industrial culture which had its own confidence and its own flavour, a flavour which is sometimes a relief from modern functionalism. It is possible that something of the same renewal of understanding and appreciation needs to take place for the poetry of the age, and I hope that this anthology will encourage it. After all, the Victorians themselves were aware of their own shortcomings before T. S. Eliot: 'It's the smell of a rose,' wrote Elizabeth Barrett Browning about the poems of Frederick Tennyson, 'rather than a rose – very sweet notwithstanding.'[4]

Certainly much Victorian poetry is sweet; but how much is it the smell of a rose, rather than a rose? Any answer to this question will depend on the historical and critical preconceptions which a reader brings to bear on the poems; and in the latter case the shaping of the critical faculties by Eliot and the others may prove to be an advantage. In much Victorian poetry (and not only in Hopkins) we can observe an original touch of thought and feeling, and a use of language which is vital, inventive, and rich in emotional and logical apprehension. When Browning ends 'By the Fire-Side' with the beautiful diminuendo of

> And the whole is well worth thinking o'er
> When autumn comes: which I mean to do
> One day, as I said before.

we recognize a rendering of the apparently casual into high and skilful art, through the pauses, the line-endings, the gradual shortening of syntactical units. And when John Davidson has portrayed, through their dramatic monologues, the six artists in a music hall, he suddenly breaks in with the epilogue –

> Under the earth are the dead
> Alive and asleep;

–so that the contrast is marvellously effective, a sudden juxtaposition of tone and language which cuts into the cheerful humanity of the rest of the poem with a profound reminder of mortality. The three heavy syllables, 'Under the earth are the dead' resonate like a bell, before the poem moves off again into speculation with 'Alive and asleep'. The words suggest spiritual qualities, which the epigraph and the prologue have already adumbrated; the poem itself becomes, taken as a whole, a direct, sensuous apprehension of men and women seen as figures in a music hall and simultaneously as figures in a divine comedy of mortality and immortality.

Not all Victorian poetry will stand up to the kind of critical examination which is practised by Eliot, Richards and their followers, but this is because it is a poetry of many different kinds. Towards the end of the century that rather over-heated poet, Francis Thompson, wrote a neo-Miltonic 'Ode for the Diamond Jubilee of Queen Victoria, 1897', which makes this variety conveniently clear. Thompson writes of seeing the great dead Victorians, 'the long Victorian line', and first the poets, led by Tennyson and Browning. Tennyson was the writer of

> many a lovely lay,
> Where Beauty did her beauties unarray
> In conscious song

and by his side went Browning, followed by the others:

> A Strength beside this Beauty, Browning went,
> With shrewd looks and intent,
> And meditating still some gnarled theme.
> Then came, somewhat apart,
> In a fastidious dream,
> Arnold, with a half-discontented calm,
> Binding up wounds, but pouring in no balm.
> The fervid breathing of Elizabeth
> Broke on Christina's gentle-taken breath.
> Rossetti, whose heart stirred within his breast
> Like lightning in a cloud . . .

This is followed by a melodramatic apparition of Coventry Patmore, and the whole disunified procession is an emphatic reminder of the extreme range and variety, even among the major poets. So an anthology which begins with John Clare and ends with Davidson and Hardy has its own problems of identity, for there are many kinds of Victorian poet. There is the poet who is continually preoccupied by the ultimate questions of man's purpose and belief, such as Tennyson, Arnold or Hardy; there is the poet whose inspiration is found in nature and the seasons; there are the whimsical and satirical poets, the tender and gentle ones; poets of the Middle Ages, poets of the Arthurian legend, poets of place, of battle, heroism, love, and loss. The last of these is important, because Victorian poets are often concerned with loss, the loss of loved ones, of loved places, of youth, of a belief in God. For the most part they looked on the Victorian city with a fascinated horror, since its formless and chaotic life denied so many opportunities for stability and love; a nostalgia for a peaceable kingdom, physically, intellectually and emotionally, is common. So they wrote, often, out of a sense of love and loss, and their work shows a great range of feeling and sentiment. Indeed, as a portrait of one kind of Victorian poet in his beliefs and practice, I would point to a biographical and critical essay by A. C. Benson on William Cory (1823–92), best known for his poem 'Heraclitus' ('They told me, Heraclitus, they told me you were dead'). Cory was a master at Eton, though a Devonian by birth, with a deep love of his native county and his old home. In Benson's words, 'His memory lingered over the vine-shaded verandah, the jessamine that grew by the balustrade of the steps, the broad-leaved myrtle that covered the wall of the little yard.' Benson himself seems to be getting a vicarious pleasure out of this nostalgia, as he does out of Cory's patriotism:

He was a lover of political and social liberty, a patriot to the marrow of his bones; he loved his country with a passionate devotion, and worshipped the heroes of his native land, statesmen, soldiers, sailors, poets, with an ardent adoration; the glory and honour of England were the breath of his nostrils.

After twenty-seven years at Eton, he retired to Devon, 'fighting bravely with regret, and feeling with sensitive sorrow the turning of the sweet page'. Benson describes his poetry as 'a singular and original contribution to the poetry of the century':

The verse is in its general characteristics of the school of Tennyson, with its equable progression, its honied epithets, its soft cadences, its gentle melody. But the poems are deeply original, because they combine a peculiar classical quality with a frank delight in the spirit of generous boyhood. For all their wealth of idealized sentiment, they never lose sight of the fuller life of the world that waits beyond the threshold of youth, the wider issues, the glory of the battle, the hopes of the patriot, the generous visions of manhood. They are full of the romance of boyish friendships, the echoes of the river and the cricket field, the ingenuous ambitions, the chivalry, the courage of youth and health, the brilliant charm of the opening world.

These extracts (which are unfair to the sustained grace and charm of Benson's essay) indicate well enough some characteristic qualities of Victorian poetry which have led to its present neglect. The patriotic and warlike sentiments seem empty, and the echoes of the river and the cricket field privileged, while the courage of youth and health and the visions of manhood are luxuries which many of the Victorians were in no position to afford. Moreover, what Benson called the 'wealth of idealized sentiment' is a common, indeed almost universal, feature of Victorian verse: events, places, encounters, failures, are used to explore the feelings with a carefully cultivated sensitivity. If the Victorians did not feel their thought, they certainly thought about their feelings. The danger is that such a sensitivity to feelings may become unhealthy, in that it prevents positive action and hopeful life. There is an example in *In Memoriam*, CI:

> Unwatched, the garden bough shall sway,
> The tender blossom flutter down,
> Unloved, that beech will gather brown,
> This maple burn itself away.

Tennyson is looking back at Somersby; his lament for the old home, and his exploration of sadness at leaving a much-loved place, is a common feature of Victorian verse. To leave a place where one has lived and been happy is to recognize that a period of one's life is irrevocably past, as Cory did, 'feeling with sensitive sorrow the turning of the sweet page', or Francis Thompson, remembering the Lancashire cricketers of his childhood:

> O my Hornby and my Barlow long ago!

This lingering over sorrow is a legacy from Keats's 'glut thy sorrow on a morning rose' in the 'Ode on Melancholy'; but with Keats the attention to the rose is somehow positive, a creative flexing of the muscles of feeling so that they become stronger, and hence more capable of appreciating the world intensely. The spirit of Tennyson's poem is less affirmative; its melancholy is caused by a concentration on what has been lost, a self-indulgent brooding over an absence. The result is what Matthew Arnold called 'a pleasing melancholy', a poetry which does not (in Arnold's crucial word) 'animate':

> I am glad you like the Gipsy Scholar, but what does it *do* for you? Homer *animates* – Shakespeare *animates* – the Gipsy Scholar at best awakens a pleasing melancholy.
>
> (Arnold to Clough, 30 November 1853)

The melancholy of Tennyson is here, as so often, a disabling and contemplating melancholy; Elizabeth Gaskell makes her own sharp and animating comment on it when she quotes it in *North and South*. There Margaret Hale has to leave her beloved Helstone, and buckle down to life in the industrial city of Milton Northern; with a masterly control of narrative and tone, Elizabeth Gaskell reveals the depth of affection which Margaret has for Helstone, but also her energy and resourcefulness, which form their own devastating comment on the Tennyson poem.

The sentiment here, and in 'The Scholar-Gipsy', may be that of a disabling melancholy, and we may find it unhelpful or even unhealthy; but it is important to realize the degree to which the presence of such sentiment determines the tone and content, and even the form of Victorian verse. Nor is sentiment invariably to be despised, or confused with sentimentality, which is an emotional reaction in excess of anything that is justified by the situation; the line is a difficult one to draw, and is (more than most critical judgments) prone to subjective assessment, but it is important to draw the line, or all sentiment becomes associated with sentimentality. Sentiment is important because it is individual: it is rooted, as its original meaning makes clear, in personal experience, and sentiment in poetry is the irreplaceable part of the original perception, the feeling and idea which make it the work of that poet alone. At the same time, feelings are what we share with others, and are evidence of our common humanity, of 'the human heart by which we live'.

Sentiment is a good servant but a bad master; it can be properly used, as I think it is in many of the poems printed here, where it becomes a quality that encourages feeling and tenderness, humanity, and individual awareness; over-indulged, or allowed to become pre-dictable, it becomes sentimental. The eclipse of the word sentiment by sentimental is a natural one, because the use of emotion in poetry so easily becomes excessive. It has certainly helped in the devaluation of Victorian poetry, which has become associated with emotion and a lack of thought; I hope to indicate through this anthology that there is a place for emotion, and that the sentiment of Victorian poetry is central to its proper functioning. No attempt to understand Victorian poetry is likely to succeed without taking this into consideration, however alien it may seem now. As I. A. Richards wrote in *Practical Criticism*:

> A widespread general inhibition of all the simpler expansive develop-ments of emotion (not only of its expression) has to be recognized among our educated population. It is a new condition not easily paral-leled in history, and though it is propagated through social convention its deeper causes are not easy to divine. To put it down, as many have done, to the excesses of the Victorians, is only to show an ignorance of the generations that preceded them. (p.269)

Richards was writing in 1929, and there is no doubt that we are more inhibited today, except in certain recognized ways, such as pop songs; his last comment is to me somewhat obscure, but he does remind us that emotion can be an expansive development. What Matthew Arnold saw as a pleasing melancholy in 'The Scholar-Gipsy' can also be seen as an authentic and moving response to the confusions of the age.

If sentiment affects the tone and content of Victorian poetry, it can also be seen to have affected its form as well. The dominance of the lyrical form, of what Benson described as 'its honied epithets, its soft cadences, its gentle melody', this dominance accords well with a certain kind of emotion, notably the sweet sadness of parting, or the tears of loss. Often rhyme, rhythm and verse-form encourage a tenderness and nostalgia: the short line in 'The Scholar-Gipsy', for instance, or the four-line verse with a short line at the end, or the ebb and flow movement of the *In Memoriam* stanza, all provide encouragement for the expression of tender feeling; their musical equivalent is a Victorian hymn tune such as John Bacchus Dykes's 'Beatitudo', where the final line sinks with an affecting fifth.

The dominance of the lyric form, and the overpowering presence of individual feeling, may have been one reason why the dramatic monologue flourished during this period. Through the dramatic monologue poets were able to explore moral questions and affecting situations without implicating themselves; through characters from the Middle Ages, or the Arthurian legends, or the seventeenth century, they saw problematical situations enacted as if on a magic lantern screen — magnified, more colourful, sometimes more simplified and at other times more complex. The dramatic monologue provided an escape from the domination of individual feeling: it also provided a form through which complicated moral situations could be unravelled, and it required a considerable amount of interpretative action on the part of the reader, who had to discover the character and situation through what was being said, and make his own judgment. It is hardly surprising that the dramatic monologue form should have been the most widely appreciated genre in the criticism of Victorian poetry in this century. It has a particular flavour, a colourful and memorable life of its own; and it accords with an attractive sense that good art involves the artist in a continual self-abnegation. T. S. Eliot's distaste for some Victorian poetry may have been due to this:

> What happens is a continual surrender of himself as he is at the moment to something which is more valuable. The progress of the artist is a continual self-sacrifice, a continual extinction of personality.
>
> ('Tradition and the Individual Talent')[5]

In contrast to this Neo-classical dictum, the Victorians inherited the Romantic idea that poetry was the spontaneous overflow of powerful feelings. From Wordsworth also they inherited the dramatic monologue, and made it their own; making their poetry acceptable, as it were, almost by accident, to twentieth-century critical opinion. But a substantial amount of Victorian poetry is distinguished by its spontaneous overflow without recourse to a *persona*, and this is underlined by the criticism of the age: one of the eminent collections was the 'English Men of Letters' series, a title scarcely imaginable now (especially as the first man was George Eliot). In the Victorian period the figures emerge from their slim volumes sharply etched: they reveal with an endearing candour their regional background and their social class; their photographs are found next to the title page.

It is with this sentiment, directness, and candour that we are dealing, therefore, as well as with the safer distancing of the dramatic monologue. Both stand in a slightly oblique position with regard to the age. We must not expect, for instance, the shared preconceptions of the literary class of the early eighteenth century, because the individual background of writers is much wider, and the assumptions about art are more subjective. The result is a poetry which in part reflects the age, but only in part; there are poems which concern themselves with social problems, or with problems of faith and doubt, but equally there are poems which do neither. Because of this the arrangement of the poems has been difficult, especially since I have avoided the simple, customary solution of printing them author by author. I have tried instead to preserve a roughly chronological order, while attempting at the same time to shape the selection into one which emphasizes the salient characteristics of each part of the period, and which suggests useful contrasts and comparisons. In its overall pattern, the collection begins and ends with song: it begins with Tennyson's magical 'The Poet's Song', in which the poet passes out of the town and into a lonely place, where he sings a melody which, Orpheus-like, captivates the living creatures around him; it ends with Hardy's 'The Darkling Thrush', that strange signal to our own century from the last afternoon of the nineteenth. Tennyson's poem celebrates the lyrical mode, and associates it with power and hope; Hardy finds a bitter contrast between the beauty of the thrush's song and the gloom of the afternoon which corresponds to his inner sense of death. Between the two songs, the hopeful and the hopeless, between 1837 and 1901, between Victoria the young queen and Victoria the aged empress, lie decades of change, years of controversy and doubt, changes of mood and temper, times of war and peace, prosperity and hardship.

I have divided the Victorian age into four sections in this anthology. The dividing lines are somewhat arbitrary, but they form convenient places for the reader to pause and consider what has gone before, and to gather breath before entering a different age; and just as any divisions are arbitrary, so the 'character' of an age is bound to be elusive. But I have thought it sensible to place some rough divisions, as follows: 1837–1851; 1851–1867; 1867–1885; 1885–1901. Curiously, there is a sense in which these are actually ages, the four ages of Victorian poetry as it develops through the century in parallel with the unfolding of the reign. Early Victorian, Mid-Victorian, High Victorian, *Fin de Siècle*, these are simplistic labels, but they do indicate something of the way in which the Victorian period changes, at least in the consciousness of poets. To speak of the period itself as changing is not only a truism, but involves an appreciation of change at many different levels, and at many different rates. Peter Vansittart has recently pointed out that at Kentford there is the grave of a shepherd boy who, in 1840, hanged himself for fear, having miscounted his sheep.[6] A reign that begins like that and ends with the imperialism of the Diamond Jubilee is not easily described; to examine the changes, period by period and class by class, would be impossible in anything but the largest survey. But it is possible, albeit subjectively and impressionistically, to detect shifts of tone, character and subject-matter in Victorian poetry.

Between 1837 and 1851 there seems to be an unsettled, exploratory feel about the poetry. There is the awareness of a new age, but there is also a looking back, in Richard Monckton Milnes's poem about Scott, and Barnes's charming recollection of his grandmother in 'Grammer's Shoes'. Barnes is remarkable for his use of dialect, but he is one of several regional poets whose work during this period celebrates the individuality of place; each of these has an unmistakable voice, from the tender strangeness of Hawker to the rapture of Anne Brontë and the intensity of Clare. During the 1840s emerges the most individual and quirky voice of the Victorian age, in the early Browning, and there is quirkiness too in the bizarre comedy of Hood. But Hood is also significant as a poet of poverty and social unrest, and the miseries of the 1840s, especially before the repeal of the Corn Laws, are found in both Hood and Elizabeth Barrett Browning. An authentic expression of disease and suffering is found in Charles Mackay, while in quite another mode Dante Gabriel Rossetti indulges a taste for religious decoration and furniture in 'The Blessed Damozel'. Art and religion, social conditions; the past, the present: the poetry of the early Victorian period points all ways.

*In Memoriam* is a landmark, not only because of its phenomenal success and Tennyson's subsequent Laureateship, but because of the reasons for that success. In many ways it is a multi-faced poem, gathering up into itself so many of the anxieties and explorings of the early Victorian period. It is a poem of hope and despair, of place and time, of the seasons, of science, of religion, above all of that muddled agnosticism which was the mid-nineteenth century's reaction to the discoveries of Geology and Natural History. *In Memoriam* touches these things with an unerring finger: its greatness lies in its authenticity as a poem of grief and despair, combined with its representational exploring of the meaning of death in the age of the Higher Criticism of the Bible. Add to this its extraordinary music, the subtle and flexible rhythms of the ABBA stanza, which so beautifully adapt themselves to the shaping which Tennyson gives them, and it is not difficult to see why *In Memoriam* is such a pre-eminent poem; after it, nineteenth-century poets have to struggle for their imaginative space.

This struggle is clear throughout the second age, from 1851 to 1867. These were years of anxiety at home and abroad, of the Crimean War and the Indian Mutiny, of Darwin's *Origin of Species* and of *Essays and Reviews*. It is seen urgently in the criticism of Matthew Arnold, and in the perplexity which is so gracefully articulated in his poetry; it is found in the contrast between the ideal and the actual, the possibility and the reality, in *Maud*, in Browning's discerning

> infinite passion, and the pain
> Of finite hearts that yearn

and in the melancholy of Christina Rossetti. Deaths and farewells are common in this period, as well as a sense of anger and frustration, in Gerald Massey, and bewilderment, in David Gray; it leads to an escape into comic verse, or into the magic of narrative or image, the fragile delicacy of Christina Rossetti or Dora Greenwell.

Upon this scene bursts Swinburne, with *Poems and Ballads* in 1866. His pagan sensuality and life-affirming energy are a landmark, as significant a turning-point in poetry as the Second Reform Bill of 1867 was in politics. It heralds an age of immense poetic achievement in terms of both volume and intensity: Swinburne's kind of energy is found in the capacity of William Morris and of Browning to sustain the long poem, and his exuberance seems to infect others. It is found in Hardy's 'When I set out for Lyonnesse', and in the ferocious gloom of James Thomson's 'The City of Dreadful Night'; it occurs in the remarkable metrics of Meredith's 'Love in the Valley', and, above all, in the genius of Gerard Manley Hopkins. In another direction, this is the period of the best comic verse of the century, with Gilbert, Calverley, and Lear.

Gradually this High Victorian exuberance and energy began to involve an enthusiasm for art and beauty: a whole generation was ready to be influenced by Pater when *Studies in the History of the Renaissance* was published in 1873, though its effect was gradual and pervasive rather than immediate. Pater's influence on Oscar Wilde, whose *Poems* were published in 1881, was confirmed by *Marius the Epicurean* in 1885. I have chosen this year to begin the fourth age of the Victorian period: not only because of Pater, but because it marks the end of Gladstone's second ministry and the beginning of the last era of Victorian politics under Salisbury and Chamberlain.

Anything after 1890 (or after Pater's *Appreciations*, 1889) is often called, not very helpfully, *fin de siècle*, and is associated with the 'aesthetic' or 'decadent' movement in literature. The truth is more complicated, not only because any such movement began before 1890 (as my date of 1885 implies), but also because the poetry of this age is much more interesting than the word 'aesthetic' suggests. It is a poetry which succeeds remarkably in focusing on its subjects: Kipling's 'Danny Deever' is an obvious example of this, and so is Lionel Johnson's lesser-known 'The Troopship'. The same can be said of John Davidson's recreations of city life. Davidson and Henley are both extraordinarily skilful at rendering the life of the streets; behind them are the languorous voices of Dowson and Johnson, the early magical Irishness of Yeats, and the poems of Hardy, so rich with a sense of the past and of death. Quiller-Couch, who touches the hem of his garment, is an interesting figure to compare with Hardy; so too is Housman, in whom the regional impulse revives, robustly but self-consciously.

With these ghosts of the past, the dead actors, the messmates, the friends beyond, and the ancestral voices, the poetry of the age of Queen Victoria comes to an end. Its progress through exploration, to anxiety, to energy, and to a complex aestheticism is one which marks an elusive, yet in places almost tangible, response to the age in which it was written.

To edit a selection of such poetry is both a test of nerve and a declaration of faith. It is a test of nerve in an ironic age to print so many poems which are not ironic; it is a declaration of faith in the value of much of the verse, major and minor, reprinted here. And at this point I would like to end on a personal note. 'Half our standards come from our first masters, and the other half from our first loves', wrote George Santayana;[7] my own introduction to poetry, and my own first loves, came from a childhood reading of *Palgrave's Golden Treasury*. It was only much later, and not without some pain, that I learnt as an undergraduate that there were other, more important criteria by which poetry should be judged, concerned with other qualities than lyricism and emotion. The making of this anthology has therefore been a return to my first loves, and I say 'loves' advisedly, because one qualification for making this selection must be a love for Victorian poetry in its many different modes and forms.

The connection goes back, in one way, beyond my childhood reading of Palgrave. My grandmother, who was born in 1866 and who was a nurse in London until her marriage in 1900, was a great lover of poetry, and especially of Tennyson. She could recite *Enoch Arden* by heart; and although that poem is not included here, I have some hope that the rest of the selection would have pleased her. She has been in my mind often during the reading of the hundreds of dusty little volumes which have passed beneath my eyes, and it is to her memory that I dedicate this book.

1982                                                        J. R. Watson

1   William S. Rubin, *Dada and Surrealist Art*, p.9.
2   T. S. Eliot, *Selected Essays*, p.287.
3   ibid., p.286.
4   *The Shorter Poems of Frederick Tennyson*, ed. Charles Tennyson, p.ix.
5   T. S. Eliot, *Selected Essays*, p.17.
6   *London Magazine*, October 1980, p.43.
7   George Santayana, *The Life of Reason*, iv. 194.

## Editor's Note

I have arranged the poems in this selection roughly in chronological order, although it has not always been possible to determine the date of composition of the work of minor poets. I have therefore exercised some freedom in arrangement, often in order to bring out similarities in technique or subject matter. Wherever possible I have used standard Victorian editions published during the poets' lifetimes.

I am very grateful to the staff of Durham University Library, Newcastle University Library, Aberdeen University Library (where there is a magnificent collection of minor Victorian verse) and the Library of the Literary and Philosophical Society of Newcastle upon Tyne.

I should also like to thank Jocelyn Burton for much encouragement and guidance, and Carol Waller for timely help in research, typing and administration.

J.R.W.

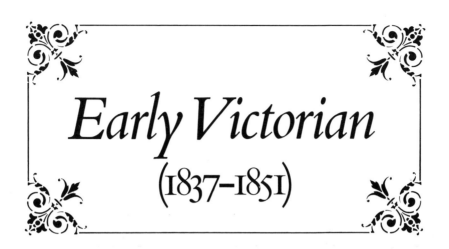

# Early Victorian
## (1837–1851)

ALFRED, LORD TENNYSON

## The Poet's Song

The rain had fallen, the Poet arose,
  He passed by the town and out of the street,
A light wind blew from the gates of the sun,
  And waves of shadow went over the wheat,
And he sat him down in a lonely place,
  And chanted a melody loud and sweet,
That made the wild-swan pause in her cloud,
  And the lark drop down at his feet.

The swallow stopped as he hunted the fly,
  The snake slipped under a spray,
The wild hawk stood with the down on his beak,
  And stared, with his foot on the prey,
And the nightingale thought, 'I have sung many songs,
  But never a one so gay,
For he sings of what the world will be
  When the years have died away.'

RICHARD MONCKTON MILNES

## Sir Walter Scott at the Tomb of the Stuarts
## in St Peter's

Eve's tinted shadows slowly fill the fane
Where Art has taken almost Nature's room,
While still two objects clear in light remain,
An alien pilgrim at an alien tomb. —

–A sculptured tomb of regal heads discrowned,·
Of one heart-worshipped, fancy-haunted, name,
Once loud on earth, but now scarce else renowned
Than as the offspring of that stranger's fame.

There lie the Stuarts! — There lingers Walter Scott!
Strange congress of illustrious thoughts and things!
A plain old moral, still too oft forgot, —
The power of Genius and the fall of Kings.

The curse on lawless Will high-planted there,
A beacon to the world, shines not for him;
He is with those who felt their life was sere,
When the full light of loyalty grew dim.

He rests his chin upon a sturdy staff,
Historic as that sceptre, theirs no more;
His gaze is fixed; his thirsty heart can quaff,
For a short hour the spirit-draughts of yore.

Each figure in its pictured place is seen,
Each fancied shape his actual vision fills,
From the long-pining, death-delivered Queen,
To the worn Outlaw of the heathery hills.

O grace of life, which shame could never mar!
O dignity, that circumstance defied!
Pure is the neck that wears the deathly scar,
And sorrow has baptised the front of pride.

But purpled mantle, and blood-crimsoned shroud,
Exiles to suffer and returns to woo,
Are gone, like dreams by daylight disallowed;
And their historian, — he is sinking too!

A few more moments and that labouring brow
Cold as those royal busts and calm will lie;
And, as on them his thoughts are resting now,
His marbled form will meet the attentive eye.

Thus, face to face, the dying and the dead,
Bound in one solemn ever-living bond,
Communed; and I was sad that ancient head
Ever should pass those holy walls beyond.


ROBERT STEPHEN HAWKER

## The Poor Man and His Parish Church
### A True Tale

The poor have hands, and feet, and eyes,
　　Flesh, and a feeling mind:
They breathe the breath of mortal sighs,
　　They are of human kind.
They weep such tears as others shed,
　　And now and then they smile:—
For sweet to them is that poor bread,
　　They win with honest toil.

The poor men have their wedding-day:
    And children climb their knee:
They have not many friends, for they
    Are in such misery.
They sell their youth, their skill, their pains,
    For hire in hill and glen:
The very blood within their veins,
    It flows for other men.

They should have roofs to call their own,
    When they grow old and bent:
Meek houses built of dark grey stone,
    Worn labour's monument.
There should they dwell, beneath the thatch,
    With threshold calm and free:
No stranger's hand should lift the latch,
    To mark their poverty.

Fast by the church those walls should stand,
    Her aisles in youth they trod:—
They have no home in all the land,
    Like that old House of God.
There, there, the Sacrament was shed,
    That gave them heavenly birth;
And lifted up the poor man's head
    With princes of the earth.

There in the chancel's voice of praise,
    Their simple vows were poured;
And angels looked with equal gaze
    On Lazarus and his Lord.
There, too, at last, they calmly sleep,
    Where hallowed blossoms bloom;
And eyes as fond and faithful weep
    As o'er the rich man's tomb.

They told me of an ancient home,
    Beside a churchyard wall,
Where roses round the porch would roam,
    And gentle jasmines fall:
There dwelt an old man, worn and blind,
    Poor, and of lowliest birth;
He seemed the last of all his kind —
    He had no friend on earth.

Men saw him till his eyes grew dim,
    At morn and evening tide
Pass, 'mid the graves, with tottering limb,
    To the grey chancel's side:

There knelt he down, and meekly prayed
  The prayer his youth had known;
Words by the old Apostles made,
  In tongues of ancient tone.

At matin-time, at evening hour,
  He bent with reverent knee:
The dial carved upon the tower
  Was not more true than he.
This lasted till the blindness fell
  In shadows round his bed;
And on those walls he loved so well,
  He looked, and they were fled.

Then would he watch, and fondly turn,
  If feet of men were there,
To tell them how his soul would yearn
  For the old place of prayer;
And some would lead him on to stand,
  While fast their tears would fall,
Until he felt beneath his hand
  The long-accustomed wall.

Then joy in those dim eyes would melt;
  Faith found the former tone;
His heart within his bosom felt
  The touch of every stone.
He died—he slept beneath the dew,
  In his own grassy mound:
The corpse, within the coffin, knew
  That calm, that holy ground.

I know not why—but when they tell
  Of houses fair and wide,
Where troops of poor men go to dwell
  In chambers side by side:—
I dream of that old cottage door,
  With garlands overgrown,
And wish the children of the poor
  Had flowers to call their own.

And when they vaunt, that in those walls
  They have their worship day,
Where the stern signal coldly calls
  The prisoned poor to pray,—
I think upon that ancient home
  Beside the churchyard wall,
Where roses round the porch would roam,
  And gentle jasmines fall.

I see the old man of my lay,
  His grey head bowed and bare;
He kneels by one dear wall to pray,
  The sunlight in his hair.
Well! they may strive, as wise men will,
  To work with wit and gold:
I think my own dear Cornwall still
  Was happier of old.

O! for the poor man's church again,
  With one roof over all;
Where the true hearts of Cornish men
  Might beat beside the wall:
The altars where, in holier days,
  Our fathers were forgiven,
Who went, with meek and faithful ways.
  Through the old aisles to heaven.


ROBERT STEPHEN HAWKER

## A Legend of the Hive

Behold those wingèd images,
  Bound for their evening bowers:
They are the nation of the bees,
  Born from the breath of flowers.
Strange people they! a mystic race,
In life, and food, and dwelling-place.

They first were seen on earth, 'tis said,
  When the rose breathes in spring:
Men thought her blushing bosom shed
  These children of the wing.
But lo! their hosts went down the wind,
Filled with the thoughts of God's own mind.

They built them houses made with hands,
  And there alone they dwell:
No man to this day understands
  The mystery of their cell.
Your mighty sages cannot see
The deep foundations of the bee.

Low in the violets' breast of blue,
  For treasured food they sink:
They know the flowers that hold the dew,
  For their small race to drink.
They glide—King Solomon might gaze
  With wonder on their awful ways.

And once—it is a grandame's tale,
  Yet filled with secret lore—
There dwelt within a woodland vale,
  Fast by old Cornwall's shore,
An ancient woman, worn and bent,
Fallen nature's mournful monument.

A home had they, the clustering race,
  Beside her garden wall:
All blossoms breathed around the place,
  And sunbeams fain would fall.
The lily loved that combe the best
Of all the valleys of the west.

But so it was, that on a day
  When summer built her bowers,
The waxen wanderers ceased to play
  Around the cottage flowers.
No hum was heard, no wing would roam:
They dwelt within their cloistered home.

This lasted long—no tongue could tell
  Their pastime or their toil;
What binds the soldier to the cell?
  Who should divide the spoil?
It lasted long—it fain would last,
Till autumn rustled on the blast.

Then sternly went that woman old,
  She sought the chancel floor,
And there, with purpose bad and bold,
  Knelt down amid the poor.
She took—she hid—that blessèd bread,
That is, what Jesu, Master, said!

She bare it to her distant home,
  She laid it by the hive:
To lure the wanderers forth to roam,
  That so her store might thrive.
'Twas a wild wish, a thought unblest,
Some evil legend of the west.

But lo! at morning tide, a sign
   For wondering eyes to trace:
They found above the bread, a shrine
   Reared by the harmless race.
They brought their walls from bud and flower,
They built bright roof and beamy tower.

Was it a dream? or did they hear,
   Float from those golden cells,
A sound as of some psaltery near,
   Or soft and silvery bells;
A low sweet psalm that grieved within,
In mournful memory of the sin?

Was it a dream? 'tis sweet no less:
   Set not the vision free,
Long let the lingering legend bless
   The nation of the bee.
So shall they bear upon their wings
A parable of sacred things.

So shall they teach, when men blaspheme
   Or sacrament or shrine,
That humbler things may fondly dream
   Of mysteries divine;
And holier hearts than his may beat
Beneath the bold blasphemer's feet.


ANNE BRONTË

## Lines Composed in a Wood on a Windy Day

My soul is awakened, my spirit is soaring,
And carried aloft on the wings of the breeze;
For, above, and around me, the wild wind is roaring
Arousing to rapture the earth and the seas.

The long withered grass in the sunshine is glancing,
The bare trees are tossing their branches on high;
The dead leaves beneath them are merrily dancing,
The white clouds are scudding across the blue sky.

I wish I could see how the ocean is lashing
The foam of its billows to whirlwinds of spray,
I wish I could see how its proud waves are dashing
And hear the wild roar of their thunder today!

ANNE BRONTË

## *The Captive Dove*

Poor restless Dove, I pity thee,
And when I hear thy plaintive moan
I'll mourn for thy captivity
And in thy woes forget mine own.

To see thee stand prepared to fly,
And flap those useless wings of thine,
And gaze into the distant sky
Would melt a harder heart than mine.

In vain! In vain! Thou canst not rise—
Thy prison roof confines thee there;
Its slender wires delude thine eyes,
And quench thy longing with despair.

O! thou wert made to wander free
In sunny mead and shady grove,
And far beyond the rolling sea
In distant climes at will to rove.

Yet hadst thou but one gentle mate
Thy little drooping heart to cheer
And share with thee thy captive state,
Thou could'st be happy even there.

Yes, even there, if listening by
One faithful dear companion stood,
While gazing on her full bright eye
Thou might'st forget thy native wood.

But thou, poor solitary dove,
Must make unheard thy joyless moan;
The heart that nature formed to love
Must pine neglected and alone.

ANNE BRONTË

## Memory

Brightly the sun of summer shone
Green fields and waving woods upon
    And soft winds wandered by.
Above, a sky of purest blue,
Around, bright flowers of loveliest hue
    Allured the gazer's eye.

But what were all these charms to me
When one sweet breath of memory
    Came gently wafting by?
I closed my eyes against the day
And called my willing soul away
    From earth and air and sky;

That I might simply fancy there
One little flower—a primrose fair
    Just opening into sight.
As in the days of infancy,
An opening primrose seemed to me
    A source of strange delight.

Sweet memory, ever smile on me;
Nature's chief beauties spring from thee,
    O, still thy tribute bring.
Still make the golden crocus shine
Among the flowers the most divine,
    The glory of the spring.

Still in the wall-flower's fragrance dwell,
And hover round the slight bluebell,
    My childhood's darling flower.
Smile on the little daisy still,
The buttercup's bright goblet fill
    With all thy former power.

Forever hang thy dreamy spell
Round golden star and heatherbell,
    And do not pass away
From sparkling frost, or wreathed snow,
And whisper when the wild winds blow
    Or rippling waters play.

Is childhood then so all divine?
Or, memory, is the glory thine
      That haloes thus the past?
Not all divine; its pangs of grief
Although perchance their stay is brief,
      Are bitter while they last.

Nor is the glory all thine own,
For on our earliest joys alone
      That holy light is cast.
With such a ray no spell of thine
Can make our later pleasures shine,
      Though long ago they passed.


ANNE BRONTË

## The Arbour


I'll rest me in this sheltered bower,
And look upon the clear blue sky
That smiles upon me through the trees,
Which stand so thickly clustering by;

And view their green and glossy leaves,
All glistening in the sunshine fair;
And list the rustling of their boughs,
So softly whispering through the air.

And while my ear drinks in the sound,
My wingèd soul shall fly away;
Reviewing long departed years
As one mild, beaming, autumn day;

And soaring on to future scenes,
Like hills and woods, and valleys green,
All basking in the summer's sun,
But distant still, and dimly seen.

Oh, list! 'tis summer's very breath
That gently shakes the rustling trees—
But look! the snow is on the ground—
How can I think of scenes like these?

'Tis but the *frost* that clears the air,
And gives the sky that lovely blue;
They're smiling in a *winter's* sun,
Those evergreens of sombre hue.

And winter's chill is on my heart—
How can I dream of future bliss?
How can my spirit soar away,
Confined by such a chain as this?

JOHN CLARE

## The Nightingale

This is the month the nightingale, clod-brown,
Is heard among the woodland shady boughs:
This is the time when, in the vale, grass-grown,
The maiden hears at eve her lover's vows,
What time the blue mist round the patient cows
Dim rises from the grass and half conceals
Their dappled hides. I hear the nightingale,
That from the little blackthorn spinney steals
To the old hazel hedge that skirts the vale,
And still unseen sings sweet. The ploughman feels
The thrilling music as he goes along,
And imitates and listens; while the fields
Lose all their paths in dusk to lead him wrong,
Still sings the nightingale her soft melodious song.

JOHN CLARE

## I Am

I am—yet what I am none cares or knows,
  My friends forsake me like a memory lost;
I am the self-consumer of my woes,
  They rise and vanish in oblivions host,
Like shadows in love—frenzied stifled throes
And yet I am, and live like vapours tost

Into the nothingness of scorn and noise,
  Into the living sea of waking dreams,
Where there is neither sense of life or joys,
  But the vast shipwreck of my life's esteems;
And e'en the dearest—that I love the best—
Are strange – nay, rather stranger than the rest.

I long for scenes where man has never trod,
  A place where woman never smiled or wept;
There to abide with my Creator, God,
  And sleep as I in childhood sweetly slept:
Untroubling and untroubled where I lie,
The grass below – above the vaulted sky.

JOHN CLARE

## A Vision

I lost the love of heaven above,
  I spurned the lust of earth below,
I felt the sweets of fancied love,
  And hell itself my only foe.

I lost earth's joys, but felt the glow
  Of heaven's flame abound in me,
Till loveliness and I did grow
  The bard of immortality.

I loved, but woman fell away;
  I hid me from her faded fame.
I snatched the sun's eternal ray
  And wrote till earth was but a name.

In every language upon earth,
  On every shore, o'er every sea,
I gave my name immortal birth
  And kept my spirit with the free.

JOHN CLARE

## *Hesperus*

Hesperus, the day is gone;
Soft falls the silent dew;
A tear is now on many a flower
And heaven lives in you.

Hesperus, the evening mild
Falls round us soft and sweet:
'Tis like the breathings of a child
When day and evening meet

Hesperus, the closing flower
Sleeps on the dewy ground;
While dews fall in a silent shower
And heaven breathes around

Hesperus, thy twinkling ray
Beams in the blue of heaven,
And tells the traveller on his way
That earth shall be forgiven.

JOHN CLARE

## *Clock-a-Clay*

In the cowslips peeps I lie,
Hidden from the buzzing fly,
While green grass beneath me lies,
Pearled wi' dew like fishes' eyes,
Here I lye, a clock-a-clay,
Waiting for the time o' day.

While grassy forests quake surprise,
And the wild wind sobs and sighs,
My gold home rocks as like to fall,
On its pillar green and tall;
When the pattering rain drives by
Clock-a-clay keeps warm and dry.

Day by day and night by night,
All the week I hide from sight;
In the cowslips peeps I lie,
In rain and dew still warm and dry;
Day and night, and night and day,
Red, black-spotted clock-a-clay.

My home it shakes in wind and showers,
Pale green pillar top't wi' flowers,
Bending at the wild wind's breath,
Till I touch the grass beneath;
Here still I live, lone clock-a-clay,
Watching for the time of day.


WILLIAM BARNES

## Evenèn in the Village

Now the light o' the west is a-turn'd to gloom,
    An' the men be at hwome vrom ground;
An' the bells be a-zendèn all down the Coombe
    From tower, their mwoansome sound.
        An' the wind is still,
        An' the house-dogs do bark,
An' the rooks be a-vled to the elems high an' dark,
    An' the water do roar at mill.

An' the flickerèn light drough the window-peäne
    Vrom the candle's dull fleäme do shoot,
An' young Jemmy the smith is a-gone down leäne,
    A-playèn his shrill-vaïced flute.
        An' the miller's man
        Do zit down at his ease
On the seat that is under the cluster o' trees,
    Wi' his pipe an' his cider can.

WILLIAM BARNES

*Be'mi'ster*

Sweet Be'mi'ster, that bist a-bound
By green an' woody hills all round,
Wi' hedges, reachèn up between
A thousan' vields o' zummer green,
Where elems' lofty heads do drow
Their sheädes vor haÿ-meakers below,
An' wild hedge-flow'rs do charm the souls
O' maïdens in their evenèn strolls.

When I o' Zunday nights wi' Jeäne
Do saunter drough a vield or leäne,
Where elder-blossoms be a-spread
Above the eltrot's milk-white head,
An' flow'rs o' blackberries do blow
Upon the brembles, white as snow,
To be outdone avore my zight
By Jeän's gaÿ frock o'dazzlèn white;

Oh! then there's nothèn that's 'ithout
Thy hills that I do ho about,—
Noo bigger pleäce, noo gaÿer town,
Beyond thy sweet bells' dyèn soun',
As they do ring, or strike the hour,
At evenèn vrom thy wold red tow'r.
No: shelter still my head, an' keep
My bwones when I do vall asleep.

WILLIAM BARNES

*Grammer's Shoes*

I do seem to zee Grammer as she did use
Vor to show us, at Chris'mas, her weddèn shoes,
An' her flat spreadèn bonnet so big an' roun'
As a girt pewter dish a-turn'd upside down;
      When we all did draw near
      In a cluster to hear
O' the merry wold soul how she did use
To walk an' to dance wi' her high-heel shoes.

She'd a gown wi' girt flowers lik' hollyhocks,
An' zome stockèns o' gramfer's a-knit wi' clocks,
An' a token she kept under lock an' key, –
A small lock ov his heäir off avor 't wer grey.
     An' her eyes wer red,
     An' she shook her head,
When we'd all a-look'd at it, an' she did use
To lock it away wi' her weddèn shoes.

She could tell us such teäles about heavy snows,
An' o' raïns an' o' floods when the waters rose
All up into the housen, an' carr'd awoy
All the bridge wi' a man an' his little bwoy;
     An' o' vog an' vrost,
     An' o' vo'k a-lost,
An' o' peärties at Chris'mas, when she did use
Vor to walk hwome wi' gramfer in high-heel shoes.

Ev'ry Chris'mas she lik'd vor the bells to ring,
An' to have in the zingers to heär em zing
The wold carols she heärd many years a-gone,
While she warm'd em zome cider avore the bron';
     An' she'd look an' smile
     An our dancèn, while
She did tell how her friends now a-gone did use
To reely wi' her in their high-heel shoes.

Ah! an' how she did like vor to deck wi' red
Holly-berries the window an' wold clock's head,
An' the clavy wi' boughs o' some bright green leaves,
An to meäke twoast an' eäle upon Chris'mas eves;
     But she's now, drough greäce,
     In a better pleäce,
Though we'll never vorget her, poor soul, nor lose
Gramfer's token ov heäir, nor her weddèn shoes.


WILLIAM BARNES

## The Shep'erd Bwoy

When the warm zummer breeze do blow over the hill,
  An' the vlock's a-spread over the ground;
When the vaïce o' the busy wold sheep dog is still,
  An' the sheep-bells do tinkle all round;
   Where noo tree vor a sheäde but the thorn is a-vound,

There, a zingèn a zong,
   Or a-whislèn among
The sheep, the young shep'erd do bide all day long.

When the storm do come up wi' a thundery cloud
   That do shut out the zunlight, an' high
Over head the wild thunder do rumble so loud.
   An' the lightnèn do flash vrom the sky,
      Where noo shelter's a-vound but his hut, that is nigh,
         There out ov all harm,
         In the dry an' the warm,
The poor little shep'erd do smile at the storm.

When the cwold winter win' do blow over the hill,
   An' the hore-vrost do whiten the grass,
An' the breath o' the no'th is so cwold, as to chill
   The warm blood ov woone's heart as do pass;
      When the ice o' the pond is so slipp'ry as glass,
         There, a-zingèn a zong,
         Or a-whislèn among
The sheep, the poor shep'erd do bide all day long.

When the shearèn's a-come, an' the shearers do pull
   In the sheep, hangèn back a-gwaïn in,
Wi' their roun' zides a-heavèn in under their wool,
   To come out all a-clipp'd to the skin;
      When the feästèn, an' zingèn, an fun do begin,
         Vor to help em, an' sheäre
         All their me'th an' good feäre,
The poor little shep'erd is sure to be there.


WILLIAM BARNES

## The Bells ov Alderburnham

While now upon the win' do zwell
   The church-bells' evenèn peal, O,
Along the bottom, who can tell
   How touch'd my heart do veel, O.
To hear ageän, as woonce they rung
In holidays when I wer young,
      Wi' merry sound
      A-ringèn round,
   The bells ov Alderburnham.

Vor when they run their gaÿest peals
   O' zome sweet day o' rest, O,
We all did ramble drough the viels,
   A-dress'd in all our best, O;
An' at the bridge or roarèn weir,
Or in the wood, or in the gleäre
         Ov open ground,
         Did hear ring round
   The bells ov Alderburnham.

They bells, that now do ring above
   The young brides at church-door, O,
Woonce rung to bless their mother's love,
   When they were brides avore, O.
An' sons in tow'r do still ring on
The merry peals o' fathers gone,
         Noo mwore to sound,
         Or hear ring round,
   The bells ov Alderburnham.

Ov happy peäirs, how soon be zome
   A-wedded an' a-peärted!
Vor woone ov jaÿ, what peals mid come
   To zome o's broken-hearted!
The stronger mid the sooner die,
The gaÿer mid the sooner sigh;
         An' who do know
         What grief's below
   The bells ov Alderburnham!

But still 'tis happiness to know
   That there's a God above us;
An' he, by day an' night, do ho
   Vor all ov us, an' love us,
An' call us to His house, to heal
Our hearts by his own Zunday peal
         Ov bells a-rung
         Vor wold an' young,
   The bells ov Alderburnham.

ROBERT BROWNING

## Home-Thoughts, from Abroad

Oh, to be in England
Now that April's there,
And whoever wakes in England
Sees, some morning, unaware,
That the lowest boughs and the brushwood sheaf
Round the elm-tree bole are in tiny leaf,
While the chaffinch sings on the orchard bough
In England—now!

And after April, when May follows,
And the whitethroat builds, and all the swallows!
Hark, where my blossomed pear-tree in the hedge
Leans to the field and scatters on the clover
Blossoms and dewdrops—at the bent spray's edge—
That's the wise thrush; he sings each song twice over,
Lest you should think he never could recapture
The first fine careless rapture!
And though the fields look rough with hoary dew,
All will be gay when noontide wakes anew
The buttercups, the little children's dower
– Far brighter than this gaudy melon-flower!

ROBERT BROWNING

## Home-Thoughts, from the Sea

Nobly, nobly Cape Saint Vincent to the North-west died away;
Sunset ran, one glorious blood-red, reeking into Cadiz Bay;
Bluish 'mid the burning water, full in face Trafalgar lay;
In the dimmest North-east distance dawned Gibraltar grand and gray;
'Here and here did England help me: how can I help England?' – say,
Whoso turns as I, this evening, turn to God to praise and pray,
While Jove's planet rises yonder, silent over Africa.

ELIZABETH BARRETT BROWNING

## The Cry of the Children

'Φεῦ, φεῦ, τί προσδέρκεσθέ μ' ὄμμασιν, τέκνα;' — Medea

Do ye hear the children weeping, O my brothers,
    Ere the sorrow comes with years?
They are leaning their young heads against their mothers,
    And *that* cannot stop their tears.
The young lambs are bleating in the meadows,
    The young birds are chirping in the nest,
The young fawns are playing with the shadows,
    The young flowers are blowing toward the west—
But the young, young children, O my brothers,
    They are weeping bitterly!
They are weeping in the playtime of the others,
    In the country of the free.

Do you question the young children in the sorrow
    Why their tears are falling so?
The old man may weep for his to-morrow
    Which is lost in Long Ago;
The old tree is leafless in the forest,
    The old year is ending in the frost,
The old wound, if stricken, is the sorest,
    The old hope is hardest to be lost:
But the young, young children, O my brothers,
    Do you ask them why they stand
Weeping sore before the bosoms of their mothers,
    In our happy Fatherland?

They look up with their pale and sunken faces,
    And their looks are sad to see,
For the man's hoary anguish draws and presses
    Down the cheeks of infancy;
'Your old earth,' they say, 'is very dreary,
    Our young feet,' they say, 'are very weak;
Few paces have we taken, yet are weary—
    'Our grave-rest is very far to seek:
Ask the aged why they weep, and not the children,
    For the outside earth is cold,
And we young ones stand without, in our bewildering,
    And the graves are for the old.

'True,' say the children, 'it may happen
 That we die before our time:
Little Alice died last year, her grave is shapen
 Like a snowball, in the rime.
We looked into the pit prepared to take her:
 Was no room for any work in the close clay!
From the sleep wherein she lieth none will wake her,
 Crying, "Get up, little Alice! it is day."
If you listen by that grave, in sun and shower,
 With your ear down, little Alice never cries;
Could we see her face, be sure we should not know her,
 For the smile has time for growing in her eyes:
And merry go her moments, lulled and stilled in
 The shroud by the kirk-chime.
It is good when it happens,' say the children,
 'That we die before our time.'

Alas, alas, the children! they are seeking
 Death in life, as best to have:
They are binding up their hearts away from breaking,
 With a cerement from the grave.
Go out, children, from the mine and from the city,
 Sing out, children, as the little thrushes do;
Pluck your handfuls of the meadow-cowslips pretty,
 Laugh aloud, to feel your fingers let them through!
But they answer, 'Are your cowslips of the meadows
 Like our weeds anear the mine?
Leave us quiet in the dark of the coal-shadows,
 From your pleasures fair and fine!

'For oh,' say the children, 'we are weary,
 And we cannot run or leap;
If we cared for any meadows, it were merely
 To drop down in them and sleep.
Our knees tremble sorely in the stooping,
 We fall upon our faces, trying to go;
And, underneath our heavy eyelids drooping
 The reddest flower would look as pale as snow.
For, all day, we drag our burden tiring
 Through the coal-dark, underground:
Or, all day, we drive the wheels of iron
 In the factories, round and round.

'For all day the wheels are droning, turning;
 Their wind comes in our faces,
Till our hearts turn, our heads with pulses burning,
 And the walls turn in their places:

Turns the sky in the high window, blank and reeling,
   Turns the long light that drops adown the wall,
Turn the black flies that crawl along the ceiling:
   All are turning, all the day, and we with all.
And all day the iron wheels are droning,
   And sometimes we could pray,
"Oh ye wheels" (breaking out in a mad moaning),
   "Stop! be silent for to-day!" '

Ay, be silent! Let them hear each other breathing
   For a moment, mouth to mouth!
Let them touch each other's hands, in a fresh wreathing
   Of their tender human youth!
Let them feel that this cold metallic motion
   Is not all the life God fashions or reveals:
Let them prove their living souls against the notion
   That they live in you, or under you, O wheels!
Still, all day, the iron wheels go onward,
   Grinding life down from its mark:
And the children's souls, which God is calling sunward,
   Spin on blindly in the dark.

Now tell the poor young children, O my brothers,
   To look up to Him and pray;
So the blessed One who blesseth all the others,
   Will bless them another day.
They answer, 'Who is God that He should hear us,
   While the rushing of the iron wheels is stirred?
When we sob aloud, the human creatures near us
   Pass by, hearing not, or answer not a word.
And *we* hear not (for the wheels in their resounding)
   Strangers speaking at the door:
Is it likely God, with angels singing round Him,
   Hears our weeping any more?

'Two words, indeed, of praying we remember,
   And at midnight's hour of harm,
"Our Father," looking upward in the chamber,
   We say softly for a charm.
We know no other words except "Our Father,"
   And we think that, in some pause of angels' song,
God may pluck them with the silence sweet to gather,
   And hold both within His right hand which is strong.
"Our Father!" If He heard us, He would surely
   (For they call Him good and mild)
Answer, smiling down the steep world very purely,
   "Come and rest with me, my child."

'But, no!' say the children, weeping faster,
    'He is speechless as a stone:
And they tell us, of His image is the master
    Who commands us to work on.
Go to!' say the children,—'up in Heaven,
   Dark, wheel-like, turning clouds are all we find.
Do not mock us; grief has made us unbelieving:
   We look up for God, but tears have made us blind.'
Do you hear the children weeping and disproving,
    O my brothers, what ye preach?
For God's possible is taught by His world's loving,
    And the children doubt of each.

And well may the children weep before you!
    They are weary ere they run;
They have never seen the sunshine, nor the glory
    Which is brighter than the sun.
They know the grief of man, without its wisdom;
   They sink in man's despair, without its calm;
Are slaves, without the liberty in Christdom,
   Are martyrs, by the pang without the palm:
Are worn as if with age, yet unretrievingly
    The harvest of its memories cannot reap,—
Are orphans of the earthly love and heavenly.
    Let them weep! let them weep!

They look up with their pale and sunken faces,
    And their look is dread to see,
For they mind you of their angels in high places,
    With eyes turned on Deity.
'How long,' they say, 'how long, O cruel nation,
   Will you stand, to move the world, on a child's heart,—
Stifle down with a mailed heel its palpitation,
   And tread onward to your throne amid the mart?
Our blood splashes upward, O gold-heaper,
    And your purple shows your path!
But the child's sob in the silence curses deeper
    Than the strong man in his wrath.'

THOMAS HOOD

## The Song of the Shirt

With fingers weary and worn,
　With eyelids heavy and red,
A Woman sat, in unwomanly rags,
　Plying her needle and thread—
　　Stitch! stitch! stitch!
In poverty, hunger, and dirt,
And still with a voice of dolorous pitch
She sang the 'Song of the Shirt'!

'Work! work! work!
While the cock is crowing aloof!
　And work—work—work,
Till the stars shine through the roof!
It's O! to be a slave
　Along with the barbarous Turk,
Where woman has never a soul to save,
　If this is Christian work!

'Work—work—work
Till the brain begins to swim;
　Work—work—work
Till the eyes are heavy and dim!
Seam, and gusset, and band,
　Band, and gusset, and seam,
Till over the buttons I fall asleep,
　And sew them on in a dream!

'Oh! Men with Sisters dear!
　Oh! Men! with Mothers and Wives!
It is not linen you're wearing out,
　But human creatures' lives!
　　Stitch—stitch—stitch,
　In poverty, hunger, and dirt,
Sewing at once, with a double thread,
　A Shroud as well as a Shirt.

'But why do I talk of Death?
　That Phantom of grisly bone,
I hardly fear his terrible shape,
　It seems so like my own—
　It seems so like my own,
　Because of the fasts I keep,
Oh! God! that bread should be so dear,
　And flesh and blood so cheap!

'Work—work—work!
    My labour never flags;
And what are its wages? A bed of straw,
    A crust of bread—and rags.
That shattered roof,—and this naked floor—
    A table—a broken chair—
And a wall so blank, my shadow I thank
    For sometimes falling there!

'Work—work—work!
From weary chime to chime,
    Work—work—work—
As prisoners work for crime!
    Band, and gusset, and seam,
    Seam, and gusset, and band,
Till the heart is sick, and the brain benumbed,
    As well as the weary hand.

'Work—work—work,
In the dull December light,
    And work—work—work,
When the weather is warm and bright—
While underneath the eaves
    The brooding swallows cling
As if to show me their sunny backs
    And twit me with the spring.

'Oh! but to breathe the breath
Of the cowslip and primrose sweet—
    With the sky above my head,
And the grass beneath my feet,
For only one short hour
    To feel as I used to feel,
Before I knew the woes of want
    And the walk that costs a meal!

'Oh but for one short hour!
    A respite however brief!
No blessed leisure for Love or Hope,
    But only time for Grief!
A little weeping would ease my heart,
    But in their briny bed
My tears must stop, for every drop
    Hinders needle and thread!'

Seam, and gusset, and band,
Band, and gusset, and seam,
    Work, work, work,
Like the Engine that works by Steam!

A mere machine of iron and wood
   That toils for Mammon's sake—
Without a brain to ponder and craze
   Or a heart to feel—and break!

With fingers weary and worn,
   With eyelids heavy and red,
A Woman sate in unwomanly rags,
   Plying her needle and thread—
     Stitch! stitch! stitch!
   In poverty, hunger, and dirt,
And still with a voice of dolorous pitch
Would that its tone could reach the Rich!—
   She sang this 'Song of the Shirt'!

THOMAS HOOD

## From *Miss Kilmansegg and Her Precious Leg*

.  .  .

Born in wealth and wealthily nursed,
Capped, papped, napped, and lapped from the first
   On the knees of Prodigality,
Her childhood was one eternal round
Of the game of going on Tickler's ground,
   Picking up gold—in reality.

With extempore carts she never played,
Or the odds and ends of a tinker's trade,
Or little dirt pies and puddings made,
   Like children happy and squalid;
The very puppet she had to pet,
Like a bait for the 'Nix my Dolly' set,
   Was a Dolly of Gold—and solid!

Gold! and gold! 'twas the burden still!
To gain the Heiress's early goodwill
   There was much corruption and bribery—
The yearly cost of her golden toys
Would have given half London's Charity Boys
And Charity Girls the annual joys
   Of a holiday dinner at Highbury.

Bon-bons she ate from the gilt *cornet*;
And gilded queens on St Bartlemy's day;
   Till her fancy was tinged by her presents—
And first a Goldfinch excited her wish,
Then a spherical bowl with its Golden fish,
   And then two Golden Pheasants.

Nay, once she squalled and screamed, like wild—
And it shows how the bias we give to a child
   Is a thing most weighty and solemn;—
But whence was wonder or blame to spring,
If little Miss K.,—after such a swing—
Made a dust for the flaming gilded thing
   On the top of the Fish-street column?


### Her Education

According to metaphysical creed,
To the earliest books that children read
   For much good or much bad they are debtors;
But before with their ABC they start,
There are things in morals as well as art,
That play a very important part—
   'Impressions before the letters.'

Dame Education begins the pile,
Mayhap in the graceful Corinthian style,
   But alas for the elevation!
If the Lady's maid or Gossip the Nurse
With a load of rubbish, or something worse,
   Have made a rotten foundation.

Even thus with little Miss Kilmansegg,
Before she learnt her E for egg,
   Ere her Governess came, or her Masters—
Teachers of quite a different kind
Had 'crammed' her beforehand, and put her mind
   In a go-cart on golden castors.

Long before her A B and C,
They had taught her by heart her L.S.D.,
   And as how she was born a great Heiress;
And as sure as London is built of bricks,
My Lord would ask her the day to fix,
To ride in a fine gilt coach and six,
   Like her Worship the Lady May'ress.

LEWIS EGERTON SMOOT MEM'L LIB
KING GEORGE, VA. 22485

Instead of stories from Edgeworth's page,
The true golden lore for our golden age,
  Or lessons from Barbauld and Trimmer,
Teaching the worth of Virtue and Health,
All that she knew was the Virtue of Wealth,
Provided by vulgar nursery stealth
  With a Book of Leaf Gold for a Primer.

The very metal of merit they told,
And praised her for being as 'good as gold'
  Till she grew as a peacock haughty;
Of money they talked the whole day round,
And weighed desert like grapes by the pound,
Till she had an idea from the very sound
  That people with naught were naughty.

They praised—poor children with nothing at all!
Lord! how you twaddle and waddle and squall,
  Like common-bred geese and ganders!
What sad little bad little figures you make
To the rich Miss K., whose plainest seed-cake
  Was stuffed with corianders!

They praised her falls, as well as her walk,
Flatterers make cream cheese of chalk,
They praised—how they praised—her very small talk,
  As if it fell from a Solon;
Or the girl who at each pretty phrase let drop
A ruby comma, a pearl full-stop,
  And an emerald semi-colon.

They praised her spirit, and now and then,
The Nurse brought her own little 'nevy' Ben,
  To play with the future May'ress,
And when he got raps, and taps, and slaps,
Scratches, and pinches, snips, and snaps,
  As if from a Tigress or Bearess,
They told him how lords would court that hand,
And always gave him to understand
    While he rubbed, poor soul!
    His carroty poll,
  That his hair had been pulled by 'a *Hairess*'.

Such were the lessons from maid and nurse,
A Governess helped to make still worse,
Giving an appetite so perverse

Fresh diet whereon to batten—
Beginning with A B C to hold
Like a royal play-bill printed in gold
   On a square of pearl-white satin.

The books to teach the verbs and nouns,
And those about countries, cities, and towns,
Instead of their sober drabs and browns,
   Were in crimson silk, with gilt edges;—
Her Butler and Enfield and Entick—in short
Her 'Early Lessons' of every sort,
   Looked like Souvenirs, Keepsakes, and Pledges.

Old Johnson shone out in as fine array
As he did one night when he went to the play;
Chambaud like a beau of King Charles's day—
   Lindley Murray in like conditions—
Each weary, unwelcome, irksome task,
Appeared in a fancy dress and a mask—
If you wish for similar copies ask
   For Howell and James's Editions.

Novels she read to amuse her mind,
But always the affluent match-making kind
   That ends with Promessi Sposi,
And a father-in-law so wealthy and grand,
He could give cheque-mate to Coutts in the Strand;
   So along with a ring and posy,
He endows the Bride with Golconda offhand,
   And gives the Groom Potosi.

Plays she perused—but she liked the best
Those comedy gentlefolks always possessed
   Of fortunes so truly romantic—
Of money so ready that right or wrong
It always is ready to go for a song,
Throwing it, going it, pitching it strong—
They ought to have purses as green and long
   As the cucumber called the Gigantic.

Then Eastern Tales she loved for the sake
Of the Purse of Oriental make,
   And the thousand pieces they put in it—
But Pastoral scenes on her heart fell cold,
For Nature with her had lost its hold,
No field but the Field of the Cloth of Gold
   Would ever have caught her foot in it.

What more? She learned to sing, and dance,
To sit on a horse, although he should prance,
And to speak a French not spoken in France
    Any more than at Babel's building—
And she painted shells, and flowers, and Turks,
But her great delight was in Fancy Works
    That are done with gold or gilding.

Gold! still gold!—the bright and the dead,
With golden beads, and gold lace, and gold thread,
She worked in gold as if for her bread.
    The metal had so undermined her—
Gold ran in her thoughts and filled her brain,
She was golden-headed as Peter's cane
    With which he walked behind her.


### Her Accident

The horse that carried Miss Kilmansegg,
And a better never lifted leg,
    Was a very rich bay, called Banker—
A horse of a breed and a mettle so rare,—
By Bullion out of an Ingot mare,—
That for action, the best of figures, and air,
    It made many good judges hanker.

And when she took a ride in the Park,
Equestrian Lord, or pedestrian Clerk,
    Was thrown in an amorous fever,
To see the heiress how well she sat,
With her groom behind her, Bob or Nat,
In green, half smothered with gold, and a hat
    With more gold lace than beaver.

And then when Banker obtained a pat,
To see how he arched his neck at that!
    He snorted with pride and pleasure!
Like the Steed in the fable so lofty and grand,
Who gave the poor Ass to understand,
That *he* didn't carry a bag of sand,
    But a burden of golden treasure.

A load of treasure?—alas! alas!
Had her horse but been fed upon English grass
   And sheltered in Yorkshire spinneys,
Had he scoured the sand with the Desert Ass,
   Or where the American whinnies,—
But a hunter from Erin's turf and gorse,
A regular thorough-bred Irish Horse,
Why, he ran away, as a matter of course,
   With a girl worth her weight in guineas!

Mayhap 'tis the trick of such pampered nags
To shy at the sight of a beggar in rags;
   But away, like the bolt of a rabbit,
Away went the horse in the madness of fright,
And away went the horsewoman mocking the sight—
Was yonder blue flash a flash of blue light,
   Or only the skirt of her habit?

Away she flies, with the groom behind,—
It looks like a race of the Calmuck kind,
   When Hymen himself is the starter:
And the Maid rides first in the four-footed strife,
Riding, striding, as if for her life,
While the Lover rides after to catch him a wife,
   Although it's catching a Tartar.

But the Groom has lost his glittering hat!
Though he does not sigh and pull up for that—
   Alas! his horse is a tit for Tatt,
   To sell to a very low bidder—
His wind is ruined, his shoulder is sprung,
Things, though a horse be well-bred and young,
   A purchaser *will* consider.

But still flies the heiress through stones and dust,
Oh, for a fall, if fall she must,
   On the gentle lap of Flora!
But still, thank Heaven! she clings to her seat—
Away! away! she could ride a dead heat
With the Dead who ride so fast and fleet,
   In the Ballad of Leonora!

Away she gallops!—it's awful work!
It's faster than Turpin's ride to York,
   On Bess that notable clipper!
She has circled the Ring!—she crosses the Park!
Mazeppa, although he was stripped so stark,
   Mazeppa couldn't outstrip her!

The fields seem running away with the folks!
The Elms are having a race for the Oaks!
   At a pace that all Jockeys disparages!
All, all is racing! the Serpentine
Seems rushing past like the 'arrowy Rhine',
The houses have got on a railway line,
   And are off like the first-class carriages!

She'll lose her life! she is losing her breath!
A cruel chase, she is chasing Death,
   As female shriekings forewarn her:
And now—as gratis as blood of Guelph—
She clears that gate, which has cleared itself
   Since then, at Hyde Park Corner!

Alas! for the hope of the Kilmanseggs!
For her head, her brains, her body, and legs,
   Her life's not worth a copper!
     Willy-nilly,
     In Piccadilly,
A hundred hearts turn sick and chilly,
   A hundred voices cry, 'Stop her!'
And one old gentleman stares and stands,
Shakes his head and lifts his hands,
   And says, 'How very improper!'

On and on!—what a perilous run!
The iron rails seem all mingling in one,
   To shut out the Green Park scenery!
And now the Cellar its dangers reveals,
She shudders—she shrieks—she's doomed, she feels,
To be torn by powers of horses and wheels,
   Like a spinner by steam machinery!

Sick with horror she shuts her eyes,
But the very stones seem uttering cries,
   As they did to that Persian daughter,
When she climbed up the steep vociferous hill,
Her little silver flagon to fill
   With the magical Golden Water!

    'Batter her! shatter her!
    Throw and scatter her!'
Shouts each stony-hearted chatterer!
    'Dash at the heavy Dover!
Spill her! kill her! tear and tatter her!
Smash her! crash her!' (the stones didn't flatter her!)
'Kick her brains out! let her blood spatter her!
   Roll on her over and over!'

For so she gathered the awful sense
Of the street in its past unmacadamized tense,
    As the wild horse overran it,—
His four heels making the clatter of six,
Like a Devil's tattoo, played with iron sticks
    On a kettle-drum of granite!

On! still on! she's dazzled with hints
Of oranges, ribbons, and coloured prints,
A Kaleidoscope jumble of shapes and tints,
    And human faces all flashing,
Bright and brief as the sparks from the flints,
    That the desperate hoof keeps dashing!

On and on! still frightfully fast!
Dover-street, Bond-street, all are past!
But—yes—no—yes!—they're down at last!
    The Furies and Fates have found them!
Down they go with a sparkle and crash,
Like a Bark that's struck by the lightning flash—
        There's a shriek—and a sob—
        And the dense dark mob
    Like a billow closes around them!

            ·   ·   ·   ·   ·

            'She breathes!'
            'She don't!'
            'She'll recover!'
            'She won't!'
    'She's stirring! she's living, by Nemesis!'
Gold, still gold! on counter and shelf
Golden dishes as plenty as delf!
Miss Kilmansegg's coming again to herself
    On an opulent goldsmith's premises!

Gold! fine gold!—both yellow and red,
Beaten, and molten—polished, and dead—
To see the gold with profusion spread
    In all forms of its manufacture!
But what avails gold to Miss Kilmansegg,
When the femoral bone of her dexter leg
    Has met with a compound fracture?

Gold may soothe Adversity's smart;
Nay, help to bind up a broken heart;
But to try it on any other part
    Were as certain a disappointment,

As if one should rub the dish and plate,
Taken out of a Staffordshire crate—
In the hope of a Golden Service of State—
With Singleton's 'Golden Ointment'.


HENRY CHOLMONDELEY PENNELL

## The Night Mail North
### (Euston Square, 1840)


Now then, take your seats! for Glasgow and the North;
Chester!—Carlisle!—Holyhead,—and the wild Firth of Forth,
    'Clap on the steam and sharp's the word,
        You men in scarlet cloth:—

    'Are there any more pas . . sengers,
    For the Night . . Mail . . to the North!'

        Are there any more passengers?
        Yes three—but they can't get in,—
Too late, too late!—How they bellow and knock,
    They might as well try to soften a rock
        As the heart of that fellow in green.

    For the Night Mail North? what ho—
    No use to struggle, you can't get through,
        My young and lusty one—
Whither away from the gorgeous town?—

'For the lake and the stream and the heather brown,
        And the double-barrelled gun!'

    For the Night Mail North, I say?—
        You, with the eager eyes—
    You with the haggard face and pale?—

'From a ruined hearth and a starving brood,
        A Crime and a felon's gaol!'

    For the Night Mail North, old man?—
        Old statue of despair—
    Why tug and strain at the iron gate?
            'My Daughter!!'

Ha! too late, too late,
She is gone, you may safely swear;
She has given you the slip, d'you hear?
She has left you alone in your wrath,—
And she's off and away, with a glorious start,
To the home of her choice, with the man of her heart,
By the Night Mail North!

.  .  .  .  .

Wh——ish, R——ush,
Wh——ish, R——ush . . .
'What's all that hullabaloo?
Keep fast the gates there—who is this
That insists on bursting through?'
A desperate man whom none may withstand,
For look, there is something clenched in his hand—
Though the bearer is ready to drop—
He waves it wildly to and fro,
And hark! how the crowd are shouting below—

'Back!'—

And back the opposing barriers go,
'*A reprieve for the Canongate murderer, Ho!*
*In the Queen's name*–

STOP.'

'*Another has confessed the crime.*'

Whish—rush—whish—rush. . . .

The Guard has caught the fluttering sheet,
Now forward and northward! fierce and fleet,
Through the mist and the dark and the driving sleet,
As if life and death were in it;
'Tis a splendid race! a race against Time,—
And a thousand to one we win it:

Look at those flitting ghosts—
The white-armed finger-posts—
If we're moving the eighth of an inch, I say,
We're going a mile a minute!
A mile a minute—for life or death—
Away, away! though it catches one's breath,
The man shall not die in his wrath:
The quivering carriages rock and reel—
Hurrah! for the rush of the grinding steel!
The thundering crank, and the mighty wheel!—

Are there any more pas . . sengers
For the Night . . Mail . . to the North?

GEORGE OUTRAM

## On Hearing a Lady Praise a Certain
## Rev. Doctor's Eyes

I cannot praise the Doctor's eyes,
I never saw his glance divine;
He always shuts them when he prays
And when he preaches he shuts mine.

ROBERT BROWNING

## My Last Duchess
### Ferrara

That's my last Duchess painted on the wall,
Looking as if she were alive. I call
That piece a wonder, now: Frà Pandolf's hands
Worked busily a day, and there she stands.
Will 't please you sit and look at her? I said
'Fra Pandolf' by design, for never read
Strangers like you that pictured countenance,
The depth and passion of its earnest glance,
But to myself they turned (since none puts by
The curtain I have drawn for you, but I)
And seemed as they would ask me, if they durst,
How such a glance came there; so, not the first
Are you to turn and ask thus. Sir, 'twas not
Her husband's presence only, called that spot
Of joy into the Duchess' cheek: perhaps
Frà Pandolf chanced to say 'Her mantle laps
Over my lady's wrist too much,' or 'Paint
Must never hope to reproduce the faint
Half-flush that dies along her throat:' such stuff
Was courtesy, she thought, and cause enough
For calling up that spot of joy. She had
A heart—how shall I say?—too soon made glad,
Too easily impressed; she liked whate'er
She looked on, and her looks went everywhere.
Sir, 'twas all one! My favour at her breast,
The dropping of the daylight in the West,
The bough of cherries some officious fool
Broke in the orchard for her, the white mule

She rode with round the terrace—all and each
Would draw from her alike the approving speech,
Or blush, at least. She thanked men,—good! but thanked
Somehow—I know not how—as if she ranked
My gift of a nine-hundred-years-old name
With anybody's gift. Who'd stoop to blame
This sort of trifling? Even had you skill
In speech—(which I have not)—to make your will
Quite clear to such an one, and say, 'Just this
Or that in you disgusts me; here you miss,
Or there exceed the mark'—and if she let
Herself be lessoned so, nor plainly set
Her wits to yours, forsooth, and made excuse,
—E'en then would be some stooping; and I choose
Never to stoop. Oh sir, she smiled, no doubt,
Whene'er I passed her; but who passed without
Much the same smile? This grew; I gave commands;
Then all smiles stopped together. There she stands
As if alive. Will 't please you rise? We'll meet
The company below, then. I repeat,
The Count your master's known munificence
Is ample warrant that no just pretence
Of mine for dowry will be disallowed;
Though his fair daughter's self, as I avowed
At starting, is my object. Nay, we'll go
Together down, sir. Notice Neptune, though,
Taming a sea-horse, thought a rarity,
Which Claus of Innsbruck cast in bronze for me!

### ROBERT BROWNING

## *Sibrandus Schafnaburgensis*

Plague take all your pedants, say I!
    He who wrote what I hold in my hand,
Centuries back was so good as to die,
    Leaving this rubbish to cumber the land;
This, that was a book in its time,
    Printed on paper and bound in leather,
Last month in the white of a matin-prime
    Just when the birds sang all together,

Into the garden I brought it to read,
   And under the arbute and laurustine
Read it, so help me grace in my need,
   From title-page to closing line.
Chapter on chapter did I count,
   As a curious traveller counts Stonehenge;
Added up the mortal amount;
   And then proceeded to my revenge.

Yonder's a plum-tree with a crevice
   An owl would build in, were he but sage;
For a lap of moss, like a fine pont-levis
   In a castle of the Middle Age,
Joins to a lip of gum, pure amber;
   When he'd be private, there might he spend
Hours alone in his lady's chamber:
   Into this crevice I dropped our friend.

Splash, went he, as under he ducked,
   —At the bottom, I knew, rain-drippings stagnate:
Next, a handful of blossoms I plucked
   To bury him with, my bookshelf's magnate;
Then I went in-doors, brought out a loaf,
   Half a cheese, and a bottle of Chablis;
Lay on the grass and forgot the oaf
   Over a jolly chapter of Rabelais.

Now, this morning, betwixt the moss
   And gum that locked our friend in limbo,
A spider had spun his web across,
   And sat in the midst with arms akimbo:
So, I took pity, for learning's sake,
   And, *de profundis, accentibus laetis,*
*Cantate!* quoth I, as I got a rake;
   And up I fished his delectable treatise.

Here you have it, dry in the sun,
   With all the binding all of a blister,
And great blue spots where the ink has run,
   And reddish streaks that wink and glister
O'er the page so beautifully yellow:
   Oh, well have the droppings played their tricks!
Did he guess how toadstools grow, this fellow?
   Here's one stuck in his chapter six!

How did he like it when the live creatures
   Tickled and toused and browsed him all over,
And worm, slug, eft, with serious features,
   Came in, each one, for his right of trover?

—When the water-beetle with great blind deaf face
  Made of her eggs the stately deposit,
And the newt borrowed just so much of the preface
  As tiled in the top of his black wife's closet?

All that life and fun and romping,
  All that frisking and twisting and coupling,
While slowly our poor friend's leaves were swamping
  And clasps were cracking and covers suppling!
As if you had carried sour John Knox
  To the play-house at Paris, Vienna or Munich,
Fastened him into a front-row box,
  And danced off the ballet with trousers and tunic.

Come, old martyr! What, torment enough is it?
  Back to my room shall you take your sweet self.
Good-bye, mother-beetle; husband-eft, *sufficit!*
  See the snug niche I have made on my shelf!
A.'s book shall prop you up, B.'s shall cover you,
  Here's C. to be grave with, or D. to be gay,
And with E. on each side, and F. right over you,
  Dry-rot at ease till the Judgment-day!

ROBERT BROWNING

## *The Bishop Orders His Tomb*
## *at Saint Praxed's Church*
### *Rome, 15—*

Vanity, saith the preacher, vanity!
Draw round my bed: is Anselm keeping back?
Nephews—sons mine . . . ah God, I know not! Well—
She, men would have to be your mother once,
Old Gandolf envied me, so fair she was!
What's done is done, and she is dead beside,
Dead long ago, and I am Bishop since,
And as she died so must we die ourselves,
And thence ye may perceive the world's a dream.
Life, how and what is it? As here I lie
In this state-chamber, dying by degrees,
Hours and long hours in the dead night, I ask
'Do I live, am I dead?' Peace, peace seems all.

Saint Praxed's ever was the church for peace;
And so, about this tomb of mine. I fought
With tooth and nail to save my niche, ye know:
—Old Gandolf cozened me, despite my care;
Shrewd was that snatch from out the corner South
He graced his carrion with, God curse the same!
Yet still my niche is not so cramped but thence
One sees the pulpit o' the epistle-side,
And somewhat of the choir, those silent seats,
And up into the aery dome where live
The angels, and a sunbeam's sure to lurk:
And I shall fill my slab of basalt there,
And 'neath my tabernacle take my rest,
With those nine columns round me, two and two,
The odd one at my feet where Anselm stands:
Peach-blossom marble all, the rare, the ripe
As fresh-poured red wine of a mighty pulse.
—Old Gandolf with his paltry onion-stone,
Put me where I may look at him! True peach,
Rosy and flawless: how I earned the prize!
Draw close: that conflagration of my church
—What then? So much was saved if aught were missed!
My sons, ye would not be my death? Go dig
The white-grape vineyard where the oil-press stood,
Drop water gently till the surface sink,
And if ye find . . . Ah God, I know not, I! . . .
Bedded in store of rotten fig-leaves soft,
And corded up in a tight olive-frail,
Some lump, ah God, of *lapis lazuli*,
Big as a Jew's head cut off at the nape,
Blue as a vein o'er the Madonna's breast . . .
Sons, all have I bequeathed you, villas, all,
That brave Frascati villa with its bath,
So, let the blue lump poise between my knees,
Like God the Father's globe on both his hands
Ye worship in the Jesu Church so gay,
For Gandolf shall not choose but see and burst!
Swift as a weaver's shuttle fleet our years:
Man goeth to the grave, and where is he?
Did I say basalt for my slab, sons? Black—
'Twas ever antique-black I meant! How else
Shall ye contrast my frieze to come beneath?
The bas-relief in bronze ye promised me,
Those Pans and Nymphs ye wot of, and perchance
Some tripod, thyrsus, with a vase or so,
The Saviour at his sermon on the mount,

Saint Praxed in a glory, and one Pan
Ready to twitch the Nymph's last garment off,
And Moses with the tables . . . but I know
Ye mark me not! What do they whisper thee,
Child of my bowels, Anselm? Ah, ye hope
To revel down my villas while I gasp
Bricked o'er with beggar's mouldy travertine
Which Gandolf from his tomb-top chuckles at!
Nay, boys, ye love me—all of jasper, then!
'Tis jasper ye stand pledged to, lest I grieve.
My bath must needs be left behind, alas!
One block, pure green as a pistachio-nut,
There's plenty jasper somewhere in the world—
And have I not Saint Praxed's ear to pray
Horses for ye, and brown Greek manuscripts,
And mistresses with great smooth marbly limbs?
—That's if ye carve my epitaph aright,
Choice Latin, picked phrase, Tully's every word,
No gaudy ware like Gandolf's second line—
Tully, my masters? Ulpian serves his need!
And then how I shall lie through centuries,
And hear the blessed mutter of the mass,
And see God made and eaten all day long,
And feel the steady candle-flame, and taste
Good strong thick stupefying incense-smoke!
For as I lie here, hours of the dead night,
Dying in state and by such slow degrees,
I fold my arms as if they clasped a crook,
And stretch my feet forth straight as stone can point,
And let the bedclothes, for a mortcloth, drop
Into great laps and folds of sculptor's-work:
And as yon tapers dwindle, and strange thoughts
Grow, with a certain humming in my ears,
About the life before I lived this life,
And this life too, popes, cardinals and priests,
Saint Praxed at his sermon on the mount,
Your tall pale mother with her talking eyes,
And new-found agate urns as fresh as day,
And marble's language, Latin pure, discreet,
—Aha, ELUCESCEBAT quoth our friend?
No Tully, said I, Ulpian at the best!
Evil and brief hath been my pilgrimage.
All *lapis*, all, sons! Else I give the Pope
My villas! Will ye ever eat my heart?
Ever your eyes were as a lizard's quick,
They glitter like your mother's for my soul,

Or ye would heighten my impoverished frieze,
Piece out its starved design, and fill my vase
With grapes, and add a vizor and a Term,
And to the tripod ye would tie a lynx
That in his struggle throws the thyrsus down,
To comfort me on my entablature
Whereon I am to lie till I must ask
'Do I live, am I dead?' There, leave me, there!
For ye have stabbed me with ingratitude
To death—ye wish it—God, ye wish it! Stone—
Gritstone, a-crumble! Clammy squares which sweat
As if the corpse they keep were oozing through—
And no more *lapis* to delight the world!
Well go! I bless ye. Fewer tapers there,
But in a row: and, going, turn your backs
—Ay, like departing altar-ministrants,
And leave me in my church, the church for peace,
That I may watch at leisure if he leers—
Old Gandolf, at me, from his onion-stone,
As still he envied me, so fair she was!

ELIZABETH BARRETT BROWNING

From *Sonnets from the Portuguese*

I

I thought once how Theocritus had sung
Of the sweet years, the dear and wished-for years,
Who each one in a gracious hand appears
To bear a gift for mortals, old or young:
And, as I mused it in his antique tongue,
I saw, in gradual vision through my tears,
The sweet, sad years, the melancholy years,
Those of my own life, who by turns had flung
A shadow across me. Straightway I was 'ware,
So weeping, how a mystic Shape did move
Behind me, and drew me backward by the hair;
And a voice said in mastery, while I strove,—
'Guess now who holds thee?'—'Death', I said. But, there,
The silver answer rang,—'Not Death, but Love.'

### XVIII

I never gave a lock of hair away
To a man, Dearest, except this to thee,
Which now upon my fingers thoughtfully,
I ring out to the full brown length and say
'Take it.' My day of youth went yesterday;
My hair no longer bounds to my foot's glee,
Nor plant I it from rose or myrtle-tree,
As girls do, any more: it only may
Now shade on two pale cheeks the mark of tears,
Taught drooping from the head that hangs aside
Through sorrow's trick. I thought the funeral-shears
Would take this first, but Love is justified,—
Take it thou,—finding pure, from all those years,
The kiss my mother left here when she died.

### XLIII

How do I love thee? Let me count the ways.
I love thee to the depth and breadth and height
My soul can reach, when feeling out of sight
For the ends of Being and ideal Grace.
I love thee to the level of everyday's
Most quiet need, by sun and candle-light.
I love thee freely, as men strive for Right;
I love thee purely, as they turn from Praise.
I love thee with the passion put to use
In my old griefs, and with my childhood's faith.
I love thee with a love I seemed to lose
With my lost saints,—I love thee with the breath,
Smiles, tears, of all my life!—and, if God choose,
I shall but love thee better after death.

### XLIV

Belovèd, thou has brought me many flowers
Plucked in the garden, all the summer through
And winter, and it seemed as if they grew
In this close room, nor missed the sun and showers.
So, in the like name of that love of ours,
Take back these thoughts which here unfolded too,
And which on warm and cold days I withdrew
From my heart's ground. Indeed, those beds and bowers

Be overgrown with bitter weeds and rue,
And wait thy weeding; yet here's eglantine,
Here's ivy!—take them, as I used to do
Thy flowers, and keep them where they shall not pine.
Instruct thine eyes to keep their colours true,
And tell thy soul their roots are left in mine.


EMILY JANE BRONTË

## R. Alcona to J. Brenzaida

Cold in the earth, and the deep snow piled above thee!
Far, far removed, cold in the dreary grave!
Have I forgot, my Only Love, to love thee,
Severed at last by Time's all-wearing wave?

Now, when alone, do my thoughts no longer hover
Over the mountains on Angora's shore;
Resting their wings where heath and fern-leaves cover
That noble heart for ever, ever more?

Cold in the earth, and fifteen wild Decembers
From those brown hills have melted into spring—
Faithful indeed is the spirit that remembers
After such years of change and suffering!

Sweet Love of youth, forgive if I forget thee
While the World's tide is bearing me along:
Sterner desires and darker hopes beset me,
Hopes which obscure but cannot do thee wrong.

No other Sun has lightened up my heaven;
No other Star has ever shone for me:
All my life's bliss from thy dear life was given—
All my life's bliss is in the grave with thee.

But when the days of golden dreams had perished
And even Despair was powerless to destroy,
Then did I learn how existence could be cherished,
Strengthened and fed without the aid of joy;

Then did I check the tears of useless passion,
Weaned my young soul from yearning after thine;
Sternly denied its burning wish to hasten
Down to that tomb already more than mine!

And even yet, I dare not let it languish,
Dare not indulge in Memory's rapturous pain;
Once drinking deep of that divinest anguish,
How could I seek the empty world again?

EMILY JANE BRONTË

## *Love and Friendship*

Love is like the wild rose-briar,
Friendship like the holly tree—
The holly is dark when the rose-briar blooms
But which will bloom most constantly?

The wild rose-briar is sweet in spring,
Its summer blossoms scent the air;
Yet wait till winter comes again
And who will call the wild-briar fair?

Then scorn the silly rose-wreath now
And deck thee with the holly's sheen,
That when December blights thy brow
He still may leave thy garland green.

EMILY JANE BRONTË

In summer's mellow midnight,
A cloudless moon shone through
Our open parlour window
And rosetrees wet with dew.

I sat in silent musing,
The soft wind waved my hair:
It told me Heaven was glorious,
And sleeping Earth was fair.

I needed not its breathing
To bring such thoughts to me,
But still it whispered lowly,
'How dark the woods will be!

'The thick leaves in my murmur
Are rustling like a dream,
And all their myriad voices
Instinct with spirit seem.'

I said, 'Go, gentle singer,
Thy wooing voice is kind,
But do not think its music
Has power to reach my mind.

'Play with the scented flower,
The young tree's supple bough,
And leave my human feelings
In their own course to flow.'

The wanderer would not leave me;
Its kiss grew warmer still—
'O come,' it sighed so sweetly,
'I'll win thee 'gainst thy will.

'Have we not been from childhood friends?
Have I not loved thee long?
As long as thou hast loved the night
Whose silence wakes my song.

'And when thy heart is laid at rest
Beneath the church-yard stone
I shall have time enough to mourn
And thou to be alone.'


EMILY JANE BRONTË


Death, that struck when I was most confiding
In my certain Faith of Joy to be,
Strike again, Time's withered branch dividing
From the fresh root of Eternity!

Leaves, upon Time's branch, were growing brightly,
Full of sap and full of silver dew;
Birds, beneath its shelter, gathered nightly;
Daily, round its flowers, the wild bees flew.

Sorrow passed and plucked the golden blossom,
Guilt stripped off the foliage in its pride;
But, within its parent's kindly bosom,
Flowed forever Life's restoring tide.

Little mourned I for the parted Gladness,
For the vacant nest and silent song;
Hope was there and laughed me out of sadness,
Whispering, 'Winter will not linger long.'

And behold, with tenfold increase blessing
Spring adorned the beauty-burdened spray;
Wind and rain and fervent heat caressing
Lavished glory on its second May.

High it rose; no wingèd grief could sweep it;
Sin was scared to distance with its shine:
Love and its own life had power to keep it
From all wrong, from every blight but thine!

Heartless Death, the young leaves droop and languish!
Evening's gentle air may still restore—
No: the morning sunshine mocks my anguish—
Time for me must never blossom more!

Strike it down, that other boughs may flourish
Where that perished sapling used to be;
Thus, at least, its mouldering corpse will nourish
That from which it sprung—Eternity.


EMILY JANE BRONTË


No coward soul is mine
No trembler in the world's storm-troubled sphere
I see Heaven's glories shine
And Faith shines equal arming me from Fear

O God within my breast
Almighty ever-present Deity
Life, that in me hast rest
As I Undying Life, have power in Thee

Vain are the thousand creeds
That move men's hearts, unutterably vain,
Worthless as withered weeds
Or idlest froth amid the boundless main

To waken doubt in one
Holding so fast by thy infinity
So surely anchored on
The steadfast rock of Immortality

With wide-embracing love
Thy spirit animates eternal years
Pervades and broods above,
Changes, sustains, dissolves, creates and rears

Though Earth and moon were gone
And suns and universes ceased to be
And thou wert left alone
Every Existence would exist in thee

There is not room for Death
Nor atom that his might could render void
Since thou art Being and Breath
And what thou art may never be destroyed.


HENRY FRANCIS LYTE

## Abide with Me

Abide with me; fast falls the eventide;
The darkness deepens; Lord, with me abide,
When other helpers fail, and comforts flee,
Help of the helpless, O abide with me.

Swift to its close ebbs out life's little day;
Earth's joys grow dim, its glories pass away;
Change and decay in all around I see:
O Thou who changest not, abide with me!

I need Thy presence every passing hour;
What but Thy grace can foil the tempter's power?
Who like Thyself my guide and stay can be?
Through cloud and sunshine, O abide with me.

I fear no foe, with Thee at hand to bless;
Ills have no weight, and tears no bitterness;
Where is death's sting? where, grave, thy victory?
I triumph still, if Thou abide with me.

Hold Thou Thy Cross before my closing eyes,
Shine through the gloom, and point me to the skies;
Heaven's morning breaks, and earth's vain shadows flee:
In life, in death, O Lord, abide with me!

ALFRED, LORD TENNYSON

## From *The Princess*

The splendour falls on castle walls
    And snowy summits old in story:
The long light shakes across the lakes,
    And the wild cataract leaps in glory.
Blow, bugle, blow, set the wild echoes flying,
Blow, bugle; answer, echoes, dying, dying, dying.

    O hark, O hear! how thin and clear,
      And thinner, clearer, farther going!
    O sweet and far from cliff and scar
      The horns of Elfland faintly blowing!
Blow, let us hear the purple glens replying:
Blow, bugle; answer, echoes, dying, dying, dying.

    O love, they die in yon rich sky,
      They faint on hill or field or river:
    Our echoes roll from soul to soul,
      And grow for ever and for ever.
Blow, bugle, blow, set the wild echoes flying,
And answer, echoes, answer, dying, dying, dying.


'There sinks the nebulous star we call the Sun,
If that hypothesis of theirs be sound'
Said Ida; 'let us down and rest; and we
Down from the lean and wrinkled precipices,
By every coppice-feathered chasm and cleft,
Dropped through the ambrosial gloom to where below
No bigger than a glow-worm shone the tent
Lamp-lit from the inner. Once she leaned on me,
Descending; once or twice she lent her hand,
And blissful palpitations in the blood,
Stirring a sudden transport rose and fell.

    But when we planted level feet, and dipped
Beneath the satin dome and entered in,
There leaning deep in broidered down we sank
Our elbows: on a tripod in the midst
A fragrant flame rose, and before us glowed
Fruit, blossom, viand, amber wine, and gold.

    Then she, 'Let some one sing to us: lightlier move
The minutes fledged with music:' and a maid,
Of those beside her, smote her harp, and sang.

'Tears, idle tears, I know not what they mean,
Tears from the depth of some divine despair
Rise in the heart, and gather to the eyes,
In looking on the happy Autumn-fields,
And thinking of the days that are no more.

'Fresh as the first beam glittering on a sail,
That brings our friends up from the underworld,
Sad as the last which reddens over one
That sinks with all we love below the verge;
So sad, so fresh, the days that are no more.

'Ah, sad and strange as in dark summer dawns
The earliest pipe of half-awakened birds
To dying ears, when unto dying eyes
The casement slowly grows a glimmering square;
So sad, so strange, the days that are no more.

.  .  .

Deep in the night I woke: she, near me, held
A volume of the Poets of her land:
There to herself, all in low tones, she read.

'Now sleeps the crimson petal, now the white;
Nor waves the cypress in the palace walk;
Nor winks the gold fin in the porphyry font:
The fire-fly wakens: waken thou with me.

Now droops the milkwhite peacock like a ghost,
And like a ghost she glimmers on to me.

Now lies the Earth all Danaë to the stars,
And all thy heart lies open unto me.

Now slides the silent meteor on, and leaves
A shining furrow, as thy thoughts in me.

Now folds the lily all her sweetness up,
And slips into the bosom of the lake:
So fold thyself, my dearest, thou, and slip
Into my bosom and be lost in me.'

I heard her turn the page; she found a small
Sweet Idyl, and once more, as low, she read:

'Come down, O maid, from yonder mountain height:
What pleasure lives in height (the shepherd sang)
In height and cold, the splendour of the hills?
But cease to move so near the Heavens, and cease
To glide a sunbeam by the blasted Pine,
To sit a star upon the sparkling spire;
And come, for Love is of the valley, come,
For Love is of the valley, come thou down
And find him; by the happy threshold, he,
Or hand in hand with Plenty in the maize,
Or red with spirted purple of the vats,
Or foxlike in the vine; nor cares to walk
With Death and Morning on the silver horns,
Nor wilt thou snare him in the white ravine,
Nor find him dropped upon the firths of ice,
That huddling slant in furrow-cloven falls
To roll the torrent out of dusky doors:
But follow; let the torrent dance thee down
To find him in the valley; let the wild
Lean-headed Eagles yelp alone, and leave
The monstrous ledges there to slope, and spill
Their thousand wreaths of dangling water-smoke,
That like a broken purpose waste in air:
So waste not thou; but come; for all the vales
Await thee; azure pillars of the hearth
Arise to thee; the children call, and I
Thy shepherd pipe, and sweet is every sound,
Sweeter thy voice, but every sound is sweet;
Myriads of rivulets hurrying through the lawn,
The moan of doves in immemorial elms,
And murmuring of innumerable bees.'

   So she low-toned; while with shut eyes I lay
Listening; then looked. Pale was the perfect face;
The bosom with long sighs laboured; and meek
Seemed the full lips, and mild the luminous eyes,
And the voice trembled and the hand. She said
Brokenly, that she knew it, she had failed
In sweet humility; had failed in all;
That all her labour was but as a block
Left in the quarry; but she still were loth,
Still still were loth to yield herself to one
That wholly scorned to help their equal rights
Against the sons of men, and barbarous laws.

DANTE GABRIEL ROSSETTI

## *The Blessed Damozel*

The blessed damozel leaned out
  From the gold bar of Heaven;
Her eyes were deeper than the depth
  Of waters stilled at even;
She had three lilies in her hand,
  And the stars in her hair were seven.

Her robe, ungirt from clasp to hem,
  No wrought flowers did adorn,
But a white rose of Mary's gift,
  For service meetly worn;
Her hair that lay along her back
  Was yellow like ripe corn.

Herseemed she scarce had been a day
  One of God's choristers;
The wonder was not yet quite gone
  From that still look of hers;
Albeit, to them she left, her day
  Had counted as ten years.

(To one, it is ten years of years.
  . . . Yet now, and in this place,
Surely she leaned o'er me—her hair
  Fell all about my face. . . .
Nothing: the autumn fall of leaves.
  The whole year sets apace.)

It was the rampart of God's house
  That she was standing on;
By God built over the sheer depth
  The which is Space begun;
So high, that looking downward thence
  She scarce could see the sun.

It lies in Heaven, across the flood
  Of ether, as a bridge.
Beneath, the tides of day and night
  With flame and darkness ridge
The void, as low as where this earth
  Spins like a fretful midge.

Heard hardly, some of her new friends
 Amid their loving games
Spake evermore among themselves
 Their virginal chaste names;
And the souls mounting up to God
 Went by her like thin flames.

And still she bowed herself and stooped
 Out of the circling charm;
Until her bosom must have made
 The bar she leaned on warm,
And the lilies lay as if asleep
 Along her bended arm.

From the fixed place of Heaven she saw
 Time like a pulse shake fierce
Through all the worlds. Her gaze still strove
 Within the gulf to pierce
Its path: and now she spoke as when
 The stars sang in their spheres.

The sun was gone now; the curled moon
 Was like a little feather
Fluttering far down the gulf; and now
 She spoke through the still weather.
Her voice was like the voice the stars
 Had when they sang together.

(Ah sweet! Even now, in that bird's song,
 Strove not her accents there,
Fain to be hearkened? When those bells
 Possessed the mid-day air,
Strove not her steps to reach my side
 Down all the echoing stair?)

'I wish that he were come to me,
 For he will come,' she said.
'Have I not prayed in Heaven?—on earth,
 Lord, Lord, has he not prayed?
Are not two prayers a perfect strength?
 And shall I feel afraid?

'When round his head the aureole clings,
 And he is clothed in white,
I'll take his hand and go with him
 To the deep wells of light;
We will step down as to a stream,
 And bathe there in God's sight.

'We two will stand beside that shrine,
     Occult, withheld, untrod,
Whose lamps are stirred continually
     With prayer sent up to God;
And see our old prayers, granted, melt
     Each like a little cloud.

'We two will lie i' the shadow of
     That living mystic tree
Within whose secret growth the Dove
     Is sometimes felt to be,
While every leaf that His plumes touch
     Saith His Name audibly.

'And I myself will teach to him,
     I myself, lying so,
The songs I sing here; which his voice
     Shall pause in, hushed and slow,
And find some knowledge at each pause,
     Or some new thing to know.'

(Alas! We two, we two, thou say'st!
     Yea, one wast thou with me
That once of old. But shall God lift
     To endless unity
The soul whose likeness with thy soul
     Was but its love for thee?)

'We two,' she said, 'will seek the groves
     Where the lady Mary is,
With her five handmaidens, whose names
     Are five sweet symphonies,
Cecily, Gertrude, Magdalen,
     Margaret and Rosalys.

'Circlewise sit they, with bound locks
     And foreheads garlanded;
Into the fine cloth white like flame
     Weaving the golden thread,
To fashion the birth-robes for them
     Who are just born, being dead.

'He shall fear, haply, and be dumb:
     Then will I lay my cheek
To his, and tell about our love,
     Not once abashed or weak:
And the dear Mother will approve
     My pride, and let me speak.

'Herself shall bring us, hand in hand,
   To Him round whom all souls
Kneel, the clear-ranged unnumbered heads
   Bowed with their aureoles;
And angels meeting us shall sing
   To their citherns and citoles.

'There will I ask of Christ the Lord
   Thus much for him and me:—
Only to live as once on earth
   With Love,—only to be,
As then awhile, for ever now
   Together, I and he.'

She gazed and listened and then said,
   Less sad of speech than mild,—
'All this is when he comes.' She ceased.
   The light thrilled towards her, filled
With angels in strong level flight.
   Her eyes prayed, and she smiled.

(I saw her smile.) But soon their path
   Was vague in distant spheres:
And then she cast her arms along
   The golden barriers,
And laid her face between her hands,
   And wept. (I heard her tears.)


CHARLES TENNYSON-TURNER

## Wind on the Corn


Full often as I rove by path or stile,
To watch the harvest ripening in the vale,
Slowly and sweetly, like a growing smile—
A smile that ends in laughter—the quick gale
Upon the breadths of gold-green wheat descends;
While still the swallow, with unbaffled grace,
About his viewless quarry dips and bends—
And all the fine excitement of the chase
Lies in the hunter's beauty: in the eclipse
Of that brief shadow, how the barley's beard
Tilts at the passing gloom, and wild-rose dips
Among the white-tops in the ditches reared:
And hedgerow's flowery breast of lacework stirs
Faintly in that full wind that rocks the outstanding firs.

CHARLES TENNYSON-TURNER

## Old Ruralities
### A Regret

With joy all relics of the past I hail;
The heath-bell, lingering in our cultured moor,
Or the dull sound of the slip-shouldered flail,
Still busy on the poor man's threshing-floor:
I love this unshorn hedgerow, which survives
Its stunted neighbours, in this farming age:
The thatch and house-leek, where old Alice lives
With her old herbal, trusting every page;
I love the spinning-wheel, which hums far down
In yon lone valley, though, from day to day,
The boom of Science shakes it from the town.
Ah! sweet old world! thou speedest fast away!
My boyhood's world! but all last looks are dear;
More touching is the death-bed than the bier!

CHARLES TENNYSON-TURNER

## Old Stephen

He served his master well from youth to age;
Who gave him then a little plot of land,
Enough a busy spirit to engage,
Too small to overtax an aged hand.
Old Stephen's memory hallows all the ground;
He made this thrifty lawn so spruce and small,
Dial and seat within its narrow bound,
And both half-hid with woodbine from the Hall.
But he is gone at last: how meek he lay
That night, and prayed his dying hours away—
When the sun rose he ceased to breathe and feel:
Day broke—his eyes were on a lovelier dawn,
While ours beheld the sweet May morning steal
Across his dial and his orphan lawn.

CHARLES MACKAY

## The Mowers
### *An Anticipation of the Cholera, 1848*

Dense on the stream the vapours lay,
Thick as wool on the cold highway;
Spongy and dim each lonely lamp
Shone o'er the streets so dull and damp;
The moonbeam could not pierce the cloud
That swathed the city like a shroud.
There stood three Shapes on the bridge alone,
Three figures by the coping stone;
Gaunt, and tall, and undefined,
Spectres built of mist and wind;
Changing ever in form and height,
But black and palpable to sight.

'This is a city fair to see,'
Whispered one of the fearful three;
'A mighty tribute it pays to me.
Into its river, winding slow,
    Thick and foul from shore to shore,
The vessels come, the vessels go,
    And teeming lands their riches pour.
It spreads beneath the murky sky
A wilderness of masonry;

'Huge, unshapely, overgrown,
Dingy brick and blackened stone.
Mammon is its chief and lord,
Monarch slavishly adored;
Mammon sitting side by side
With Pomp, and Luxury, and Pride;
Who call his large dominions theirs,
Nor dream a portion is Despair's.

'Countless thousands bend to me
    In rags and purple, in hovel and hall,
And pay the tax of misery
    With tears, and blood, and spoken gall.
Whenever they cry
For aid to die,
I give them courage to dare the worst,
And leave their ban on a world accurst.

I show them the river so black and deep,
They take the plunge, they sink to sleep;
I show them poison, I show them rope,
They rush to death without a hope.
Poison, and rope, and pistol ball,
Welcome either, welcome all!
I am the lord of the teeming town—
*I mow them down, I mow them down!*'

'Aye thou art great, but greater I,'
The second spectre made reply;
'Thou rulest with a frown austere,
Thy name is synonym of Fear.
But I, despotic and hard as thou,
Have a laughing lip, an open brow.
I build a temple in every lane,
I have a palace in every street;
And the victims throng to the doors amain,
And wallow like swine beneath my feet.
To me the strong man gives his health,
The wise man reason, the rich man wealth,
Maids their virtue, youth its charms,
And mothers the children in their arms.
Thou art a slayer of mortal men—
Thou of the unit, I of the ten;
Great thou art, but greater I,
To decimate humanity.
'Tis *I* am the lord of the teeming town—
*I mow them down, I mow them down!*'

Vain boasters to exult at death,'
   The third replied, 'so feebly done;
I ope my jaws, and with a breath
   Slay thousands while you think of one.
All the blood that Caesar spilled,
   All that Alexander drew,
All the hosts by "glory" killed,
   From Agincourt to Waterloo,
Compared with those whom I have slain,
Are but a river to the main.

'I brew disease in stagnant pools,
   And wandering here, disporting there,
Favoured much by knaves and fools,
   I poison streams, I taint the air;
I shake from my locks the spreading pest,
I keep the typhus at my behest;
In filth and slime
I crawl, I climb,

I find the workman at his trade,
  I blow on his lips, and down he lies;
I look in the face of the ruddiest maid,
    And straight the fire forsakes her eyes—
    She droops, she sickens, and she dies;
I stint the growth of babes new born,
Or shear them off like standing corn;
I rob the sunshine of its glow,
I poison all the winds that blow;
Whenever they pass they suck my breath,
And freight their wings with certain death.
'Tis *I* am the lord of the crowded town—
*I mow them down, I mow them down!*

'But great as we are, there cometh one
  Greater than you—greater than I,
To aid the deeds that shall be done,
To end the work that we've begun,
  And thin this thick humanity.
I see his footmarks east and west,
  I hear his tread in the silence fall,

'He shall not sleep, he shall not rest—
  He comes to aid us one and all.
Were men as wise as men might be,
They would not work for you, for me,
For him that cometh over the sea;
But they will not heed the warning voice.
The Cholera comes, rejoice! rejoice!
*He* shall be lord of the swarming town,
*And mow them down, and mow them down!'*


CHARLES MACKAY

## The Poor Man's Sunday Walk

The morning of our rest has come,
  The sun is shining clear;
I see it on the steeple-top:
  Put on your shawl, my dear,
And let us leave the smoky town,
  The dense and stagnant lane,
And take our children by the hand
  To see the fields again.

I've pined for air the live-long week;
    For the smell of new-mown hay;
For a pleasant, quiet, country walk,
    On a sunny Sabbath day.

Our parish church is cold and damp;
I need the air and sun;
We'll sit together on the grass,
    And see the children run.
We'll watch them gathering buttercups,
    Or cowslips in the dell,
Or listen to the cheerful sounds
    Of the far-off village bell;
And thank our God with grateful hearts,
    Though in the fields we pray;
And bless the healthful breeze of heaven,
    On a sunny Sabbath day.

I'm weary of the stifling room,
    Where all the week we're pent;
Of the alley filled with wretched life,
    And odours pestilent.
And long once more to see the fields,
    And the grazing sheep and beeves;
To hear the lark amid the clouds,
    And the wind among the leaves;
And all the sounds that glad the air
    On green hills far away:—
The sounds that breathe of Peace and Love,
    On a sunny Sabbath day.

For somehow, though they call it wrong,
    In church I cannot kneel
With half the natural thankfulness
    And piety I feel,
When out, on such a day as this,
    I lie upon the sod,
And think that every leaf and flower
    Is grateful to its God:
That I, who feel the blessing more,
    Should thank him more than they,
That I can elevate my soul
    On a sunny Sabbath day.

Put on your shawl, and let us go;—
    For one day let us think
Of something else than daily care,
    Of toil, and meat, and drink:

For one day let our children sport
  And feel their limbs their own;
For one day let us quite forget
  The grief that we have known:—
Let us forget that we are poor;
  And, basking in the ray,
Thank God that we can still enjoy
  A sunny Sabbath day.

CHARLES MACKAY

## The Three Preachers

There are three preachers, ever preaching,
  Filled with eloquence and power:—
One is old, with locks of white,
Skinny as an anchorite;
  And he preaches every hour
With a shrill fanatic voice,
  And a bigot's fiery scorn:—
'BACKWARD! ye presumptuous nations;
  Man to misery is born!
Born to drudge, and sweat, and suffer—
  Born to labour and to pray;
BACKWARD! Ye presumptuous nations—
  Back!—be humble and obey!'

The second is a milder preacher;
  Soft he talks as if he sung;
Sleek and slothful is his look,
And his words, as from a book,
  Issue glibly from his tongue.
With an air of self-content,
  High he lifts his fair white hands:
'STAND YE STILL! ye restless nations;
  And be happy, all ye lands!
Fate is law, and law is perfect;
  If ye meddle, ye will mar;
Change is rash, and ever was so:
  We are happy as we are.'

Mightier is the younger preacher,
  Genius flashes from his eyes;
And the crowds who hear his voice,
Give him, while their souls rejoice,
  Throbbing bosoms for replies.
Awed they listen, yet elated,
  While his stirring accents fall:—
'FORWARD! ye deluded nations,
  Progress is the rule of all:
Man was made for healthful effort;
  Tyranny has crushed him long;
He shall march from good to better,
  And do battle with the wrong.

'Standing still is childish folly,
  Going backward is a crime:
None should patiently endure
Any ill that he can cure;
  ONWARD! keep the march of Time.
Onward! while a wrong remains
  To be conquered by the right;
While Oppression lifts a finger
  To affront us by his might;
While an error clouds the reason
  Of the universal heart,
Or a slave awaits his freedom,
  Action is the wise man's part.

'Lo! the world is rich in blessings:
  Earth and Ocean, flame and wind,
Have unnumbered secrets still,
To be ransacked when you will,
  For the service of mankind.
Science is a child as yet,
  And her power and scope shall grow,
And her triumphs in the future
  Shall diminish toil and woe;
Shall extend the bounds of pleasure
  With an ever-widening ken,
And of woods and wildernesses
  Make the homes of happy men.

'ONWARD!—there are ills to conquer,
  Daily wickedness is wrought,
Tyranny is swoln with Pride,
Bigotry is deified,
  Error interwined with Thought.

Vice and Misery ramp and crawl;—
   Root them out, their day has passed;
Goodness is alone immortal;
   Evil was not made to last:
ONWARD! and all Earth shall aid us
   Ere our peaceful flag be furled.'—
And the preaching of this preacher
   Stirs the pulses of the world.


ARTHUR HUGH CLOUGH

## *Duty*


Duty—that's to say, complying,
   With whate'er's expected here;
On your unknown cousin's dying,
   Straight be ready with the tear;
Upon etiquette relying,
Unto usage nought denying,
Lend your waist to be embraced,
   Blush not even, never fear;
Claims of kith and kin connection,
   Claims of manners honour still,
Ready money of affection
   Pay, whoever drew the bill.
With the form conforming duly,
Senseless what it meaneth truly,
Go to church—the world require you,
   To balls—the world require you too,
And marry—papa and mamma desire you,
   And your sisters and schoolfellows do.
Duty—'tis to take on trust
What things are good, and right, and just;
   And whether indeed they be or be not,
   Try not, test not, feel not, see not:
   'Tis walk and dance, sit down and rise
   By leading, opening ne'er your eyes;
Stunt sturdy limbs that Nature gave,
And be drawn in a Bath chair along to the grave.
'Tis the stern and prompt suppressing,
   As an obvious deadly sin,
All the questing and the guessing
   Of the soul's own soul within:

'Tis the coward acquiescence
   In a destiny's behest,
To a shade by terror made,
Sacrificing, aye, the essence
   Of all that's truest, noblest, best:
'Tis the blind non-recognition
   Or of goodness, truth, or beauty,
Save by precept and submission;
   Moral blank, and moral void,
   Life at very birth destroyed.
Atrophy, exinanition!
Duty!
Yea, by duty's prime condition
   Pure nonentity of duty!

ARTHUR HUGH CLOUGH

## Sic Itur

As, at a railway junction, men
Who came together, taking then
One the train up, one down, again

Meet never! Ah, much more as they
Who take one street's two sides, and say
Hard parting words, but walk one way:

Though moving other mates between,
While carts and coaches intervene,
Each to the other goes unseen;

Yet seldom, surely, shall there lack
Knowledge they walk not back to back,
But with an unity of track,

Where common dangers each attend,
And common hopes their guidance lend
To light them to the self-same end.

Whether he then shall cross to thee,
Or thou go thither, or it be
Some midway point, ye yet shall see

Each other, yet again shall meet.
Ah, joy! when with the closing street,
Forgivingly at last ye greet!

ARTHUR HUGH CLOUGH

## *Say Not the Struggle Nought Availeth*

Say not, the struggle nought availeth,
   The labour and the wounds are vain,
The enemy faints not, nor faileth,
   And as things have been they remain.

If hopes were dupes, fears may be liars;
   It may be, in yon smoke concealed,
Your comrades chase e'en now the fliers,
   And, but for you, possess the field.

For while the tired waves, vainly breaking,
   Seem here no painful inch to gain,
Far back, through creeks and inlets making,
   Comes silent, flooding in, the main.

And not by eastern windows only,
   When daylight comes, comes in the light,
In front, the sun climbs slow, how slowly,
   But westward, look, the land is bright.

ARTHUR HUGH CLOUGH

## From *Amours de Voyage*

### *Canto I*

#### I  Claude to Eustace

Dear Eustatio, I write that you may write me an answer,
Or at the least to put us again *en rapport* with each other.
Rome disappoints me much,— St Peter's, perhaps, in especial;
Only the Arch of Titus and view from the Lateran please me:
This, however, perhaps is the weather, which truly is horrid.
Greece must be better, surely; and yet I am feeling so spiteful,
That I could travel to Athens, to Delphi, and Troy, and Mount Sinai,
Though but to see with my eyes that these are vanity also.
   Rome disappoints me much; I hardly as yet understand, but
*Rubbishy* seems the word that most exactly would suit it.
All the foolish destructions, and all the sillier savings,
All the incongruous things of past incompatible ages,
Seem to be treasured up here to make fools of present and future.

Would to Heaven the old Goths had made a cleaner sweep of it!
Would to Heaven some new ones would come and destroy these churches!
However, one can live in Rome as also in London.
It is a blessing, no doubt, to be rid, at least for a time, of
All one's friends and relations,—yourself (forgive me!) included,—
All the *assujettissement* of having been what one has been,
What one thinks one is, or thinks that others suppose one;
Yet, in despite of all, we turn like fools to the English.
Vernon has been my fate; who is here the same that you knew him,—
Making the tour, it seems, with friends of the name of Trevellyn.


### II  Claude to Eustace

Rome disappoints me still; but I shrink and adapt myself to it.
Somehow a tyrannous sense of a superincumbent oppression
Still, wherever I go, accompanies ever, and makes me
Feel like a tree (shall I say?) buried under a ruin of brickwork.
Rome, believe me, my friend, is like its own Monte Testaceo,
Merely a marvellous mass of broken and castaway wine-pots.
Ye gods! what do I want with this rubbish of ages departed,
Things that nature abhors, the experiments that she has failed in?
What do I find in the Forum? An archway and two or three pillars.
Well, but St Peter's? Alas, Bernini has filled it with sculpture!
No one can cavil, I grant, at the size of the great Coliseum.
Doubtless the notion of grand and capacious and massive amusement,
This the old Romans had; but tell me, is this an idea?
Yet of solidity much, but of splendour little is extant:
'Brickwork I found thee, and marble I left thee!' their Emperor vaunted;
'Marble I thought thee, and brickwork I find thee!' the Tourist may answer.


### From *Canto II*

### I  Claude to Eustace

What do the people say, and what does the government do?—you
Ask, and I know not at all. Yet fortune will favour your hopes; and
I, who avoided it all, am fated, it seems, to describe it.
I, who nor meddle nor make in politics,—I who sincerely
Put not my trust in leagues nor any suffrage by ballot,
Never predicted Parisian millenniums, never beheld a
New Jerusalem coming down dressed like a bride out of heaven
Right on the Place de la Concorde,—I, nevertheless, let me say it,
Could in my soul of souls, this day, with the Gaul at the gates shed
One true tear for thee, thou poor little Roman Republic;
What, with the German restored, with Sicily safe to the Bourbon,

Not leave one poor corner for native Italian exertion?
France, it is foully done! and you, poor foolish England,—
You, who a twelvemonth ago said nations must choose for themselves, you
Could not, of course, interfere,—you, now, when a nation has chosen—
Pardon this folly! The *Times* will, of course, have announced the occasion,
Told you the news of to-day; and although it was slightly in error
When it proclaimed as a fact the Apollo was sold to a Yankee,
You may believe when it tells you the French are at Civita Vecchia.

### II   Claude to Eustace

*Dulce* it is, and *decorum*, no doubt, for the country to fall,—to
Offer one's blood an oblation to Freedom, and die for the Cause; yet
Still, individual culture is also something, and no man
Finds quite distinct the assurance that he of all others is called on,
Or would be justified even, in taking away from the world that
Precious creature, himself. Nature sent him here to abide here;
Else why send him at all? Nature wants him still, it is likely;
On the whole, we are meant to look after ourselves; it is certain
Each has to eat for himself, digest for himself, and in general
Care for his own dear life, and see to his own preservation;
Nature's intentions, in most things uncertain, in this are decisive;
Which, on the whole, I conjecture the Romans will follow, and I shall.
   So we cling to our rocks like limpets; Ocean may bluster,
Over and under and round us; we open our shells to imbibe our
Nourishment, close them again, and are safe, fulfilling the purpose
Nature intended,—a wise one, of course, and a noble, we doubt not.
Sweet it may be and decorous, perhaps, for the country to die; but,
On the whole, we conclude the Romans won't do it, and I sha'n't.

### V   Claude to Eustace

Yes, we are fighting at last, it appears. This morning as usual,
*Murray*, as usual, in hand, I enter the Caffè Nuovo;
Seating myself with a sense as it were of a change in the weather,
Not understanding, however, but thinking mostly of Murray,
And, for to-day is their day, of the Campidoglio Marbles;
*Caffè-latte!* I call to the waiter,—and *Non c' è latte,*
This is the answer he makes me, and this is the sign of a battle.
So I sit; and truly they seem to think anyone else more
Worthy than me of attention. I wait for my milkless *nero*,
Free to observe undistracted all sorts and sizes of persons,
Blending civilian and soldier in strangest costume, coming in, and
Gulping in hottest haste, still standing, their coffee,—withdrawing
Eagerly, jangling a sword on the steps, or jogging a musket
Slung to the shoulder behind. They are fewer, moreover, than usual,

Much and silenter far; and so I begin to imagine
Something is really afloat. Ere I leave, the Caffè is empty,
Empty too the streets, in all its length the Corso
Empty, and empty I see to my right and left the Condotti.

   Twelve o'clock, on the Pincian Hill, with lots of English,
Germans, Americans, French,—the Frenchmen, too, are protected,—
So we stand in the sun, but afraid of a probable shower;
So we stand and stare, and see, to the left of St Peter's,
Smoke, from the cannon, white,—but that is at intervals only,—
Black, from a burning house, we suppose, by the Cavalleggieri;
And we believe we discern some lines of men descending
Down through the vineyard-slopes, and catch a bayonet gleaming.
Every ten minutes, however,—in this there is no misconception,—
Comes a great white puff from behind Michel Angelo's dome, and
After a space the report of a real big gun,—not the Frenchman's!—
That must be doing some work. And so we watch and conjecture.

   Shortly, an Englishman comes, who says he has been to St Peter's,
Seen the Piazza and troops, but that is all he can tell us;
So we watch and sit, and, indeed, it begins to be tiresome.—
All this smoke is outside; when it has come to the inside,
It will be time, perhaps, to descend and retreat to our houses.

   Half-past one, or two. The report of small arms frequent,
Sharp and savage indeed; that cannot all be for nothing:
So we watch and wonder; but guessing is tiresome, very.
Weary of wondering, watching, and guessing, and gossiping idly,
Down I go, and pass through the quiet streets with the knots of
National Guards patrolling, and flags hanging out at the windows,
English, American, Danish,—and, after offering to help an
Irish family moving *en masse* to the Maison Serny,
After endeavouring idly to minister balm to the trembling
Quinquagenarian fears of two lone British spinsters,
Go to make sure of my dinner before the enemy enter.
But by this there are signs of stragglers returning; and voices
Talk, though you don't believe it, of guns and prisoners taken;
And on the walls you read the first bulletin of the morning.—
That is all that I saw, and all I know of the battle.


### VI   Claude to Eustace

VICTORY! VICTORY!—Yes! ah, yes, thou republican Zion,
Truly the kings of the earth are gathered and gone by together;
Doubtless they marvelled to witness such things, were astonished,
      and so forth.
Victory! Victory! Victory!—Ah, but it is, believe me,
Easier, easier far, to intone the chant of the martyr
Than to indite any paean of any victory. Death may
Sometimes be noble; but life, at the best, will appear an illusion.

While the great pain is upon us, it is great; when it is over,
Why, it is over. The smoke of the sacrifice rises to heaven,
Of a sweet savour, no doubt, to Somebody; but on the altar,
Lo, there is nothing remaining but ashes and dirt and ill odour.
 So it stands, you perceive; the labial muscles that swelled with
Vehement evolution of yesterday Marseillaises,
Articulations sublime of defiance and scorning, to-day col-
Lapse and languidly mumble, while men and women and papers
Scream and re-scream to each other the chorus of Victory. Well, but
I am thankful they fought, and glad that the Frenchmen were beaten.

### VII   Claude to Eustace

So, I have seen a man killed! An experience that, among others!
Yes, I suppose I have; although I can hardly be certain,
And in a court of justice could never declare I had seen it.
But a man was killed, I am told, in a place where I saw
Something; a man was killed, I am told, and I saw something.
 I was returning home from St Peter's; Murray, as usual,
Under my arm, I remember; had crossed the St Angelo bridge; and
Moving towards the Condotti, had got to the first barricade, when
Gradually, thinking still of St Peter's, I became conscious
Of a sensation of movement opposing me,—tendency this way
(Such as one fancies may be in a stream when the wave of the tide is
Coming and not yet come,—a sort of noise and retention);
So I turned, and, before I turned, caught sight of stragglers
Heading a crowd, it is plain, that is coming behind that corner.
Looking up, I see windows filled with heads; the Piazza,
Into which you remember the Ponte St Angelo enters,
Since I passed, has thickened with curious groups; and now the
Crowd is coming, has turned, has crossed that last barricade, is
Here at my side. In the middle they drag at something. What is it?
Ha! bare swords in the air, held up? There seem to be voices
Pleading and hands putting back; official, perhaps; but the swords are
Many, and bare in the air. In the air? they descend; they are smiting,
Hewing, chopping—At what? In the air once more upstretched? And—
Is it blood that's on them? Yes, certainly blood! Of whom, then?
Over whom is the cry of this furor of exultation?
 While they are skipping and screaming, and dancing their caps on
  the points of
Swords and bayonets, I to the outskirts back, and ask a
Mercantile-seeming bystander, 'What is it?' and he, looking always
That way, makes me answer, 'A Priest, who was trying to fly to
The Neapolitan army,'—and thus explains the proceeding.

You didn't see the dead man? No;—I began to be doubtful;
I was in black myself, and didn't know what mightn't happen,—
But a National Guard close by me, outside of the hubbub,
Broke his sword with slashing a broad hat covered with dust,—and
Passing away from the place with Murray under my arm, and
Stooping, I saw through the legs of the people the legs of a body.

   You are the first, do you know, to whom I have mentioned the matter.
Whom should I tell it to else?—these girls?—the Heavens forbid it!—
Quidnuncs at Monaldini's?—Idlers upon the Pincian?

   If I rightly remember, it happened on that afternoon when
Word of the nearer approach of a new Neapolitan army
First was spread. I began to bethink me of Paris Septembers,
Thought I could fancy the look of that old 'Ninety-two. On that evening
Three or four, or, it may be, five, of these people were slaughtered.
Some declared they had, one of them, fired on a sentinel; others
Say they were only escaping; a Priest, it is currently stated,
Stabbed a National Guard on the very Piazza Colonna:
History, Rumour of Rumours, I leave to thee to determine!

   But I am thankful to say the government seems to have strength to
Put it down; it has vanished, at least; the place is most peaceful.
Through the Trastevere walking last night, at nine of the clock, I
Found no sort of disorder; I crossed by the Island-bridges,
So by the narrow streets to the Ponte Rotto, and onwards
Thence by the Temple of Vesta, away to the great Coliseum,
Which at the full of the moon is an object worthy a visit.

### VIII  Georgina Trevellyn to Louisa——

Only think, dearest Louisa, what fearful scenes we have witnessed!—

.    .    .    .    .

George has just seen Garibaldi, dressed up in a long white cloak, on
Horseback, riding by, with his mounted negro behind him:
This is a man, you know, who came from America with him,
Out of the woods, I suppose, and uses a *lasso* in fighting,
Which is, I don't quite know, but a sort of noose, I imagine;
This he throws on the heads of the enemy's men in a battle,
Pulls them into his reach, and then most cruelly kills them:
Mary does not believe, but we heard it from an Italian.
Mary allows she was wrong about Mr Claude *being selfish*;
He was *most* useful and kind on the terrible thirtieth of April.
Do not write here any more; we are starting directly for Florence:
We should be off to-morrow, if only Papa could get horses;
All have been seized everywhere for the use of this dreadful Mazzini.

MATTHEW ARNOLD

## *Isolation. To Marguerite*

We were apart; yet, day by day,
I bade my heart more constant be.
I bade it keep the world away,
And grow a home for only thee;
Nor feared but thy love likewise grew,
Like mine, each day, more tried, more true.

The fault was grave! I might have known,
What far too soon, alas! I learned—
The heart can bind itself alone,
And faith may oft be unreturned.
Self-swayed our feelings ebb and swell—
Thou lov'st no more;—Farewell! Farewell!

Farewell!—and thou, thou lonely heart,
Which never yet without remorse
Even for a moment didst depart
From thy remote and spherèd course
To haunt the place where passions reign—
Back to thy solitude again!

Back! with the conscious thrill of shame
Which Luna felt, that summer-night,
Flash through her pure immortal frame,
When she forsook the starry height
To hang over Endymion's sleep
Upon the pine-grown Latmian steep.

Yet she, chaste queen, had never proved
How vain a thing is mortal love,
Wandering in Heaven, far removed.
But thou hast long had place to prove
This truth—to prove, and make thine own:
'Thou hast been, shalt be, art, alone.'

Or, if not quite alone, yet they
Which touch thee are unmating things—
Ocean and clouds and night and day;
Lorn autumns and triumphant springs;
And life, and others' joy and pain,
And love, if love, of happier men.

Of happier men—for they, at least,
Have *dreamed* two human hearts might blend
In one, and were through faith released
From isolation without end
Prolonged; nor knew, although not less
Alone than thou, their loneliness.

MATTHEW ARNOLD

## *To Marguerite.—Continued*

Yes! in the sea of life enisled,
With echoing straits between us thrown,
Dotting the shoreless watery wild,
We mortal millions live *alone*.
The islands feel the enclasping flow,
And then their endless bounds they know.

But when the moon their hollows lights,
And they are swept by balms of spring,
And in their glens, on starry nights,
The nightingales divinely sing;
And lovely notes, from shore to shore,
Across the sounds and channels pour—

Oh! then a longing like despair
Is to their farthest caverns sent;
For surely once, they feel, we were
Parts of a single continent!
Now round us spreads the watery plain—
Oh might our marges meet again!

Who ordered, that their longing's fire
Should be, as soon as kindled, cooled?
Who renders vain their deep desire?—
A God, a God their severance ruled!
And bade betwixt their shores to be
The unplumbed salt, estranging sea.

CHARLES KINGSLEY

## The Watchman

'Watchman, what of the night?'
  'The stars are out in the sky;
And the merry round moon will be rising soon,
  For us to go sailing by.'

'Watchman, what of the night?'
  'The tide flows in from the sea;
There's water to float a little cockboat
  Will carry such fishers as we.'

'Watchman, what of the night?'
  'The night is a fruitful time;
When to many a pair are born children fair,
  To be christened at morning chime.'


CHARLES MACKAY

## Louise on the Door-Step

Half-past three in the morning!
  And no one in the street
But me, on the sheltering door-step
  Resting my weary feet:
Watching the rain-drops patter
  And dance where the puddles run,
As bright in the flaring gaslight
  As dewdrops in the sun.

There's a light upon the pavement—
  It shines like a magic glass,
And there are faces in it
  That look at me and pass.
Faces—ah! well remembered
  In the happy Long Ago,
When my garb was white as lilies,
  And my thoughts as pure as snow.

Faces! ah, yes! I see them—
  One, two, and three—and four—
That come in the gust of tempests,
  And go on the winds that bore.

Changeful and evanescent,
  They shine 'mid storm and rain,
Till the terror of their beauty
  Lies deep upon my brain.

One of them frowns; *I* know him,
  With his thin long snow-white hair,—
Cursing his wretched daughter
  That drove him to despair.
And the other, with wakening pity
  In her large tear-streaming eyes,
Seems as she yearned toward me,
  And whispered 'Paradise'.

They pass,—they melt in the ripples,
  And I shut mine eyes, that burn,
To escape another vision
  That follows where'er I turn—
The face of a false deceiver
  That lives and lies; ah, me!
Though I see it in the pavement,
  Mocking my misery!

They are gone!—all three!—quite vanished!
  Let nothing call them back!
For I've had enough of phantoms,
  And my heart is on the rack!
God help me in my sorrow;
  But *there*,—in the wet, cold stone,
Smiling in heavenly beauty,
  I see my lost, mine own!

There, on the glimmering pavement,
  With eyes as blue as morn,
Floats by the fair-haired darling
  Too soon from my bosom torn.
She clasps her tiny fingers—
  She calls me sweet and mild,
And says that my God forgives me
  For the sake of my little child.

I will go to her grave to-morrow,
  And pray that I may die;
And I hope that my God will take me
  Ere the days of my youth go by.
For I am old in anguish,
  And long to be at rest,
With my little babe beside me,
  And the daisies on my breast.

ALFRED, LORD TENNYSON

## From *In Memoriam A. H. H.*
### *Obiit* MDCCCXXXIII

Strong Son of God, immortal Love,
    Whom we, that have not seen thy face,
    By faith, and faith alone, embrace,
Believing where we cannot prove;

Thine are these orbs of light and shade;
    Thou madest Life in man and brute;
    Thou madest Death; and lo, thy foot
Is on the skull which thou hast made.

Thou wilt not leave us in the dust:
    Thou madest man, he knows not why,
    He thinks he was not made to die;
And thou hast made him: thou art just.

Thou seemest human and divine,
    The highest, holiest manhood, thou:
    Our wills are ours, we know not how;
Our wills are ours, to make them thine.

Our little systems have their day;
    They have their day and cease to be:
    They are but broken lights of thee,
And thou, O Lord, art more than they.

We have but faith: we cannot know;
    For knowledge is of things we see;
    And yet we trust it comes from thee,
A beam in darkness: let it grow.

Let knowledge grow from more to more,
    But more of reverence in us dwell;
    That mind and soul, according well,
May make one music as before.

But vaster. We are fools and slight;
    We mock thee when we do not fear:
    But help thy foolish ones to bear;
Help thy vain worlds to bear thy light.

Forgive what seemed my sin in me;
    What seemed my worth since I began;
    For merit lives from man to man,
And not from man, O Lord, to thee.

Forgive my grief for one removed,
    Thy creature, whom I found so fair.
      I trust he lives in thee, and there
I find him worthier to be loved.

Forgive these wild and wandering cries,
    Confusions of a wasted youth;
      Forgive them where they fail in truth,
And in thy wisdom make me wise.

I

I held it truth, with him who sings
    To one clear harp in divers tones,
      That men may rise on stepping-stones
Of their dead selves to higher things.

But who shall so forecast the years
    And find in loss a gain to match?
      Or reach a hand through time to catch
The far-off interest of tears?

Let Love clasp Grief lest both be drowned,
    Let darkness keep her raven gloss:
      Ah, sweeter to be drunk with loss,
To dance with death, to beat the ground,

Than that the victor Hours should scorn
    The long result of love, and boast,
      'Behold the man that loved and lost,
But all he was is overworn.'

II

Old Yew, which graspest at the stones
    That name the under-lying dead,
      Thy fibres net the dreamless head,
Thy roots are wrapped about the bones.

The seasons bring the flower again,
    And bring the firstling to the flock;
      And in the dusk of thee, the clock
Beats out the little lives of men.

Oh not for thee the glow, the bloom,
    Who changest not in any gale,
      Nor branding summer suns avail
To touch thy thousand years of gloom:

And gazing on thee, sullen tree,
    Sick for thy stubborn hardihood,
    I seem to fail from out my blood
And grow incorporate into thee.


## VII

Dark house, by which once more I stand
    Here in the long unlovely street,
    Doors, where my heart was used to beat
So quickly, waiting for a hand,

A hand that can be clasped no more—
    Behold me, for I cannot sleep,
    And like a guilty thing I creep
At earliest morning to the door.

He is not here; but far away
    The noise of life begins again,
    And ghastly through the drizzling rain
On the bald street breaks the blank day.


## IX

Fair ship, that from the Italian shore
    Sailest the placid ocean-plains
    With my lost Arthur's loved remains,
Spread thy full wings, and waft him o'er.

So draw him home to those that mourn
    In vain; a favourable speed
    Ruffle thy mirrored mast, and lead
Through prosperous floods his holy urn.

All night no ruder air perplex
    Thy sliding keel, till Phosphor, bright
    As our pure love, through early light
Shall glimmer on the dewy decks.

Sphere all your lights around, above;
    Sleep, gentle heavens, before the prow;
    Sleep, gentle winds, as he sleeps now,
My friend, the brother of my love;

My Arthur, whom I shall not see
    Till all my widowed race be run;
    Dear as the mother to the son,
More than my brothers are to me.

X

I hear the noise about thy keel;
    I hear the bell struck in the night:
    I see the cabin-window bright;
I see the sailor at the wheel.

Thou bring'st the sailor to his wife,
    And travelled men from foreign lands;
    And letters unto trembling hands;
And, thy dark freight, a vanished life.

So bring him: we have idle dreams:
    This look of quiet flatters thus
    Our home-bred fancies: O to us,
The fools of habit, sweeter seems

To rest beneath the clover sod,
    That takes the sunshine and the rains,
    Or where the kneeling hamlet drains
The chalice of the grapes of God;

Than if with thee the roaring wells
    Should gulf him fathom-deep in brine;
    And hands so often clasped in mine,
Should toss with tangle and with shells.


XI

Calm is the morn without a sound,
    Calm as to suit a calmer grief,
    And only through the faded leaf
The chestnut pattering to the ground:

Calm and deep peace on this high wold,
    And on these dews that drench the furze,
    And all the silvery gossamers
That twinkle into green and gold:

Calm and still light on yon great plain
    That sweeps with all its autumn bowers,
    And crowded farms and lessening towers,
To mingle with the bounding main:

Calm and deep peace in this wide air,
    These leaves that redden to the fall;
    And in my heart, if calm at all,
If any calm, a calm despair:

Calm on the seas, and silver sleep,
    And waves that sway themselves in rest,
    And dead calm in that noble breast
Which heaves but with the heaving deep.


### XIV

If one should bring me this report,
    That thou hadst touched the land to-day,
    And I went down unto the quay,
And found thee lying in the port;

And standing, muffled round with woe,
    Should see thy passengers in rank
    Come stepping lightly down the plank,
And beckoning unto those they know;

And if along with these should come
    The man I held as half-divine;
    Should strike a sudden hand in mine,
And ask a thousand things of home;

And I should tell him all my pain,
    And how my life had drooped of late,
    And he should sorrow o'er my state
And marvel what possessed my brain;

And I perceived no touch of change,
    No hint of death in all his frame,
    But found him all in all the same,
I should not feel it to be strange.


### XV

To-night the winds begin to rise
    And roar from yonder dropping day:
    The last red leaf is whirled away,
The rooks are blown about the skies;

The forest cracked, the waters curled,
    The cattle huddled on the lea;
    And wildly dashed on tower and tree
The sunbeam strikes along the world:

And but for fancies, which aver
    That all thy motions gently pass
    Athwart a plane of molten glass,
I scarce could brook the strain and stir

That makes the barren branches loud;
 And but for fear it is not so,
 The wild unrest that lives in woe
Would dote and pore on yonder cloud

That rises upward always higher,
 And onward drags a labouring breast,
 And topples round the dreary west,
A looming bastion fringed with fire.


## XVII

Thou comest, much wept for: such a breeze
 Compelled thy canvas, and my prayer
 Was as the whisper of an air
To breathe thee over lonely seas.

For I in spirit saw thee move
 Through circles of the bounding sky,
 Week after week: the days go by:
Come quick, thou bringest all I love.

Henceforth, wherever thou may'st roam,
 My blessing, like a line of light,
 Is on the waters day and night,
And like a beacon guards thee home.

So may whatever tempest mars
 Mid–ocean, spare thee, sacred bark;
 And balmy drops in summer dark
Slide from the bosom of the stars.

So kind an office hath been done,
 Such precious relics brought by thee;
 The dust of him I shall not see
Till all my widowed race be run.


## XVIII

'Tis well; 'tis something; we may stand
 Where he in English earth is laid,
 And from his ashes may be made
The violet of his native land.

'Tis little; but it looks in truth
 As if the quiet bones were blest
 Among familiar names to rest
And in the places of his youth.

Come then, pure hands, and bear the head
    That sleeps or wears the mask of sleep,
    And come, whatever loves to weep,
And hear the ritual of the dead.

Ah yet, even yet, if this might be,
    I, falling on his faithful heart,
    Would breathing through his lips impart
The life that almost dies in me;

That dies not, but endures with pain,
    And slowly forms the firmer mind,
    Treasuring the look it cannot find,
The words that are not heard again.


XIX

The Danube to the Severn gave
    The darkened heart that beat no more;
    They laid him by the pleasant shore,
And in the hearing of the wave.

There twice a day the Severn fills;
    The salt sea-water passes by,
    And hushes half the babbling Wye,
And makes a silence in the hills.

The Wye is hushed nor moved along,
    And hushed my deepest grief of all,
    When filled with tears that cannot fall,
I brim with sorrow drowning song.

The tide flows down, the wave again
    Is vocal in its wooded walls;
    My deeper anguish also falls,
And I can speak a little then.


XXII

The path by which we twain did go,
    Which led by tracts that pleased us well,
    Through four sweet years arose and fell,
From flower to flower, from snow to snow:

And we with singing cheered the way,
    And, crowned with all the season lent,
    From April on to April went,
And glad at heart from May to May:

But where the path we walked began
    To slant the fifth autumnal slope,
    As we descended following Hope,
There sat the Shadow feared of man;

Who broke our fair companionship,
    And spread his mantle dark and cold,
    And wrapped thee formless in the fold,
And dulled the murmur on thy lip,

And bore thee where I could not see
    Nor follow, though I walk in haste,
    And think, that somewhere in the waste
The Shadow sits and waits for me.


### XXVIII

The time draws near the birth of Christ:
    The moon is hid; the night is still;
    The Christmas bells from hill to hill
Answer each other in the mist.

Four voices of four hamlets round,
    From far and near, on mead and moor,
    Swell out and fail, as if a door
Were shut between me and the sound:

Each voice four changes on the wind,
    That now dilate, and now decrease,
    Peace and goodwill, goodwill and peace,
Peace and goodwill, to all mankind.

This year I slept and woke with pain,
    I almost wished no more to wake,
    And that my hold on life would break
Before I heard those bells again:

But they my troubled spirit rule,
    For they controlled me when a boy;
    They bring me sorrow touched with joy,
The merry merry bells of Yule.


### XXIX

With such compelling cause to grieve
    As daily vexes household peace,
    And chains regret to his decease,
How dare we keep our Christmas-eve;

Which brings no more a welcome guest
    To enrich the threshold of the night
    With showered largess of delight
In dance and song and game and jest?

Yet go, and while the holly boughs
    Entwine the cold baptismal font
    Make one wreath more for Use and Wont,
That guard the portals of the house;

Old sisters of a day gone by,
    Gray nurses, loving nothing new;
    Why should they miss their yearly due
Before their time? They too will die.


### XXX

With trembling fingers did we weave
    The holly round the Christmas hearth;
    A rainy cloud possessed the earth,
And sadly fell our Christmas-eve.

At our old pastimes in the hall
    We gambolled, making vain pretence
    Of gladness, with an awful sense
Of one mute Shadow watching all.

We paused: the winds were in the beech:
    We heard them sweep the winter land;
    And in a circle hand-in-hand
Sat silent, looking each at each.

Then echo-like our voices rang;
    We sung, though every eye was dim,
    A merry song we sang with him
Last year: impetuously we sang:

We ceased: a gentler feeling crept
    Upon us: surely rest is meet:
    'They rest,' we said, 'their sleep is sweet,'
And silence followed, and we wept.

Our voices took a higher range;
    Once more we sang: 'They do not die
    Nor lose their mortal sympathy,
Nor change to us, although they change;

'Rapt from the fickle and the frail
    With gathered power, yet the same,
    Pierces the keen seraphic flame
From orb to orb, from veil to veil.'

Rise, happy morn, rise, holy morn,
    Draw forth the cheerful day from night:
    O Father, touch the east, and light
The light that shone when Hope was born.

### XXXI

When Lazarus left his charnel-cave,
    And home to Mary's house returned,
    Was this demanded—if he yearned
To hear her weeping by his grave?

'Where wert thou, brother, those four days?'
    There lives no record of reply,
    Which telling what it is to die
Had surely added praise to praise.

From every house the neighbours met,
    The streets were filled with joyful sound,
    A solemn gladness even crowned
The purple brows of Olivet.

Behold a man raised up by Christ!
    The rest remaineth unrevealed;
    He told it not; or something sealed
The lips of that Evangelist.

### L

Be near me when my light is low,
    When the blood creeps, and the nerves prick
    And tingle; and the heart is sick,
And all the wheels of Being slow.

Be near me when the sensuous frame
    Is racked with pangs that conquer trust;
    And Time, a maniac scattering dust,
And Life, a Fury slinging flame.

Be near me when my faith is dry,
    And men the flies of latter spring,
    That lay their eggs, and sting and sing
And weave their petty cells and die.

Be near me when I fade away,
　　To point the term of human strife,
　　And on the low dark verge of life
The twilight of eternal day.


### LIV

Oh yet we trust that somehow good
　　Will be the final goal of ill,
　　To pangs of nature, sins of will,
Defects of doubt, and taints of blood;

That nothing walks with aimless feet;
　　That not one life shall be destroyed,
　　Or cast as rubbish to the void,
When God hath made the pile complete;

That not a worm is cloven in vain;
　　That not a moth with vain desire
　　Is shrivelled in a fruitless fire,
Or but subserves another's gain.

Behold, we know not anything;
　　I can but trust that good shall fall
　　At last—far off—at last, to all,
And every winter change to spring.

So runs my dream: but what am I?
　　An infant crying in the night:
　　An infant crying for the light:
And with no language but a cry.


### LV

The wish, that of the living whole
　　No life may fail beyond the grave,
　　Derives it not from what we have
The likest God within the soul?

Are God and Nature then at strife,
　　That Nature lends such evil dreams?
　　So careful of the type she seems
So careless of the single life;

That I, considering everywhere
　　Her secret meaning in her deeds,
　　And finding that of fifty seeds
She often brings but one to bear,

I falter where I firmly trod,
    And falling with my weight of cares
    Upon the great world's altar-stairs
That slope through darkness up to God,

I stretch lame hands of faith, and grope,
    And gather dust and chaff, and call
    To what I feel is Lord of all,
And faintly trust the larger hope.


### LVI

'So careful of the type?' but no.
    From scarped cliff and quarried stone
    She cries, 'A thousand types are gone:
I care for nothing, all shall go.

'Thou makest thine appeal to me:
    I bring to life, I bring to death:
    The spirit does but mean the breath:
I know no more.' And he, shall he,

Man, her last work, who seemed so fair,
    Such splendid purpose in his eyes,
    Who rolled the psalm to wintry skies,
Who built him fanes of fruitless prayer,

Who trusted God was love indeed
    And love Creation's final law—
    Though Nature, red in tooth and claw
With ravine, shrieked against his creed—

Who loved, who suffered countless ills,
    Who battled for the True, the Just,
    Be blown about the desert dust,
Or sealed within the iron hills?

No more? A monster then, a dream,
    A discord. Dragons of the prime,
    That tare each other in their slime,
Were mellow music matched with him.

O life as futile, then, as frail!
    O for thy voice to soothe and bless!
    What hope of answer, or redress?
Behind the veil, behind the veil.

LVII

Peace; come away: the song of woe
    Is after all an earthly song:
    Peace; come away: we do him wrong
To sing so wildly: let us go.

Come; let us go: your cheeks are pale;
    But half my life I leave behind:
    Methinks my friend is richly shrined;
But I shall pass; my work will fail.

Yet in these ears, till hearing dies,
    One set slow bell will seem to toll
    The passing of the sweetest soul
That ever looked with human eyes.

I hear it now, and o'er and o'er,
    Eternal greetings to the dead;
    And 'Ave, Ave, Ave,' said,
'Adieu, adieu' for evermore.


LXXVIII

Again at Christmas did we weave
    The holly round the Christmas hearth;
    The silent snow possessed the earth,
And calmly fell our Christmas-eve:

The yule-clog sparkled keen with frost,
    No wing of wind the region swept,
    But over all things brooding slept
The quiet sense of something lost.

As in the winters left behind,
    Again our ancient games had place,
    The mimic picture's breathing grace,
And dance and song and hoodman-blind.

Who showed a token of distress?
    No single tear, no mark of pain:
    O sorrow, then can sorrow wane?
O grief, can grief be changed to less?

O last regret, regret can die!
    No—mixed with all this mystic frame,
    Her deep relations are the same,
But with long use her tears are dry.

## LXXXIII

Dip down upon the northern shore,
    O sweet new-year delaying long;
    Thou doest expectant nature wrong;
Delaying long, delay no more.

What stays thee from the clouded noons,
    Thy sweetness from its proper place?
    Can trouble live with April days,
Or sadness in the summer moons?

Bring orchis, bring the foxglove spire,
    The little speedwell's darling blue,
    Deep tulips dashed with fiery dew,
Laburnums, dropping-wells of fire.

O thou, new-year, delaying long,
    Delayest the sorrow in my blood,
    That longs to burst a frozen bud
And flood a fresher throat with song.


## LXXXVI

Sweet after showers, ambrosial air,
    That rollest from the gorgeous gloom
    Of evening over brake and bloom
And meadow, slowly breathing bare

The round of space, and rapt below
    Through all the dewy-tasselled wood,
    And shadowing down the horned flood
In ripples, fan my brows and blow

The fever from my cheek, and sigh
    The full new life that feeds thy breath
    Throughout my frame, till Doubt and Death,
Ill brethren, let the fancy fly

From belt to belt of crimson seas
    On leagues of odour streaming far,
    To where in yonder orient star
A hundred spirits whisper 'Peace'.

## LXXXVII

I passed beside the reverend walls
    In which of old I wore the gown;
    I roved at random through the town,
And saw the tumult of the halls;

And heard once more in college fanes
    The storm their high–built organs make,
    And thunder–music, rolling, shake
The prophet blazoned on the panes;

And caught once more the distant shout,
    The measured pulse of racing oars
    Among the willows; paced the shores
And many a bridge, and all about

The same gray flats again, and felt
    The same, but not the same; and last
    Up that long walk of limes I passed
To see the rooms in which he dwelt.

Another name was on the door:
    I lingered; all within was noise
    Of songs, and clapping hands, and boys
That crashed the glass and beat the floor;

Where once we held debate, a band
    Of youthful friends, on mind and art,
    And labour, and the changing mart,
And all the framework of the land;

When one would aim an arrow fair,
    But send it slackly from the string;
    And one would pierce an outer ring,
And one an inner, here and there;

And last the master–bowman, he,
    Would cleave the mark. A willing ear
    We lent him. Who, but hung to hear
The rapt oration flowing free

From point to point, with power and grace
    And music in the bounds of law,
    To those conclusions when we saw
The God within him light his face,

And seem to lift the form, and glow
    In azure orbits heavenly-wise;
    And over those ethereal eyes
The bar of Michael Angelo.


LXXXIX

Witch-elms that counterchange the floor
    Of this flat lawn with dusk and bright;
    And thou, with all thy breadth and height
Of foliage, towering sycamore;

How often, hither wandering down,
    My Arthur found your shadows fair,
    And shook to all the liberal air
The dust and din and steam of town:

He brought an eye for all he saw;
    He mixed in all our simple sports;
    They pleased him, fresh from brawling courts
And dusty purlieus of the law.

O joy to him in this retreat,
    Immantled in ambrosial dark,
    To drink the cooler air, and mark
The landscape winking through the heat:

O sound to rout the brood of cares,
    The sweep of scythe in morning dew,
    The gust that round the garden flew,
And tumbled half the mellowing pears!

O bliss, when all in circle drawn
    About him, heart and ear were fed
    To hear him, as he lay and read
The Tuscan poets on the lawn:

Or in the all-golden afternoon
    A guest, or happy sister, sung,
    Or here she brought the harp and flung
A ballad to the brightening moon:

Nor less it pleased in livelier moods,
    Beyond the bounding hill to stray,
    And break the livelong summer day
With banquet in the distant woods;

Whereat we glanced from theme to theme,
    Discussed the books to love or hate,
    Or touched the changes of the state,
Or threaded some Socratic dream;

But if I praised the busy town,
    He loved to rail against it still,
    For 'ground in yonder social mill
We rub each other's angles down,

'And merge' he said 'in form and gloss
    The picturesque of man and man.'
    We talked: the stream beneath us ran,
The wine-flask lying couched in moss.

Or cooled within the glooming wave;
    And last, returning from afar,
    Before the crimson-circled star
Had fallen into her father's grave,

And brushing ankle-deep in flowers,
    We heard behind the woodbine veil
    The milk that bubbled in the pail,
And buzzings of the honied hours.


## XCV

By night we lingered on the lawn,
    For underfoot the herb was dry;
    And genial warmth; and o'er the sky
The silvery haze of summer drawn;

And calm that let the tapers burn
    Unwavering: not a cricket chirred:
    The brook alone far-off was heard,
And on the board the fluttering urn:

And bats went round in fragrant skies,
    And wheeled or lit the filmy shapes
    That haunt the dusk, with ermine capes
And woolly breasts and beaded eyes;

While now we sang old songs that pealed
    From knoll to knoll, where, couched at ease,
    The white kine glimmered, and the trees
Laid their dark arms about the field.

But when those others, one by one,
  Withdrew themselves from me and night,
  And in the house light after light
Went out, and I was all alone,

A hunger seized my heart; I read
  Of that glad year which once had been,
  In those fallen leaves which kept their green,
The noble letters of the dead:

And strangely on the silence broke
  The silent-speaking words, and strange
  Was love's dumb cry defying change
To test his worth; and strangely spoke

The faith, the vigour, bold to dwell
  On doubts that drive the coward back,
  And keen through wordy snares to track
Suggestion to her inmost cell.

So word by word, and line by line,
  The dead man touched me from the past,
  And all at once it seemed at last
The living soul was flashed on mine,

And mine in this was wound, and whirled
  About empyreal heights of thought,
  And came on that which is, and caught
The deep pulsations of the world,

Aeonian music measuring out
  The steps of Time—the shocks of Chance—
  The blows of Death. At length my trance
Was cancelled, stricken through with doubt.

Vague words! but ah, how hard to frame
  In matter-moulded forms of speech,
  Or even for intellect to reach
Through memory that which I became:

Till now the doubtful dusk revealed
  The knolls once more where, couched at ease,
  The white kine glimmered, and the trees
Laid their dark arms about the field:

And sucked from out the distant gloom
  A breeze began to tremble o'er
  The large leaves of the sycamore,
And fluctuate all the still perfume,

And gathering freshlier overhead,
   Rocked the full-foliaged elms, and swung
   The heavy-folded rose, and flung
The lilies to and fro, and said

'The dawn, the dawn,' and died away;
   And East and West, without a breath,
   Mixed their dim lights, like life and death,
To broaden into boundless day.

### XCIX

Risest thou thus, dim dawn, again,
   So loud with voices of the birds,
   So thick with lowings of the herds,
Day, when I lost the flower of men;

Who tremblest through thy darkling red
   On yon swollen brook that bubbles fast
   By meadows breathing of the past,
And woodlands holy to the dead;

Who murmurest in the foliaged eaves
   A song that slights the coming care,
   And autumn laying here and there
A fiery finger on the leaves;

Who wakenest with thy balmy breath
   To myriads on the genial earth,
   Memories of bridal, or of birth,
And unto myriads more, of death.

O wheresoever those may be,
   Betwixt the slumber of the poles,
   To-day they count as kindred souls;
They know me not, but mourn with me.

### C

I climb the hill: from end to end
   Of all the landscape underneath,
   I find no place that does not breathe
Some gracious memory of my friend;

No gray old grange, or lonely fold,
   Or low morass and whispering reed,
   Or simple stile from mead to mead,
Or sheepwalk up the windy wold;

Nor hoary knoll of ash and haw
    That hears the latest linnet trill,
    Nor quarry trenched along the hill
And haunted by the wrangling daw;

Nor runlet tinkling from the rock;
    Nor pastoral rivulet that swerves
    To left and right through meadowy curves,
That feed the mothers of the flock;

But each has pleased a kindred eye,
    And each reflects a kindlier day;
    And, leaving these, to pass away,
I think once more he seems to die.

## CI

Unwatched, the garden bough shall sway,
    The tender blossom flutter down,
    Unloved, that beech will gather brown,
This maple burn itself away;

Unloved, the sun-flower, shining fair,
    Ray round with flames her disk of seed,
    And many a rose-carnation feed
With summer spice the humming air;

Unloved, by many a sandy bar,
    The brook shall babble down the plain,
    At noon or when the lesser wain
Is twisting round the polar star;

Uncared for, gird the windy grove,
    And flood the haunts of hern and crake;
    Or into silver arrows break
The sailing moon in creek and cove;

Till from the garden and the wild
    A fresh association blow
    And year by year the landscape grow
Familiar to the stranger's child;

As year by year the labourer tills
    His wonted glebe, or lops the glades;
    And year by year our memory fades
From all the circle of the hills.

## CII

We leave the well-belovèd place
    Where first we gazed upon the sky;
    The roofs, that heard our earliest cry,
Will shelter one of stranger race.

We go, but ere we go from home,
    As down the garden-walks I move,
    Two spirits of a diverse love
Contend for loving masterdom.

One whispers, 'Here thy boyhood sung
    Long since its matin song, and heard
    The low love-language of the bird
In native hazels tassel-hung.'

The other answers, 'Yea, but here
    Thy feet have strayed in after hours
    With thy lost friend among the bowers,
And this hath made them trebly dear.'

These two have striven half the day,
    And each prefers his separate claim,
    Poor rivals in a losing game,
That will not yield each other way.

I turn to go: my feet are set
    To leave the pleasant fields and farms;
    They mix in one another's arms
To one pure image of regret.

## CIV

The time draws near the birth of Christ;
    The moon is hid, the night is still;
    A single church below the hill
Is pealing, folded in the mist.

A single peal of bells below,
    That wakens at this hour of rest
    A single murmur in the breast,
That these are not the bells I know.

Like strangers' voices here they sound,
    In lands where not a memory strays,
    Nor landmark breathes of other days,
But all is new unhallowed ground.

CV

To-night ungathered let us leave
    This laurel, let this holly stand:
    We live within the stranger's land,
And strangely falls our Christmas-eve.

Our father's dust is left alone
    And silent under other snows:
    There in due time the woodbine blows,
The violet comes, but we are gone.

No more shall wayward grief abuse
    The genial hour with mask and mime;
    For change of place, like growth of time,
Has broke the bond of dying use.

Let cares that petty shadows cast,
    By which our lives are chiefly proved,
    A little spare the night I loved,
And hold it solemn to the past.

But let no footstep beat the floor,
    Nor bowl of wassail mantle warm;
    For who would keep an ancient form
Through which the spirit breathes no more?

Be neither song, nor game, nor feast;
    Nor harp be touched, nor flute be blown;
    No dance, no motion, save alone
What lightens in the lucid east

Of rising worlds by yonder wood.
    Long sleeps the summer in the seed;
    Run out your measured arcs, and lead
The closing cycle rich in good.


CVI

Ring out, wild bells, to the wild sky,
    The flying cloud, the frosty light:
    The year is dying in the night;
Ring out, wild bells, and let him die.

Ring out the old, ring in the new,
    Ring, happy bells, across the snow:
    The year is going, let him go;
Ring out the false, ring in the true.

Ring out the grief that saps the mind,
    For those that here we see no more;
    Ring out the feud of rich and poor,
Ring in redress to all mankind.

Ring out a slowly dying cause,
    And ancient forms of party strife;
    Ring in the nobler modes of life,
With sweeter manners, purer laws.

Ring out the want, the care, the sin,
    The faithless coldness of the times;
    Ring out, ring out my mournful rhymes,
But ring the fuller minstrel in.

Ring out false pride in place and blood,
    The civic slander and the spite;
    Ring in the love of truth and right,
Ring in the common love of good.

Ring out old shapes of foul disease;
    Ring out the narrowing lust of gold;
    Ring out the thousand wars of old,
Ring in the thousand years of peace.

Ring in the valiant man and free,
    The larger heart, the kindlier hand;
    Ring out the darkness of the land,
Ring in the Christ that is to be.

## CVII

It is the day when he was born,
    A bitter day that early sank
    Behind a purple-frosty bank
Of vapour, leaving night forlorn.

The time admits not flowers or leaves
    To deck the banquet. Fiercely flies
    The blast of North and East, and ice
Makes daggers at the sharpened eaves,

And bristles all the brakes and thorns
    To yon hard crescent, as she hangs
    Above the wood which grides and clangs
Its leafless ribs and iron horns

Together, in the drifts that pass
    To darken on the rolling brine
    That breaks the coast. But fetch the wine,
Arrange the board and brim the glass;

Bring in great logs and let them lie,
    To make a solid core of heat;
    Be cheerful-minded, talk and treat
Of all things even as he were by;

We keep the day. With festal cheer,
    With books and music, surely we
    Will drink to him, whate'er he be,
And sing the songs he loved to hear.

## CXV

Now fades the last long streak of snow,
    Now burgeons every maze of quick
    About the flowering squares, and thick
By ashen roots the violets blow.

Now rings the woodland loud and long,
    The distance takes a lovelier hue,
    And drowned in yonder living blue
The lark becomes a sightless song.

Now dance the lights on lawn and lea,
    The flocks are whiter down the vale,
    And milkier every milky sail
On winding stream or distant sea;

Where now the seamew pipes, or dives
    In yonder greening gleam, and fly
    The happy birds, that change their sky
To build and brood; that live their lives

From land to land; and in my breast
    Spring wakens too; and my regret
    Becomes an April violet,
And buds and blossoms like the rest.

## CXVIII

Contemplate all this work of Time,
    The giant labouring in his youth;
    Nor dream of human love and truth,
As dying Nature's earth and lime;

But trust that those we call the dead
    Are breathers of an ampler day
    For ever nobler ends. They say,
The solid earth whereon we tread

In tract of fluent heat began,
    And grew to seeming-random forms,
    The seeming prey of cyclic storms,
Till at the last arose the man;

Who throve and branched from clime to clime,
    The herald of a higher race,
    And of himself in higher place,
If so he type this work of time

Within himself, from more to more;
    Or, crowned with attributes of woe
    Like glories, move his course, and show
That life is not as idle ore,

But iron dug from central gloom,
    And heated hot with burning fears,
    And dipped in baths of hissing tears,
And battered with the shocks of doom

To shape and use. Arise and fly
    The reeling Faun, the sensual feast;
    Move upward, working out the beast,
And let the ape and tiger die.


CXXI

Sad Hesper o'er the buried sun
    And ready, thou, to die with him,
    Thou watchest all things ever dim
And dimmer, and a glory done:

The team is loosened from the wain,
    The boat is drawn upon the shore;
    Thou listenest to the closing door,
And life is darkened in the brain.

Bright Phosphor, fresher for the night,
    By thee the world's great work is heard
    Beginning, and the wakeful bird;
Behind thee comes the greater light:

The market boat is on the stream,
    And voices hail it from the brink;
    Thou hear'st the village hammer clink,
And see'st the moving of the team.

Sweet Hesper-Phosphor, double name
    For what is one, the first, the last,
    Thou, like my present and my past,
Thy place is changed; thou art the same.

### CXXIV

That which we dare invoke to bless;
    Our dearest faith; our ghastliest doubt;
    He, They, One, All; within, without;
The Power in darkness whom we guess;

I found Him not in world or sun,
    Or eagle's wing, or insect's eye;
    Nor through the questions men may try,
The petty cobwebs we have spun:

If e'er when faith had fallen asleep,
    I heard a voice 'believe no more'
    And heard an ever-breaking shore
That tumbled in the Godless deep;

A warmth within the breast would melt
    The freezing reason's colder part,
    And like a man in wrath the heart
Stood up and answered 'I have felt.'

No, like a child in doubt and fear:
    But that blind clamour made me wise;
    Then was I as a child that cries,
But, crying, knows his father near;

And what I am beheld again
    What is, and no man understands;
    And out of darkness came the hands
That reach through nature, moulding men.

### CXXX

Thy voice is on the rolling air;
    I hear thee where the waters run;
    Thou standest in the rising sun,
And in the setting thou art fair.

What art thou then? I cannot guess;
 But though I seem in star and flower
 To feel thee some diffusive power,
I do not therefore love thee less:

My love involves the love before;
 My love is vaster passion now;
 Though mixed with God and Nature thou,
I seem to love thee more and more.

Far off thou art, but ever nigh;
 I have thee still, and I rejoice;
 I prosper, circled with thy voice;
I shall not lose thee though I die.

### CXXXI

O living will that shalt endure
 When all that seems shall suffer shock,
 Rise in the spiritual rock,
Flow through our deeds and make them pure,

That we may lift from out of dust
 A voice as unto him that hears,
 A cry above the conquered years
To one that with us works, and trust,

With faith that comes of self-control,
 The truths that never can be proved
 Until we close with all we loved,
And all we flow from, soul in soul.

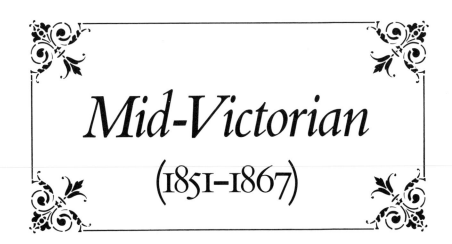

# Mid-Victorian
## (1851–1867)

## MATTHEW ARNOLD

### *Dover Beach*

The sea is calm to-night.
The tide is full, the moon lies fair
Upon the straits;—on the French coast the light
Gleams and is gone; the cliffs of England stand,
Glimmering and vast, out in the tranquil bay.
Come to the window, sweet is the night-air!
Only, from the long line of spray
Where the sea meets the moon-blanched land,
Listen! you hear the grating roar
Of pebbles which the waves draw back, and fling,
At their return, up the high strand,
Begin, and cease, and then again begin,
With tremulous cadence slow, and bring
The eternal note of sadness in.

Sophocles long ago
Heard it on the Aegaean, and it brought
Into his mind the turbid ebb and flow
Of human misery; we
Find also in the sound a thought,
Hearing it by this distant northern sea.

The Sea of Faith
Was once, too, at the full, and round earth's shore
Lay like the folds of a bright girdle furled.
But now I only hear
Its melancholy, long, withdrawing roar,
Retreating, to the breath
Of the night-wind, down the vast edges drear
And naked shingles of the world.

Ah, love, let us be true
To one another! for the world, which seems
To lie before us like a land of dreams,
So various, so beautiful, so new,
Hath really neither joy, nor love, nor light,
Nor certitude, nor peace, nor help for pain;
And we are here as on a darkling plain
Swept with confused alarms of struggle and flight,
Where ignorant armies clash by night.

MATTHEW ARNOLD

## *The Scholar-Gipsy*

Go, for they call you, shepherd, from the hill;
  Go, shepherd, and untie the wattled cotes!
    No longer leave thy wistful flock unfed,
  Nor let thy bawling fellows rack their throats,
    Nor the cropped herbage shoot another head.
      But when the fields are still,
  And the tired men and dogs all gone to rest,
    And only the white sheep are sometimes seen
    Cross and recross the strips of moon-blanched green,
Come, shepherd, and again begin the quest!

Here, where the reaper was at work of late—
  In this high field's dark corner, where he leaves
    His coat, his basket, and his earthen cruse,
  And in the sun all morning binds the sheaves,
    Then here, at noon, comes back his stores to use—
      Here will I sit and wait,
  While to my ear from uplands far away
    The bleating of the folded flocks is borne,
    With distant cries of reapers in the corn—
All the live murmur of a summer's day.

Screened is this nook o'er the high, half-reaped field,
  And here till sun-down, shepherd! will I be.
    Through the thick corn the scarlet poppies peep,
  And round green roots and yellowing stalks I see
    Pale pink convolvulus in tendrils creep;
      And air-swept lindens yield
  Their scent, and rustle down their perfumed showers
    Of bloom on the bent grass where I am laid,
    And bower me from the August sun with shade;
And the eye travels down to Oxford's towers.

And near me on the grass lies Glanvil's book—
  Come, let me read the oft-read tale again!
    The story of the Oxford scholar poor,
  Of pregnant parts and quick inventive brain,
    Who, tired of knocking at preferment's door,
      One summer-morn forsook
  His friends, and went to learn the gipsy-lore,
    And roamed the world with that wild brotherhood,
    And came, as most men deemed, to little good,
But came to Oxford and his friends no more.

But once, years after, in the country-lanes,
  Two scholars, whom at college erst he knew,
    Met him, and of his way of life enquired;
  Whereat he answered, that the gipsy-crew,
    His mates, had arts to rule as they desired
      The workings of men's brains,
  And they can bind them to what thoughts they will.
    'And I,' he said, 'the secret of their art,
      When fully learned, will to the world impart;
  But it needs heaven-sent moments for this skill.'

This said, he left them, and returned no more.—
  But rumours hung about the country-side,
    That the lost Scholar long was seen to stray,
  Seen by rare glimpses, pensive and tongue-tied,
    In hat of antique shape, and cloak of grey,
      The same the gipsies wore.
  Shepherds had met him on the Hurst in spring,
    At some lone alehouse in the Berkshire moors,
      On the warm ingle-bench, the smock-frocked boors
  Had found him seated at their entering,

But, 'mid their drink and clatter, he would fly.
  And I myself seem half to know thy looks,
    And put the shepherds, wanderer! on thy trace;
  And boys who in lone wheatfields scare the rooks
    I ask if thou hast passed their quiet place;
      Or in my boat I lie
  Moored to the cool bank in the summer-heats,
    'Mid wide grass meadows which the sunshine fills,
      And watch the warm, green-muffled Cumner hills,
  And wonder if thou haunt'st their shy retreats.

For most, I know, thou lov'st retired ground!
  Thee at the ferry Oxford riders blithe,
    Returning home on summer-nights, have met
  Crossing the stripling Thames at Bab-lock-hithe,
    Trailing in the cool stream thy fingers wet,
      As the punt's rope chops round;
  And leaning backward in a pensive dream,
    And fostering in thy lap a heap of flowers
      Plucked in shy fields and distant Wychwood bowers,
  And thine eyes resting on the moonlit stream.

And then they land, and thou art seen no more!—
  Maidens, who from the distant hamlets come
    To dance around the Fyfield elm in May,
  Oft through the darkening fields have seen thee roam,
    Or cross a stile into the public way.

Oft thou hast given them store
Of flowers—the frail-leafed, white anemony,
Dark bluebells drenched with dews of summer eves,
And purple orchises with spotted leaves—
But none hath words she can report of thee.

And, above Godstow Bridge, when hay-time's here
In June, and many a scythe in sunshine flames,
Men who through those wide fields of breezy grass
Where black-winged swallows haunt the glittering Thames,
To bathe in the abandoned lasher pass,
Have often passed thee near
Sitting upon the river bank o'ergrown;
Marked thine outlandish garb, thy figure spare,
Thy dark vague eyes, and soft abstracted air—
But, when they came from bathing, thou wast gone!

At some lone homestead in the Cumner hills,
Where at her open door the housewife darns,
Thou hast been seen, or hanging on a gate
To watch the threshers in the mossy barns.
Children, who early range these slopes and late
For cresses from the rills,
Have known thee eying, all an April-day,
The springing pastures and the feeding kine;
And marked thee, when the stars come out and shine,
Through the long dewy grass move slow away.

In autumn, on the skirts of Bagley Wood—
Where most the gipsies by the turf-edged way
Pitch their smoked tents, and every bush you see
With scarlet patches tagged and shreds of grey,
Above the forest-ground called Thessaly—
The blackbird, picking food,
Sees thee, nor stops his meal, nor fears at all;
So often has he known thee past him stray,
Rapt, twirling in thy hand a withered spray,
And waiting for the spark from heaven to fall.

And once, in winter, on the causeway chill
Where home through flooded fields foot-travellers go,
Have I not passed thee on the wooden bridge,
Wrapped in thy cloak and battling with the snow,
Thy face toward Hinksey and its wintry ridge?
And thou hast climbed the hill,
And gained the white brow of the Cumner range;

Turned once to watch, while thick the snowflakes fall,
The line of festal light in Christ-Church hall—
Then sought thy straw in some sequestered grange.

But what—I dream! Two hundred years are flown
Since first thy story ran through Oxford halls,
And the grave Glanvil did the tale inscribe
That thou wert wandered from the studious walls
To learn strange arts, and join a gipsy-tribe;
And thou from earth art gone
Long since, and in some quiet churchyard laid—
Some country-nook, where o'er thy unknown grave
Tall grasses and white flowering nettles wave,
Under a dark, red-fruited yew-tree's shade.

—No, no, thou hast not felt the lapse of hours!
For what wears out the life of mortal men?
'Tis that from change to change their being rolls;
'Tis that repeated shocks, again, again,
Exhaust the energy of strongest souls
And numb the elastic powers.
Till having used our nerves with bliss and teen,
And tired upon a thousand schemes our wit,
To the just-pausing Genius we remit
Our worn-out life, and are—what we have been.

Thou hast not lived, why should'st thou perish, so?
Thou had'st *one* aim, *one* business, *one* desire;
Else wert thou long since numbered with the dead!
Else hadst thou spent, like other men, thy fire!
The generations of thy peers are fled,
And we ourselves shall go;
But thou possessest an immortal lot,
And we imagine thee exempt from age
And living as thou liv'st on Glanvil's page,
Because thou had'st—what we, alas! have not.

For early didst thou leave the world, with powers
Fresh, undiverted to the world without,
Firm to their mark, not spent on other things;
Free from the sick fatigue, the languid doubt,
Which much to have tried, in much been baffled, brings.
O life unlike to ours!
Who fluctuate idly without term or scope,
Of whom each strives, nor knows for what he strives,
And each half lives a hundred different lives;
Who wait like thee, but not, like thee, in hope.

Thou waitest for the spark from heaven! and we,
  Light half-believers of our casual creeds,
    Who never deeply felt, nor clearly willed,
  Whose insight never has borne fruit in deeds,
    Whose vague resolves never have been fulfilled;
      For whom each year we see
  Breeds new beginnings, disappointments new;
    Who hesitate and falter life away,
    And lose to-morrow the ground won to-day—
  Ah! do not we, wanderer! await it too?

Yes, we await it!—but it still delays,
  And then we suffer! and amongst us one,
    Who most has suffered, takes dejectedly
  His seat upon the intellectual throne;
    And all his store of sad experience he
      Lays bare of wretched days;
  Tells us his misery's birth and growth and signs,
    And how the dying spark of hope was fed,
    And how the breast was soothed, and how the head,
  And all his hourly varied anodynes.

This for our wisest! and we others pine,
  And wish the long unhappy dream would end,
    And waive all claim to bliss, and try to bear;
  With closed-lipped patience for our only friend,
    Sad patience, too near neighbour to despair—
      But none has hope like thine!
  Thou through the fields and through the woods dost stray,
    Roaming the country-side, a truant boy,
    Nursing thy project in unclouded joy,
  And every doubt long blown by time away.

O born in days when wits were fresh and clear,
  And life ran gaily as the sparkling Thames;
    Before this strange disease of modern life,
  With its sick hurry, its divided aims,
    Its heads o'ertaxed, its palsied hearts, was rife—
      Fly hence, our contact fear!
  Still fly, plunge deeper in the bowering wood!
    Averse, as Dido did with gesture stern
    From her false friend's approach in Hades turn,
  Wave us away, and keep thy solitude!

Still nursing the unconquerable hope,
  Still clutching the inviolable shade,
    With a free, onward impulse brushing through,
  By night, the silvered branches of the glade—

Far on the forest-skirts, where none pursue,
  On some mild pastoral slope
Emerge, and resting on the moonlit pales
  Freshen thy flowers as in former years
  With dew, or listen with enchanted ears,
From the dark dingles, to the nightingales!

But fly our paths, our feverish contact fly!
  For strong the infection of our mental strife,
    Which, though it gives no bliss, yet spoils for rest;
  And we should win thee from thy own fair life,
    Like us distracted, and like us unblest.
      Soon, soon thy cheer would die,
  Thy hopes grow timorous, and unfixed thy powers,
    And thy clear aims be cross and shifting made;
    And then thy glad perennial youth would fade,
Fade, and grow old at last, and die like ours.

Then fly our greetings, fly our speech and smiles!
  —As some grave Tyrian trader, from the sea,
    Descried at sunrise an emerging prow
  Lifting the cool-haired creepers stealthily,
    The fringes of a southward-facing brow
      Among the Aegaean isles;
  And saw the merry Grecian coaster come,
    Freighted with amber grapes, and Chian wine,
    Green, bursting figs, and tunnies steeped in brine—
And knew the intruders on his ancient home,

The young light-hearted masters of the waves—
  And snatched his rudder, and shook out more sail;
    And day and night held on indignantly
  O'er the blue Midland waters with the gale,
    Betwixt the Syrtes and soft Sicily,
      To where the Atlantic raves
  Outside the western straits; and unbent sails
    There, where down cloudy cliffs, through sheets of foam,
    Shy traffickers, the dark Iberians come;
And on the beach undid his corded bales.

MATTHEW ARNOLD

## Stanzas from the Grande Chartreuse

Through Alpine meadows soft-suffused
With rain, where thick the crocus blows,
Past the dark forges long disused,
The mule-track from Saint Laurent goes.
The bridge is crossed, and slow we ride,
Through forest, up the mountain-side.

The autumnal evening darkens round,
The wind is up, and drives the rain;
While, hark! far down, with strangled sound
Doth the Dead Guier's stream complain,
Where that wet smoke, among the woods,
Over his boiling cauldron broods.

Swift rush the spectral vapours white
Past limestone scars with ragged pines,
Showing—then blotting from our sight!—
Halt—through the cloud-drift something shines!
High in the valley, wet and drear,
The huts of Courrerie appear.

*Strike leftward!* cries our guide; and higher
Mounts up the stony forest-way.
At last the encircling trees retire;
Look! through the showery twilight grey
What pointed roofs are these advance?—
A palace of the Kings of France?

Approach, for what we seek is here!
Alight, and sparely sup, and wait
For rest in this outbuilding near;
Then cross the sward and reach that gate.
Knock; pass the wicket! Thou art come
To the Carthusians' world-famed home.

The silent courts, where night and day
Into their stone-carved basins cold
The splashing icy fountains play—
The humid corridors behold!
Where, ghostlike in the deepening night,
Cowled forms brush by in gleaming white.

The chapel, where no organ's peal
Invests the stern and naked prayer—
With penitential cries they kneel
And wrestle; rising then, with bare
And white uplifted faces stand,
Passing the Host from hand to hand;

Each takes, and then his visage wan
Is buried in his cowl once more.
The cells!—the suffering Son of Man
Upon the wall—the knee-worn floor—
And where they sleep, that wooden bed,
Which shall their coffin be, when dead!

The library, where tract and tome
Not to feed priestly pride are there,
To hymn the conquering march of Rome,
Nor yet to amuse, as ours are!
They paint of souls the inner strife,
Their drops of blood, their death in life.

The garden, overgrown—yet mild,
See, fragrant herbs are flowering there!
Strong children of the Alpine wild
Whose culture is the brethren's care;
Of human tasks their only one,
And cheerful works beneath the sun.

Those halls, too, destined to contain
Each its own pilgrim-host of old,
From England, Germany, or Spain—
All are before me! I behold
The House, the Brotherhood austere!
—And what am I, that I am here?

For rigorous teachers seized my youth,
And purged its faith, and trimmed its fire,
Showed me the high, white star of Truth,
There bade me gaze, and there aspire.
Even now their whispers pierce the gloom:
*What dost thou in this living tomb?*

Forgive me, masters of the mind!
At whose behest I long ago
So much unlearnt, so much resigned—
I come not here to be your foe!
I seek these anchorites, not in ruth,
To curse and to deny your truth;

Not as their friend, or child, I speak!
But as, on some far northern strand,
Thinking of his own Gods, a Greek
In pity and mournful awe might stand
Before some fallen Runic stone—
For both were faiths, and both are gone.

Wandering between two worlds, one dead,
The other powerless to be born,
With nowhere yet to rest my head,
Like these, on earth I wait forlorn.
Their faith, my tears, the world deride—
I come to shed them at their side.

Oh, hide me in your gloom profound,
Ye solemn seats of holy pain!
Take me, cowled forms, and fence me round,
Till I possess my soul again;
Till free my thoughts before me roll,
Not chafed by hourly false control!

For the world cries your faith is now
But a dead time's exploded dream;
My melancholy, sciolists say,
Is a passed mode, an outworn theme—
As if the world had ever had
A faith, or sciolists been sad!

Ah, if it *be* passed, take away,
At least, the restlessness, the pain;
Be man henceforth no more a prey
To these out-dated stings again!
The nobleness of grief is gone—
Ah, leave us not the fret alone!

But—if you cannot give us ease—
Last of the race of them who grieve
Here leave us to die out with these
Last of the people who believe!
Silent, while years engrave the brow;
Silent—the best are silent now.

Achilles ponders in his tent,
The kings of modern thought are dumb;
Silent they are, though not content,
And wait to see the future come.
They have the grief men had of yore,
But they contend and cry no more.

Our fathers watered with their tears
This sea of time whereon we sail,
Their voices were in all men's ears
Who passed within their puissant hail.
Still the same ocean round us raves,
But we stand mute, and watch the waves.

For what availed it, all the noise
And outcry of the former men?—
Say, have their sons achieved more joys,
Say, is life lighter now than then?
The sufferers died, they left their pain—
The pangs which tortured them remain.

What helps it now, that Byron bore,
With haughty scorn which mocked the smart,
Through Europe to the Aetolian shore
The pageant of his bleeding heart?
That thousands counted every groan,
And Europe made his woe her own?

What boots it, Shelley! that the breeze
Carried thy lovely wail away,
Musical through Italian trees
Which fringe thy soft blue Spezzian bay?
Inheritors of thy distress
Have restless hearts one throb the less?

Or are we easier, to have read,
O Obermann! the sad, stern page,
Which tells us how thou hidd'st thy head
From the fierce tempest of thine age
In the lone brakes of Fontainebleau,
Or chalets near the Alpine snow?

Ye slumber in your silent grave!—
The world, which for an idle day
Grace to your mood of sadness gave,
Long since hath flung her weeds away.
The eternal trifler breaks your spell;
But we—we learnt your lore too well!

Years hence, perhaps, may dawn an age,
More fortunate, alas! than we,
Which without hardness will be sage,
And gay without frivolity.
Sons of the world, oh, speed those years;
But, while we wait, allow our tears!

Allow them! We admire with awe
The exulting thunder of your race;
You give the universe your law,
You triumph over time and space!
Your pride of life, your tireless powers,
We laud them, but they are not ours.

We are like children reared in shade
Beneath some old-world abbey wall,
Forgotten in a forest-glade,
And secret from the eyes of all.
Deep, deep the greenwood round them waves,
Their abbey, and its close of graves!

But, where the road runs near the stream,
Oft through the trees they catch a glance
Of passing troops in the sun's beam—
Pennon, and plume, and flashing lance!
Forth to the world those soldiers fare,
To life, to cities, and to war!

And through the wood, another way,
Faint bugle-notes from far are borne,
Where hunters gather, staghounds bay,
Round some fair forest-lodge at morn.
Gay dames are there, in sylvan green;
Laughter and cries—those notes between!

The banners flashing through the trees
Make their blood dance and chain their eyes;
That bugle-music on the breeze
Arrests them with a charmed surprise.
Banner by turns and bugle woo:
*Ye shy recluses, follow too!*

O children, what do ye reply?—
'Action and pleasure, will ye roam
Through these secluded dells to cry
And call us?—but too late ye come!
Too late for us your call ye blow,
Whose bent was taken long ago.

'Long since we pace this shadowed nave;
We watch those yellow tapers shine,
Emblems of hope over the grave,
In the high altar's depth divine;
The organ carries to our ear
Its accents of another sphere.

'Fenced early in this cloistral round
  Of reverie, of shade, of prayer,
How should we grow in other ground?
  How can we flower in foreign air?
—Pass, banners, pass, and bugles, cease;
  And leave our desert to its peace!'


COVENTRY PATMORE

## From *The Angel in the House*

### The Cathedral Close

Once more I came to Sarum Close,
  With joy half memory, half desire,
And breathed the sunny wind that rose
  And blew the shadows o'er the Spire,
And tossed the lilac's scented plumes,
  And swayed the chestnut's thousand cones,
And filled my nostrils with perfumes,
  And shaped the clouds in waifs and zones,
And wafted down the serious strain
  Of Sarum bells, when, true to time,
I reached the Dean's, with heart and brain
  That trembled to the trembling chime.

'Twas half my home, six years ago.
  The six years had not altered it:
Red-brick and ashlar, long and low,
  With dormers and with oriels lit.
Geranium, lychnis, rose arrayed
  The windows, all wide open thrown;
And some one in the Study played
  The Wedding-March of Mendelssohn.
And there it was I last took leave:
  'Twas Christmas: I remembered now
The cruel girls, who feigned to grieve,
  Took down the evergreens; and how
The holly into blazes woke
  The fire, lighting the large, low room
A dim, rich lustre of old oak
  And crimson velvet's glowing gloom.

No change had touched Dean Churchill: kind,
  By widowhood more than 'winters bent,
And settled in a cheerful mind,
  As still forecasting heaven's content.
Well might his thoughts be fixed on high,
  Now she was there! Within her face
Humility and dignity
  Were met in a most sweet embrace.
She seemed expressly sent below
  To teach our erring minds to see
The rhythmic change of time's swift flow
  As part of still eternity.
Her life, all honour, observed, with awe
  Which cross experience could not mar,
The fiction of the Christian law
  That all men honourable are;
And so her smile at once conferred
  High flattery and benign reproof;
And I, a rude boy, strangely stirred,
  Grew courtly in my own behoof.
The years, so far from doing her wrong,
  Anointed her with gracious balm,
And made her brows more and more young
  With wreaths of amaranth and palm.

Was this her eldest, Honor; prude,
  Who would not let me pull the swing;
Who, kissed at Christmas, called me rude,
  And, sobbing low, refused to sing?
How changed! In shape no slender Grace,
  But Venus; milder than the dove;
Her mother's air; her Norman face;
  Her large sweet eyes, clear lakes of love.
Mary I knew. In former time
  Ailing and pale, she thought that bliss
Was only for a better clime,
  And, heavenly overmuch, scorned this.
I, rash with theories of the right,
  Which stretched the tether of my Creed,
But did not break it, held delight
  Half discipline. We disagreed.
She told the Dean I wanted grace.
  Now she was kindest of the three,
And soft wild roses decked her face.
  And, what, was this my Mildred, she
To herself and all a sweet surprise?

My Pet, who romped and rolled a hoop?
  I wondered where those daisy eyes
    Had found their touching curve and droop.

Unmannerly times! But now we sat
    Stranger than strangers; till I caught
And answered Mildred's smile; and that
    Spread to the rest, and freedom brought.
The Dean talked little, looking on,
    Of three such daughters justly vain.
What letters they had had from Bonn,
    Said Mildred, and what plums from Spain!
By Honor I was kindly tasked
    To excuse my never coming down
From Cambridge; Mary smiled and asked
    Were Kant and Goethe yet outgrown?
And, pleased, we talked the old days o'er;
    And, parting, I for pleasure sighed.
To be there as a friend, (since more),
    Seemed then, seems still, excuse for pride;
For something that abode endued
    With temple-like repose, an air
Of life's kind purposes pursued
    With ordered freedom sweet and fair.
A tent pitched in a world not right
    It seemed, whose inmates, every one,
On tranquil faces bore the light
    Of duties beautifully done,
And humbly, though they had few peers,
    Kept their own laws, which seemed to be
The fair sum of six thousand years'
    Traditions of civility.

## Love at Large

Whene'er I come where ladies are,
    How sad soever I was before,
Though like a ship frost-bound and far
    Withheld in ice from the ocean's roar,
Third-wintered in that dreadful dock,
    With stiffened cordage, sails decayed,
And crew that care for calm and shock
    Alike, too dull to be dismayed,
Yet, if I come where ladies are,
    How sad soever I was before,
Then is my sadness banished far,
    And I am like that ship no more;

Or like that ship if the ice-field splits,
  Burst by the sudden polar Spring,
And all thank God with their warming wits,
  And kiss each other and dance and sing,
And hoist fresh sails, that make the breeze
  Blow them along the liquid sea,
Out of the North, where life did freeze,
  Into the haven where they would be.

### Sahara

I stood by Honor and the Dean,
  They seated in the London train.
A month from her! yet this had been,
  Ere now, without such bitter pain.
But neighbourhood makes parting light,
  And distance remedy has none;
Alone, she near, I felt as might
  A blind man sitting in the sun;
She near, all for the time was well;
  Hope's self, when we were far apart,
With lonely feeling, like the smell
  Of heath on mountains, filled my heart.
To see her seemed delight's full scope,
  And her kind smile, so clear of care,
Even then, though darkening all my hope,
  Gilded the cloud of my despair.

She had forgot to bring a book.
  I lent one; blamed the print for old;
And did not tell her that she took
  A Petrarch worth its weight in gold.
I hoped she'd lose it; for my love
  Was grown so dainty, high, and nice,
It prized no luxury above
  The sense of fruitless sacrifice.

The bell rang, and, with shrieks like death,
  Link catching link, the long array,
With ponderous pulse and fiery breath,
  Proud of its burthen, swept away;
And through the lingering crowd I broke,
  Sought the hill-side, and thence, heart-sick,
Beheld far off, the little smoke
  Along the landscape kindling quick.

What should I do, where should I go,
  Now she was gone, my love! for mine
She was, whatever here below
  Crossed or usurped my right divine.
Life, without her, was vain and gross,
  The glory from the world was gone,
And on the gardens of the Close
  As on Sahara shone the sun.
Oppressed with her departed grace,
  My thoughts on ill surmises fed;
The harmful influence of the place
  She went to filled my soul with dread.
She, mixing with the people there,
  Might come back altered, having caught
The foolish, fashionable air
  Of knowing all, and feeling nought.
Or, giddy with her beauty's praise,
  She'd scorn our simple country life,
Its wholesome nights and tranquil days,
  And would not deign to be my Wife.
'My Wife,' 'my Wife,' ah, tenderest word!
  How oft, as fearful she might hear,
Whispering that name of 'Wife,' I heard
  The chiming of the inmost sphere.

I passed the home of my regret.
  The clock was striking in the hall,
And one sad window open yet,
  Although the dews began to fall.
Ah, distance showed her beauty's scope!
  How light of heart and innocent
That loveliness which sickened hope
  And wore the world for ornament!
How perfectly her life was framed;
  And, thought of in that passionate mood,
How her affecting graces shamed
  The vulgar life that was but good!

I wondered, would her bird be fed,
  Her rose plots watered, she not by;
Loading my breast with angry dread
  Of light, unlikely injury.
So, filled with love and fond remorse,
  I paced the Close, its every part
Endowed with reliquary force
  To heal and raise from death my heart.

How tranquil and unsecular
    The precinct! Once, through yonder gate,
I saw her go, and knew from far
    Her love-lit form and gentle state.
Her dress had brushed this wicket; here
    She turned her face, and laughed, with light
Like moonbeams on a wavering mere.
    Weary beforehand of the night,
I went; the blackbird, in the wood,
    Talked by himself, and eastward grew
In heaven the symbol of my mood,
    Where one bright star engrossed the blue.

### The County Ball

Well, Heaven be thanked my first-love failed,
    As, Heaven be thanked, our first-loves do!
Thought I, when Fanny past me sailed,
    Loved once, for what I never knew,
Unless for colouring in her talk,
    When cheeks and merry mouth would show
Three roses on a single stalk,
    The middle wanting room to blow,
And forward ways, that charmed the boy
    Whose love-sick mind, misreading fate,
Scarce hoped that any Queen of Joy
    Could ever stoop to be his mate.

But there danced she, who from the leaven
    Of ill preserved my heart and wit
All unawares, for she was heaven,
    Others at best but fit for it.
One of those lovely things she was
    In whose least action there can be
Nothing so transient but it has
    An air of immortality.
I marked her step, with peace elate,
    Her brow more beautiful than morn,
Her sometime look of girlish state
    Which sweetly waived its right to scorn;
The giddy crowd, she grave the while,
    Although, as 'twere beyond her will,
Around her mouth the baby smile,
    That she was born with, lingered still.
Her ball-dress seemed a breathing mist,
    From the fair form exhaled and shed,
Raised in the dance with arm and wrist
    All warmth and light, unbraceleted.

Her motion, feeling 'twas beloved,
  The pensive soul of tune expressed,
And, oh, what perfume, as she moved,
  Came from the flowers in her breast!
How sweet a tongue the music had!
  'Beautiful Girl,' it seemed to say,
'Though all the world were vile and sad,
  'Dance on; let innocence be gay.'
Ah, none but I discerned her looks,
  When in the throng she passed me by,
For love is like a ghost, and brooks
  Only the chosen seer's eye;
And who but she could e'er divine
  The halo and the happy trance,
When her bright arm reposed on mine,
  In all the pauses of the dance!

Whilst so her beauty fed my sight,
  And whilst I lived in what she said,
Accordant airs, like all delight
  Most sweet when noted least, were played;
And was it like the Pharisee
  If I in secret bowed my face
With joyful thanks that I should be,
  Not as were many, but with grace,
And fortune of well-nurtured youth,
  And days no sordid pains defile,
And thoughts accustomed to the truth,
  Made capable of her fair smile?

Charles Barton followed down the stair,
  To talk with me about the Ball,
And carp at all the people there.
  The Churchills chiefly stirred his gall:
'Such were the Kriemhiles and Isondes
  You stormed about at Trinity!
Nothing at heart but handsome Blondes!
  Folk say that you and Fanny Fry—'
'They err! Good-night! Here lies my course,
  Through Wilton.' Silence blest my ears,
And, weak at heart with vague remorse,
  A passing poignancy of tears
Attacked mine eyes. By pale and park
  I rode, and ever seemed to see,
In the transparent starry dark,
  That splendid brow of chastity,
That soft and yet subduing light,

At which, as at the sudden moon,
I held my breath, and thought 'how bright!'
That guileless beauty in its noon,
Compelling tribute of desires
Ardent as day when Sirius reigns,
Pure as the permeating fires
That smoulder in the opal's veins.


GERALD MASSEY

## All's Right with the World

Sweet Phosphor tricks to a smile the brow of heaven,
Dawn's golden springs surge into floods of day,
Lush-leavy woods break into singing, Earth
From dewy dark rolls round her balmy side,
And all goes right, and merrily, with the world.

Spring with a tender beauty clothes the earth,
Happy, and jewelled like a sumptuous Bride,
As though she knew no sorrow—held no grave:
No glory dims for all the hearts that break,
And all goes right, and merrily, with the world.

Birds sing as sweetly on the blossomed boughs,
Suns mount as royally their sapphire throne,
Stars bud in gorgeous gloom, and harvests yield,
As though man nestled in the lap of Love:
All, all goes right, and merrily, with the world.

But slip this silken-folded mask aside,
And lo, Hell welters at our very feet!
The Poor are murdered body and soul, the Rich
In Pleasure's chalice melt their pearl of life!
Ay, all goes right, and merrily, with the world.

Lean out into the looming Future, mark
The battle roll across the night to come!
'See how we right our Wrongs at last,' Revenge
Writes with red radiance on the midnight heaven:
Yet, all goes right, and merrily, with the world.

So Sodom, grim old Reveller! went to death.
Voluptuous Music throbbed through all her courts,
Mirth wantoned at her heart, one pulse before
Fire-tongues told out her bloody tale of wrong,—
And all went right, and merrily, with the world.


GERALD MASSEY

## O Lay Thy Hand in Mine, Dear!

O lay thy hand in mine, dear!
   We're growing old, we're growing old;
But Time hath brought no sign, dear,
   That hearts grow cold, that hearts grow cold.
'Tis long, long since our new love
   Made life divine, made life divine;
But age enricheth true love,
   Like noble wine, like noble wine.

And lay thy cheek to mine, dear,
   And take thy rest, and take thy rest;
Mine arms around thee twine, dear,
   And make thy nest, and make thy nest.
A many cares are pressing
   On this dear head, on this dear head;
But Sorrow's hands in blessing
   Are surely laid, are surely laid.

O lean thy life on mine, dear!
   'Twill shelter thee, 'twill shelter thee.
Thou wert a winsome vine, dear,
   On my young tree, on my young tree:
And so, till boughs are leafless,
   And Song-birds flown, and Song-birds flown,
We'll twine, then lay us, griefless,
   Together down, together down.

GERALD MASSEY

## *The Worker*

I care not a curse though from birth he inherit
　The tear-bitter bread and the stingings of scorn,
If the man be but one of God's nobles in spirit,—
　Though penniless, richly-souled,—heartsome, though worn—
And will not for golden bribe lout it or flatter,
　But clings to the Right aye, as steel to the pole:
He may sweat at the plough, loom, or anvil, no matter,
　I'll own him the man that is dear to my soul.

His hand may be hard, and his raiment be tattered,
　On straw-pallet nightly his weary limbs rest;
If his brow wear the stamp of a spirit unfettered,
　I'm mining at once for the gems in his breast.
Give me the true man, who will fear not nor falter,
　Though Want be his guerdon, the Workhouse his goal,
Till his heart has burnt out upon Liberty's Altar:
　For this is the man I hold dear to my soul.

True hearts, in this brave world of blessings and beauty,
　Will scorn the poor splendour of losel and lurker;
Toil is creation's crown, worship is duty,
　And greater than Gods in old days is the Worker.
For us the wealth-laden world laboureth ever;
　For us harvests ripen, winds blow, waters roll;
And him who gives back in his might of endeavour,
　I'll cherish,—a man ever dear to my soul.

GERALD MASSEY

## *Desolate*

The Day goes down red darkling,
　The moaning waves dash out the light,
And there is not a star of hope sparkling
　On the threshold of my night.

Wild winds of Autumn go wailing
　Up the valley and over the hill,
Like yearning Ghosts round the world sailing,
　In search of the old love still.

A fathomless sea is rolling
  O'er the wreck of the bravest bark;
And my pain-muffled heart is tolling,
  Its dumb-peal down in the dark.

The waves of a mighty sorrow
  Have whelmèd the pearl of my life:
And there cometh to me no morrow
  Shall solace this desolate strife.

Gone are the last faint flashes,
  Set is the sun of my years;
And over a few poor ashes
  I sit in my darkness and tears.


ROBERT BROWNING

## A Toccata of Galuppi's

Oh Galuppi, Baldassaro, this is very sad to find!
I can hardly misconceive you; it would prove me deaf and blind;
But although I take your meaning, 'tis with such a heavy mind!

Here you come with your old music, and here's all the good it brings.
What, they lived once thus at Venice where the merchants were the kings,
Where Saint Mark's is, where the Doges used to wed the sea with rings?

Ay, because the sea's the street there; and 'tis arched by . . . what you call
. . . Shylock's bridge with houses on it, where they kept the carnival:
I was never out of England—it's as if I saw it all.

Did young people take their pleasure when the sea was warm in May?
Balls and masks begun at midnight, burning ever to mid-day,
When they made up fresh adventures for the morrow, do you say?

Was a lady such a lady, cheeks so round and lips so red,—
On her neck the small face buoyant, like a bell-flower on its bed,
O'er the breast's superb abundance where a man might base his head?

Well, and it was graceful of them—they'd break talk off and afford
—She, to bite her mask's black velvet—he, to finger on his sword,
While you sat and played Toccatas, stately at the clavichord?

What? Those lesser thirds so plaintive, sixths diminished, sigh on sigh,
Told them something? Those suspensions, those solutions—'Must we die?'
Those commiserating sevenths—'Life might last! we can but try!'

'Were you happy?'—'Yes'—'And are you still as happy?'—'Yes. And you?'
—'Then, more kisses!'—'Did *I* stop them, when a million seemed so few?'
Hark, the dominant's persistence till it must be answered to!

So, an octave struck the answer. Oh, they praised you, I dare say!
'Brave Galuppi! that was music! good alike at grave and gay!
'I can always leave off talking when I hear a master play!'

Then they left you for their pleasure: till in due time, one by one,
Some with lives that came to nothing, some with deeds as well undone,
Death stepped tacitly and took them where they never see the sun.

But when I sit down to reason, think to take my stand nor swerve,
While I triumph o'er a secret wrung from nature's close reserve,
In you come with your cold music till I creep through every nerve.

Yes, you, like a ghostly cricket, creaking where a house was burned:
'Dust and ashes, dead and done with, Venice spent what Venice earned.
The soul, doubtless, is immortal—where a soul can be discerned.

'Yours for instance: you know physics, something of geology,
Mathematics are your pastime; souls shall rise in their degree;
Butterflies may dread extinction,—you'll not die, it cannot be!

'As for Venice and her people, merely born to bloom and drop,
Here on earth they bore their fruitage, mirth and folly were the crop:
What of soul was left, I wonder, when the kissing had to stop?

'Dust and ashes!' So you creak it, and I want the heart to scold.
Dear dead women, with such hair, too—what's become of all the gold
Used to hang and brush their bosoms? I feel chilly and grown old.

ELIZABETH BARRETT BROWNING

## The Best Thing in the World

What's the best thing in the world?
June-rose, by May-dew impearled;
Sweet south-wind, that means no rain;
Truth, not cruel to a friend;
Pleasure, not in haste to end;
Beauty, not self-decked and curled
Till its pride is over-plain;
Light, that never makes you wink;

Memory, that gives no pain;
Love, when, *so*, you're loved again.
What's the best thing in the world?
—Something out of it, I think.

WILLIAM BARNES

## *My Orcha'd in Linden Lea*

'Ithin the woodlands, flow'ry gleäded,
   By the woak tree's mossy root,
The sheenèn grass-bleädes, timber-sheäded,
   Now do quiver under voot;
An' birds do whissle over head,
An' water's bubblèn in its bed,
An' there vor me the apple tree
Do leän down low in Linden Lea.

When leaves that leätely wer a-springèn
   Now do feäde 'ithin the copse,
An' païnted birds do hush their zingèn
   Up upon the timber's tops;
An' brown-leav'd fruit's a-turnèn red,
In cloudless zunsheen, over head,
Wi' fruit vor me, the apple tree
Do leän down low in Linden Lea.

Let other vo'k meäke money vaster
   In the aïr o' dark-room'd towns,
I don't dread a peevish meäster;
   Though noo man do heed my frowns,
I be free to goo abrode,
Or teäke ageän my hwomeward road
To where, vor me, the apple tree
Do leän down low in Linden Lea.

WILLIAM BARNES

## *The Leäne*

They do zay that a travellèn chap
  Have a-put in the newspeäper now,
That the bit o' green ground on the knap
  Should be all a-took in vor the plough.
He do fancy 'tis easy to show
  That we can be but stunpolls at best,
Vor to leäve a green spot where a flower can grow,
  Or a voot-weary walker mid rest.
'Tis hedge-grubbèn, Thomas, an' ledge-grubbèn,
    Never a-done
While a sov'rèn mwore's to be won.

The road, he do zay, is so wide
  As 'tis wanted vor travellers' wheels,
As if all that did travel did ride,
  An' did never get galls on their heels.
He would leäve sich a thin strip o' groun',
  That, if a man's veet in his shoes
Wer a-burnèn an' zore, why he coulden zit down
  But the wheels would run over his tooes.
Vor 'tis meäke money, Thomas, an' teäke money,
    What's zwold an' bought
Is all that is worthy o' thought.

Years agoo the leäne-zides did bear grass,
  Vor to pull wi' the geeses' red bills,
That did hiss at the vo'k that did pass,
  Or the bwoys that pick'd up their white quills.
But shortly, if vower or vive
  Ov our goslèns do creep vrom the agg
They must mwope in the geärden, mwore dead than alive,
  In a coop, or a-tied by the lag.
Vor to catch at land, Thomas, an' snatch at land,
    Now is the plan;
Meäke money wherever you can.

The childern wull soon have noo pleäce
  Vor to plaÿ in, an' if they do grow,
They wull have a thin musheroom feäce,
  Wi' their bodies so sumple as dough.
But a man is a-meäde ov a child,
  An' his limbs do grow worksome by plaÿ;
An' if the young child's little body's a-spweil'd,
  Why, the man's wull the sooner decaÿ.

But wealth is wo'th now mwore than health is wo'th;
   Let it all goo,
If't 'ull bring but a sov'rèn or two.

Vor to breed the young fox or the heäre,
  We can gi'e up whole eäcres o' ground,
But the greens be a-grudg'd, vor to rear
  Our young childern up healthy an' sound,
Why, there woont be a-left the next age
  A green spot where their veet can goo free;
'An' the goocoo wull soon be committed to cage
  Vor a trespass in zomebody's tree.
Vor 'tis lockèn up, Thomas, an' blockèn up,
   Stranger or brother,
Men mussen come nigh woone another.

Woone day I went in at a geäte,
  Wi' my child, where an echo did sound,
An' the owner come up, an' did reäte
  Me as if I would car off his ground.
But his vield an' the grass wer-a-let,
  An' the damage that he could a-took
Wer at mwost that the while I did open the geäte
  I did rub roun' the eye on the hook.
But 'tis drevèn out, Thomas', an' hevèn out.
   Trample noo grounds,
Unless you be after the hounds.

Ah! the Squiër o' Culver-dell Hall
  Were as diff'rent as light is vrom dark,
Wi' zome vo'k that, as evenèn did vall,
  Had a-broke drough long grass in his park;
Vor he went, wi' a smile, vor to meet
  Wi' the trespassers while they did pass,
An' he zaid, 'I do fear you'll catch cwold in your veet,
  You've a-walk'd drough so much o' my grass.'
His mild words, Thomas, cut em like swords, Thomas,
   Newly a-whet,
An' went vurder wi' them than a dreat.

WILLIAM BARNES

## A Wife A-Praïs'd

'Twer May, but ev'ry leaf wer dry
All day below a sheenèn sky;
The zun did glow wi' yollow gleäre,
An' cowslips blow wi' yollow gleäre,
Wi' graegles' bells a-droopèn low,
An' bremble boughs a-stoopèn low;
While culvers in the trees did coo
    Above the vallèn dew.

An' there, wi' heäir o' glossy black,
Bezide your neck an' down your back,
You rambled gaÿ a-bloomèn feäir;
By boughs o' maÿ a-bloomèn feäir;
An' while the birds did twitter nigh,
An' water weäves did glitter nigh,
You gather'd cowslips in the lew,
    Below the vallèn dew.

An' now, while you've a-been my bride
As years o' flow'rs ha' bloom'd an' died,
Your smilèn feäce ha' been my jaÿ;
Your soul o'greäce ha' been my jaÿ;
An' wi' my evenèn rest a-come,
An' zunsheen to the west a-come,
I'm glad to teäke my road to you
    Vrom vields o' vallèn dew.

An' when the raïn do wet the maÿ,
A-bloomèn where we woonce did straÿ,
An' win' do blow along so vast,
An' streams do flow along so vast;
Ageän the storms so rough abroad,
An' angry tongues so gruff abroad,
The love that I do meet vrom you
    Is lik' the vallèn dew.

An' you be sprack's a bee on wing,
In search ov honey in the Spring:
The dawn-red sky do meet ye up;
The birds vu'st cry do meet ye up;
An' wi' your feäce a-smilèn on,
An' busy hands a-tweilèn on,
You'll vind zome useful work to do
    Until the vallèn dew.

WILLIAM BARNES

## The Wife A-Lost

Since I noo mwore do zee your feäce,
    Up steärs or down below,
I'll zit me in the lwonesome pleäce,
    Where flat-bough'd beech do grow:
Below the beeches' bough, my love,
    Where you did never come,
An' I don't look to meet ye now,
    As I do look at hwome.

Since you noo mwore be at my zide,
    In walks in zummer het,
I'll go alwone where mist do ride,
    Drough trees a drippèn wet:
Below the raïn-wet bough, my love,
    Where you did never come,
An' I don't grieve to miss ye now,
    As I do grieve at home.

Since now bezide my dinner-bwoard
    Your vaïce do never sound,
I'll eat the bit I can avword,
    A-vield upon the ground;
Below the darksome bough, my love,
    Where you did never dine,
An' I don't grieve to miss ye now,
    As I at hwome do pine.

Since I do miss your vaïce an' feäce
    In praÿer at eventide,
I'll praÿ wi' woone said vaïce vor greäce
    To goo where you do bide;
Above the tree an' bough, my love,
    Where you be gone avore,
An' be a-waïtèn vor me now,
    To come vor evermwore.

ALFRED, LORD TENNYSON

## From *Maud*

### VIII

She came to the village church,
And sat by a pillar alone;
An angel watching an urn
Wept over her, carved in stone;
And once, but once, she lifted her eyes,
And suddenly, sweetly, strangely blushed
To find they were met by my own;
And suddenly, sweetly, my heart beat stronger
And thicker, until I heard no longer
The snow-banded, dilettante,
Delicate-handed priest intone;
And thought, is it pride, and mused and sighed
'No surely, now it cannot be pride'.

### IX

I was walking a mile,
More than a mile from the shore,
The sun looked out with a smile
Betwixt the cloud and the moor
And riding at set of day
Over the dark moor land,
Rapidly riding far away,
She waved to me with her hand.
There were two at her side,
Something flashed in the sun,
Down by the hill I saw them ride,
In a moment they were gone:
Like a sudden spark
Struck vainly in the night,
Then returns the dark
With no more hope of light.

### XVII

Go not, happy day,
  From the shining fields,
Go not, happy day,
  Till the maiden yields.

Rosy is the West,
　Rosy is the South,
Roses are her cheeks,
　And a rose her mouth
When the happy Yes
　Falters from her lips,
Pass and blush the news
　Over glowing ships;
Over blowing seas,
　Over seas at rest,
Pass the happy news,
　Blush it through the West;
Till the red man dance
　By his red cedar-tree,
And the red man's babe
　Leap, beyond the sea.
Blush from West to East,
　Blush from East to West,
Till the West is East,
　Blush it through the West.
Rosy is the West,
　Rosy is the South,
Roses are her cheeks,
　And a rose her mouth.


XVIII

I have led her home, my love, my only friend.
There is none like her, none.
And never yet so warmly ran my blood
And sweetly, on and on
Calming itself to the long-wished-for end,
Full to the banks, close on the promised good.

None like her, none.
Just now the dry-tongued laurels' pattering talk
Seemed her light foot along the garden walk,
And shook my heart to think she comes once more;
But even then I heard her close the door,
The gates of Heaven are closed, and she is gone.

There is none like her, none.
Nor will be when our summers have deceased.
O, art thou sighing for Lebanon
In the long breeze that streams to thy delicious East,
Sighing for Lebanon,
Dark cedar, though thy limbs have here increased,

Upon a pastoral slope as fair,
And looking to the South, and fed
With honeyed rain and delicate air,
And haunted by the starry head
Of her whose gentle will has changed my fate,
And made my life a perfumed altar-flame;
And over whom thy darkness must have spread
With such delight as theirs of old, thy great
Forefathers of the thornless garden, there
Shadowing the snow-limbed Eve from whom she came.

Here will I lie, while these long branches sway,
And you fair stars that crown a happy day
Go in and out as if at merry play,
Who am no more so all forlorn,
As when it seemed far better to be born
To labour and the mattock-hardened hand,
Than nursed at ease and brought to understand
A sad astrology, the boundless plan
That makes you tyrants in your iron skies,
Innumerable, pitiless, passionless eyes,
Cold fires, yet with power to burn and brand
His nothingness into man.

But now shine on, and what care I,
Who in this stormy gulf have found a pearl
The countercharm of space and hollow sky,
And do accept my madness, and would die
To save from some slight shame one simple girl.

Would die; for sullen-seeming Death may give
More life to Love than is or ever was
In our low world, where yet 'tis sweet to live.
Let no one ask me how it came to pass;
It seems that I am happy, that to me
A livelier emerald twinkles in the grass,
A purer sapphire melts into the sea.

Not die; but live a life of truest breath,
And teach true life to fight with mortal wrongs.
O, why should Love, like men in drinking-songs,
Spice his fair banquet with the dust of death?
Make answer, Maud my bliss,
Maud made my Maud by that long loving kiss,
Life of my life, wilt thou not answer this?
'The dusky strand of Death inwoven here
With dear Love's tie, makes Love himself more dear.'

Is that enchanted moan only the swell
Of the long waves that roll in yonder bay?
And hark the clock within, the silver knell
Of twelve sweet hours that past in bridal white,
And died to live, long as my pulses play;
But now by this my love has closed her sight
And given false death her hand, and stolen away
To dreamful wastes where footless fancies dwell
Among the fragments of the golden day.
May nothing there her maiden grace affright!
Dear heart, I feel with thee the drowsy spell.
My bride to be, my evermore delight,
My own heart's heart, my ownest own, farewell;
It is but for a little space I go:
And ye meanwhile far over moor and fell
Beat to the noiseless music of the night!
Has our whole earth gone nearer to the glow
Of your soft splendours that you look so bright?
*I* have climbed nearer out of lonely Hell.
Beat, happy stars, timing with things below,
Beat with my heart more blest than heart can tell,
Blest, but for some dark undercurrent woe
That seems to draw—but it shall not be so:
Let all be well, be well.

### XXII

Come into the garden, Maud,
    For the black bat, night, has flown,
Come into the garden, Maud,
    I am here at the gate alone;
And the woodbine spices are wafted abroad,
    And the musk of the rose is blown.

For a breeze of morning moves,
    And the planet of Love is on high,
Beginning to faint in the light that she loves
    On a bed of daffodil sky,
To faint in the light of the sun she loves,
    To faint in his light, and to die.

All night have the roses heard
    The flute, violin, bassoon;
All night has the casement jessamine stirred
    To the dancers dancing in tune;
Till a silence fell with the waking bird,
    And a hush with the setting moon.

I said to the lily, 'There is but one
  With whom she has heart to be gay.
When will the dancers leave her alone?
  She is weary of dance and play.'
Now half to the setting moon are gone,
  And half to the rising day;
Low on the sand and loud on the stone
  The last wheel echoes away.

I said to the rose, 'The brief night goes
  In babble and revel and wine.
O young lord-lover, what sighs are those,
  For one that will never be thine?
But mine, but mine,' so I sware to the rose,
  'For ever and ever, mine.'

And the soul of the rose went into my blood,
  As the music clashed in the hall;
And long by the garden lake I stood,
  For I heard your rivulet fall
From the lake to the meadow and on to the wood,
  Our wood, that is dearer than all;

From the meadow your walks have left so sweet
  That whenever a March-wind sighs
He sets the jewel-print of your feet
  In violets blue as your eyes,
To the woody hollows in which we meet
  And the valleys of Paradise.

The slender acacia would not shake
  One long milk-bloom on the tree;
The white lake-blossom fell into the lake
  As the pimpernel dozed on the lea;
But the rose was awake all night for your sake,
  Knowing your promise to me;
The lilies and roses were all awake,
  They sighed for the dawn and thee.

Queen rose of the rosebud garden of girls,
  Come hither, the dances are done,
In gloss of satin and glimmer of pearls,
  Queen lily and rose in one;
Shine out, little head, sunning over with curls,
  To the flowers, and be their sun.

There has fallen a splendid tear
From the passion-flower at the gate.
She is coming, my dove, my dear;
She is coming, my life, my fate;
The red rose cries, 'She is near, she is near;'
And the white rose weeps, 'She is late;'
The larkspur listens, 'I hear, I hear;'
And the lily whispers, 'I wait.'

She is coming, my own, my sweet;
Were it ever so airy a tread,
My heart would hear her and beat,
Were it earth in an earthy bed;
My dust would hear her and beat,
Had I lain for a century dead;
Would start and tremble under her feet,
And blossom in purple and red.


ROBERT BROWNING

## By the Fire-Side

How well I know what I mean to do
When the long dark autumn-evenings come:
And where, my soul, is thy pleasant hue?
With the music of all thy voices, dumb
In life's November too!

I shall be found by the fire, suppose,
O'er a great wise book as beseemeth age,
While the shutters flap as the cross-wind blows
And I turn the page, and I turn the page,
Not verse now, only prose!

Till the young ones whisper, finger on lip,
'There he is at it, deep in Greek:
Now then, or never, out we slip
To cut from the hazels by the creek
A mainmast for our ship!'

I shall be at it indeed, my friends:
Greek puts already on either side
Such a branch-work forth as soon extends
To a vista opening far and wide,
And I pass out where it ends.

The outside-frame, like your hazel-trees:
   But the inside-archway widens fast,
And a rarer sort succeeds to these,
   And we slope to Italy at last
And youth, by green degrees.

I follow wherever I am led,
   Knowing so well the leader's hand:
Oh woman-country, wooed not wed,
   Loved all the more by earth's male-lands,
Laid to their hearts instead!

Look at the ruined chapel again
   Half way up in the Alpine gorge!
Is that a tower, I point you plain,
   Or is it a mill, or an iron-forge
Breaks solitude in vain?

A turn, and we stand in the heart of things;
   The woods are round us, heaped and dim;
From slab to slab how it slips and springs,
   The thread of water single and slim,
Through the ravage some torrent brings!

Does it feed the little lake below?
   That speck of white just on its marge
Is Pella; see, in the evening-glow,
   How sharp the silver spear-heads charge
When Alp meets heaven in snow!

On our other side is the straight-up rock;
   And a path is kept 'twixt the gorge and it
By boulder-stones where lichens mock
   The marks on a moth, and small ferns fit
Their teeth to the polished block.

Oh the sense of the yellow mountain-flowers,
   And thorny balls, each three in one,
The chestnuts throw on our path in showers!
   For the drop of the woodland fruit's begun
These early November hours,

That crimson the creeper's leaf across
   Like a splash of blood, intense, abrupt,
O'er a shield else gold from rim to boss,
   And lay it for show on the fairy-cupped
Elf-needled mat of moss,

By the rose-flesh mushrooms, undivulged
   Last evening—nay, in to-day's first dew
Yon sudden coral nipple bulged,
   Where a freaked fawn-coloured flaky crew
Of toadstools peep indulged.

And yonder, at foot of the fronting ridge
   That takes the turn to a range beyond,
Is the chapel reached by the one-arched bridge
   Where the water is stopped in a stagnant pond
Danced over by the midge.

The chapel and bridge are of stone alike,
   Blackish-grey and mostly wet;
Cut hemp-stalks steep in the narrow dyke.
   See here again, how the lichens fret
And the roots of the ivy strike!

Poor little place, where its one priest comes
   On a festa-day, if he comes at all,
To the dozen folk from their scattered homes,
   Gathered within that precinct small
By the dozen ways one roams—

To drop from the charcoal-burners' huts,
   Or climb from the hemp-dressers' low shed,
Leave the grange where the woodman stores his nuts,
   Or the wattled cote where the fowlers spread
Their gear on the rock's bare juts.

It has some pretension too, this front,
   With its bit of fresco half-moon-wise
Set over the porch, Art's early wont:
   'Tis John in the Desert, I surmise,
But has borne the weather's brunt—

Not from the fault of the builder, though,
   For a pent-house properly projects
Where three carved beams make a certain show,
   Dating—good thought of our architect's—
'Five, six, nine, he lets you know.

And all day long a bird sings there,
   And a stray sheep drinks at the pond at times;
The place is silent and aware;
   It has had its scenes, its joys and crimes,
But that is its own affair.

My perfect wife, my Leonor,
  Oh heart, my own, oh eyes, mine too,
Whom else could I dare look backward for,
  With whom beside should I dare pursue
The path grey heads abhor?

For it leads to a crag's sheer edge with them;
  Youth, flowery all the way, there stops—
Not they; age threatens and they contemn,
  Till they reach the gulf wherein youth drops,
One inch from life's safe hem!

With me, youth led . . . I will speak now,
  No longer watch you as you sit
Reading by fire-light, that great brow
  And the spirit-small hand propping it,
Mutely, my heart knows how—

When, if I think but deep enough,
  You are wont to answer, prompt as rhyme;
And you, too, find without rebuff
  Response your soul seeks many a time
Piercing its fine flesh-stuff.

My own, confirm me! If I tread
  This path back, is it not in pride
To think how little I dreamed it led
  To an age so blest that, by its side,
Youth seems the waste instead?

My own, see where the years conduct!
  At first, 'twas something our two souls
Should mix as mists do; each is sucked
  In each now: on, the new stream rolls,
Whatever rocks obstruct.

Think, when our one soul understands
  The great Word which makes all things new,
When earth breaks up and heaven expands,
  How will the change strike me and you
In the house not made with hands?

Oh I must feel your brain prompt mine,
  Your heart anticipate my heart,
You must be just before, in fine,
  See and make me see, for your part,
New depths of the divine!

But who could have expected this
   When we two drew together first
Just for the obvious human bliss,
   To satisfy life's daily thirst
With a thing men seldom miss?

Come back with me to the first of all,
   Let us lean and love it over again,
Let us now forget and now recall,
   Break the rosary in a pearly rain,
And gather what we let fall!

What did I say?— that a small bird sings
   All day long, save when a brown pair
Of hawks from the wood float with wide wings
   Strained to a bell: 'gainst noon-day glare
You count the streaks and rings.

But at afternoon or almost eve
   'Tis better; then the silence grows
To that degree, you half believe
   It must get rid of what it knows,
Its bosom does so heave.

Hither we walked then, side by side,
   Arm in arm and cheek to cheek,
And still I questioned or replied,
   While my heart, convulsed to really speak,
Lay choking in its pride.

Silent the crumbling bridge we cross,
   And pity and praise the chapel sweet,
And care about the fresco's loss,
   And wish for our souls a like retreat,
And wonder at the moss.

Stoop and kneel on the settle under,
   Look through the window's grated square:
Nothing to see! For fear of plunder,
   The cross is down and the altar bare,
As if thieves don't fear thunder.

We stoop and look in through the grate,
   See the little porch and rustic door,
Read duly the dead builder's date;
   Then cross the bridge that we crossed before,
Take the path again—but wait!

Oh moment, one and infinite!
　　The water slips o'er stock and stone;
The West is tender, hardly bright:
　　How grey at once is the evening grown—
One star, its chrysolite!

We two stood there with never a third,
　　But each by each, as each knew well:
The sights we saw and the sounds we heard,
　　The lights and the shades made up a spell
Till the trouble grew and stirred.

Oh, the little more, and how much it is!
　　And the little less, and what worlds away!
How a sound shall quicken content to bliss,
　　Or a breath suspend the blood's best play,
And life be a proof of this!

Had she willed it, still had stood the screen
　　So slight, so sure, 'twixt my love and her:
I could fix her face with a guard between,
　　And find her soul as when friends confer,
Friends—lovers that might have been.

For my heart had a touch of the woodland-time,
　　Wanting to sleep now over its best.
Shake the whole tree in the summer-prime,
　　But bring to the last leaf no such test!
'Hold the last fast!' runs the rhyme.

For a chance to make your little much,
　　To gain a lover and lose a friend,
Venture the tree and a myriad such,
　　When nothing you mar but the year can mend:
But a last leaf—fear to touch!

Yet should it unfasten itself and fall
　　Eddying down till it find your face
At some slight wind—best chance of all!
　　Be your heart henceforth its dwelling-place
You trembled to forestall!

Worth how well, those dark grey eyes,
　　That hair so dark and dear, how worth
That a man should strive and agonize,
　　And taste a veriest hell on earth
For the hope of such a prize!

You might have turned and tried a man,
  Set him a space to weary and wear,
And prove which suited more your plan,
  His best of hope or his worst despair,
Yet end as he began.

But you spared me this, like the heart you are,
  And filled my empty heart at a word.
If two lives join, there is oft a scar,
  They are one and one, with a shadowy third;
One near one is too far.

A moment after, and hands unseen
  Were hanging the night around us fast;
But we knew that a bar was broken between
  Life and life: we were mixed at last
In spite of the mortal screen.

The forests had done it; there they stood;
  We caught for a moment the powers at play:
They had mingled us so, for once and good,
  Their work was done—we might go or stay,
They relapsed to their ancient mood.

How the world is made for each of us!
  How all we perceive and know in it
Tends to some moment's product thus,
  When a soul declares itself—to wit,
By its fruit, the thing it does!

Be hate that fruit or love that fruit,
  It forwards the general deed of man,
And each of the Many helps to recruit
  The life of the race by a general plan;
Each living his own, to boot.

I am named and known by that moment's feat;
  There took my station and degree;
So grew my own small life complete,
  As nature obtained her best of me—
One born to love you, sweet!

And to watch you sink by the fire-side now
  Back again, as you mutely sit
Musing by fire-light, that great brow
  And the spirit-small hand propping it,
Yonder, my heart knows how!

So, earth has gained by one man the more,
    And the gain of earth must be heaven's gain too;
And the whole is well worth thinking o'er
    When autumn comes: which I mean to do
      One day, as I said before.


ROBERT BROWNING

## Two in the Campagna

I wonder do you feel to-day
    As I have felt since, hand in hand,
We sat down on the grass, to stray
    In spirit better through the land,
This morn of Rome and May?

For me, I touched a thought, I know,
    Has tantalized me many times,
(Like turns of thread the spiders throw
    Mocking across our path) for rhymes
To catch at and let go.

Help me to hold it! First it left
    The yellowing fennel, run to seed
There, branching from the brickwork's cleft,
    Some old tomb's ruin: yonder weed
Took up the floating weft,

Where one small orange cup amassed
    Five beetles,—blind and green they grope
Among the honey-meal: and last,
    Everywhere on the grassy slope
I traced it. Hold it fast!

The champaign with its endless fleece
    Of feathery grasses everywhere!
Silence and passion, joy and peace,
    An everlasting wash of air—
Rome's ghost since her decease.

Such life here, through such lengths of hours,
    Such miracles performed in play,
Such primal naked forms of flowers,
    Such letting nature have her way
While heaven looks from its towers!

How say you? Let us, O my dove,
 Let us be unashamed of soul,
As earth lies bare to heaven above!
 How is it under our control
To love or not to love?

I would that you were all to me,
 You that are just so much, no more.
Nor yours nor mine, nor slave nor free!
 Where does the fault lie? What the core
O' the wound, since wound must be?

I would I could adopt your will,
 See with your eyes, and set my heart
Beating by yours, and drink my fill
 At your soul's springs,—your part my part
In life, for good and ill.

No. I yearn upward, touch you close,
 Then stand away. I kiss your cheek,
Catch your soul's warmth,—I pluck the rose
 And love it more than tongue can speak—
Then the good minute goes.

Already how am I so far
 Out of that minute? Must I go
Still like the thistle-ball, no bar,
 Onward, whenever light winds blow,
Fixed by no friendly star?

Just when I seemed about to learn!
 Where is the thread now? Off again!
The old trick! Only I discern—
 Infinite passion, and the pain
Of finite hearts that yearn.


ELIZABETH BARRETT BROWNING

## A Musical Instrument


What was he doing, the great god Pan,
 Down in the reeds by the river?
Spreading ruin and scattering ban,
Splashing and paddling with hoofs of a goat,
And breaking the golden lilies afloat
 With the dragon-fly on the river.

He tore out a reed, the great god Pan,
    From the deep cool bed of the river:
The limpid water turbidly ran,
And the broken lilies a-dying lay,
And the dragon-fly had fled away,
    Ere he brought it out of the river.

High on the shore sat the great god Pan
    While turbidly flowed the river;
And hacked and hewed as a great god can,
With his hard bleak steel at the patient reed,
Till there was not a sign of the leaf indeed
    To prove it fresh from the river.

He cut it short, did the great god Pan,
    (How tall it stood in the river!)
Then drew the pith, like the heart of a man,
Steadily from the outside ring,
And notched the poor dry empty thing
    In holes, as he sat by the river.

'This is the way,' laughed the great god Pan
    (Laughed while he sat by the river),
'The only way, since gods began
To make sweet music, they could succeed.'
Then, dropping his mouth to a hole in the reed,
    He blew in power by the river.

Sweet, sweet, sweet, O Pan!
    Piercing sweet by the river!
Blinding sweet, O great god Pan!
The sun on the hill forgot to die,
And the lilies revived, and the dragon-fly
    Came back to dream on the river.

Yet half a beast is the great god Pan,
    To laugh as he sits by the river,
Making a poet out of a man:
The true gods sigh for the cost and pain,—
For the reed which grows nevermore again
    As a reed with the reeds in the river.

ROBERT STEPHEN HAWKER

## The Butterfly

Bird of the moths! that radiant wing
  Hath borne thee from thine earthly lair;
Thou revellest on the breath of spring,
  A graceful shape of woven air!

The glories of the earth are thine,
  The joyful breeze, the balmy sky;
For thee the starry roses shine,
  And violets in their valleys sigh.

Yet was the scene as soft and bright
  When thou wert low in wormy rest:
The skies of summer gushed with light,
  The blossoms breathed on Nature's breast.

But thou that gladness didst not share,
  A cave restrained that shadowy form;
In vain did fragrance fill the air,
  Dew soften and the sunbeams warm.

Dull was thy day—a living death,
  Till the great change in glory came,
And thou, a thing of life and breath,
  Didst cleave the air with quivering frame!

My son! my son! read, mark, and learn
  This parable of summer skies,
Until thy trusting spirit yearn,
  Like the bright moth, to rush and rise.

Lo! round and near, a mightier scene,
  With hues that flesh may not behold;
There all things glow with loveliest mien,
  And earthly forms have heavenly mould!

Oh! for that place of paths divine,
  By the freed soul in rapture trod;
The upper air, the fields that shine,
  For ever in the light of God!

CHARLES KINGSLEY

## *Airly Beacon*

Airly Beacon, Airly Beacon;
  Oh the pleasant sight to see
Shires and towns from Airly Beacon,
  While my love climbed up to me!

Airly Beacon, Airly Beacon;
  Oh the happy hours we lay
Deep in fern on Airly Beacon,
  Courting through the summer's day!

Airly Beacon, Airly Beacon;
  Oh the weary haunt for me,
All alone on Airly Beacon,
  With his baby on my knee!

CHARLES KINGSLEY

## *The Three Fishers*

Three fishers went sailing away to the West,
  Away to the West as the sun went down;
Each thought on the woman who loved him the best,
  And the children stood watching them out of the town;
  For men must work, and women must weep,
  And there's little to earn, and many to keep,
    Though the harbour bar be moaning.

Three wives sat up in the lighthouse tower,
  And they trimmed the lamps as the sun went down;
They looked at the squall, and they looked at the shower,
  And the night-rack came rolling up ragged and brown.
  But men must work, and women must weep,
  Though storms be sudden, and waters deep,
    And the harbour bar be moaning.

Three corpses lay out on the shining sands
  In the morning gleam as the tide went down,
And the women are weeping and wringing their hands
  For those who will never come home to the town;
  For men must work, and women must weep,
  And the sooner it's over, the sooner to sleep;
    And good-bye to the bar and its moaning.


CHARLES KINGSLEY

## The Last Buccaneer

Oh England is a pleasant place for them that's rich and high,
But England is a cruel place for such poor folks as I;
And such a port for mariners I ne'er shall see again
As the pleasant Isle of Avès beside the Spanish main.

There were forty craft in Avès that were both swift and stout,
All furnished well with small arms and cannons round about;
And a thousand men in Avès made laws so fair and free
To choose their valiant captains and obey them loyally.

Thence we sailed against the Spaniard with his hoards of plate and gold,
Which he rung with cruel tortures from Indian folk of old;
Likewise the merchant captains, with hearts as hard as stone,
Who flog men and keel-haul them, and starve them to the bone.

Oh the palms grew high in Avès, and fruits that shone like gold,
And the colibris and parrots they were gorgeous to behold;
And the negro maids to Avès from bondage fast did flee,
To welcome gallant sailors, a-sweeping in from sea.

Oh sweet it was in Avès to hear the landward breeze,
A-swing with good tobacco in a net between the trees,
With a negro lass to fan you, while you listened to the roar
Of the breakers on the reef outside, that never touched the shore.

But Scripture saith, an ending to all fine things must be;
So the King's ships sailed on Avès, and quite put down were we.
All day we fought like bulldogs, but they burst the booms at night;
And I fled in a piragua, sore wounded, from the fight.

Nine days I floated starving, and a negro lass beside
Till for all I tried to cheer her, the poor young thing she died;
But as I lay a gasping, a Bristol sail came by,
And brought me home to England here, to beg until I die.

And now I'm old and going—I'm sure I can't tell where;
One comfort is, this world's so hard, I can't be worse off there:
If I might but be a sea-dove, I'd fly across the main,
To the pleasant Isle of Avès, to look at it once again.

CHARLES KINGSLEY

## The Sands of Dee

'Oh, Mary, go and call the cattle home,
    And call the cattle home,
    And call the cattle home,
Across the sands of Dee.'
The western wind was wild and dark with foam,
    And all alone went she.

The western tide crept up along the sand,
    And o'er and o'er the sand,
    And round and round the sand
As far as eye could see.
The rolling mist came down and hid the land,
    And never home came she.

'Oh! is it weed, or fish, or floating hair—
    A tress of golden hair,
    A drownèd maiden's hair,
Above the nets at sea?'
Was never salmon yet that shone so fair
    Among the stakes of Dee.

They rowed her in across the rolling foam,
    The cruel, crawling foam,
    The cruel, hungry foam,
To her grave beside the sea,
But still the boatmen hear her call the cattle home,
    Across the sands of Dee.

JEAN INGELOW

## *The High Tide on the Coast of Lincolnshire, 1571*

The old mayor climbed the belfry tower,
  The ringers ran by two, by three;
'Pull, if ye never pulled before;
  Good ringers, pull your best,' quoth he,
'Play uppe, play uppe, O Boston bells!
Ply all your changes, all your swells,
    Play uppe "The Brides of Enderby".'

Men say it was a stolen tyde—
  The Lord that sent it, He knows all;
But in myne ears doth still abide
  The message that the bells let fall:
And there was nought of strange, beside
The flights of mews and peewits pied
    By millions crouched on the old sea wall.

I sat and spun within the doore,
  My thread brake off, I raised myne eyes;
The level sun, like ruddy ore,
  Lay sinking in the barren skies;
And dark against day's golden death
She moved where Lindis wandereth,
My sonne's faire wife, Elizabeth.

'Cusha! Cusha! Cusha!' calling,
Ere the early dews were falling,
Farre away I heard her song.
'Cusha! Cusha!' all along;
Where the reedy Lindis floweth,
    Floweth, floweth,
From the meads where melick groweth
Faintly came her milking song—

'Cusha! Cusha! Cusha!' calling,
'For the dews will soone be falling;
Leave your meadow grasses mellow,
    Mellow, mellow;
Quit your cowslips, cowslips yellow;
Come uppe Whitefoot, come uppe Lightfoot;
Quit the stalks of parsley hollow,
    Hollow, hollow;
Come uppe Jetty, rise and follow,
From the clovers lift your head;

Come uppe Whitefoot, come uppe Lightfoot,
Come uppe Jetty, rise and follow,
Jetty, to the milking shed.'

If it be long, ay, long ago,
   When I beginne to think howe long,
Againe I hear the Lindis flow,
   Swift as an arrowe, sharpe and strong;
And all the aire, it seemeth mee,
Bin full of floating bells (sayth shee),
That ring the tune of Enderby.

Alle fresh the level pasture lay,
   And not a shadowe mote be seene,
Save where full fyve good miles away
   The steeple towered from out the greene;
And lo! the great bell farre and wide
Was heard in all the country side
That Saturday at eventide.

The swanherds where their sedges are
   Moved on in sunset's golden breath,
The shepherde lads I heard afarre,
   And my sonne's wife, Elizabeth;
Till floating o'er the grassy sea
Came downe that kyndly message free,
The 'Brides of Mavis Enderby'.

Then some looked uppe into the sky,
   And all along where Lindis flows
To where the goodly vessels lie,
   And where the lordly steeple shows.
They sayde, 'And why should this thing be?
What danger lowers by land or sea?
They ring the tune of Enderby!

'For evil news from Mablethorpe,
   Of pyrate galleys warping down;
For shippes ashore beyond the scorpe,
   They have not spared to wake the towne:
But while the west bin red to see,
And storms be none, and pyrates flee,
Why ring "The Brides of Enderby"?'

I looked without, and lo! my sonne
   Came riding downe with might and main:
He raised a shout as he drew on,
   Till all the welkin rang again,

'Elizabeth! Elizabeth!'
(A sweeter woman ne'er drew breath
Than my sonne's wife, Elizabeth.)

'The olde sea wall (he cried) is downe,
    The rising tide comes on apace,
And boats adrift in yonder towne
    Go sailing uppe the market-place.'
He shook as one that looks on death:
'God save you, mother!' straight he saith;
'Where is my wife, Elizabeth?'

'Good sonne, where Lindis winds away,
    With her two bairns I marked her long;
And ere yon bells beganne to play
    Afar I heard her milking song.'
He looked across the grassy lea,
To right, to left, 'Ho Enderby!'
They rang 'The Brides of Enderby'!

With that he cried and beat his breast;
    For, lo! along the river's bed
A mighty eygre reared his crest,
    And uppe the Lindis raging sped.
It swept with thunderous noises loud;
Shaped like a curling snow-white cloud,
Or like a demon in a shroud.

And rearing Lindis backward pressed
    Shook all her trembling bankes amaine;
Then madly at the eygre's breast
    Flung uppe her weltering walls again.
Then bankes came down with ruin and rout—
Then beaten foam flew round about—
Then all the mighty floods were out.

So farre, so fast the eygre drave,
    The heart had hardly time to beat,
Before a shallow seething wave
    Sobbed in the grasses at oure feet:
The feet had hardly time to flee
Before it brake against the knee,
And all the world was in the sea.

Upon the roofe we sate that night,
    The noise of bells went sweeping by;
I marked the lofty beacon light
    Stream from the church tower, red and high—

A lurid mark and dread to see;
And awesome bells they were to mee,
That in the dark rang 'Enderby'.

They rang the sailor lads to guide
   From roofe to roofe who fearless rowed;
And I—my sonne was at my side,
   And yet the ruddy beacon glowed;
And yet he moaned beneath his breath,
'O come in life, or come in death!
O lost! my love, Elizabeth.'

And didst thou visit him no more?
   Thou didst, thou didst, my daughter deare;
The waters laid thee at his doore,
   Ere yet the early dawn was clear.
Thy pretty bairns in fast embrace,
The lifted sun shone on thy face,
Downe drifted to thy dwelling-place.

That flow strewed wrecks about the grass,
   That ebbe swept out the flocks to sea;
A fatal ebbe and flow, alas!
   To manye more than myne and mee:
But each will mourn his own (she saith).
And sweeter woman ne'er drew breath
Than my sonne's wife, Elizabeth.

I shall never hear her more
By the reedy Lindis shore,
'Cusha! Cusha! Cusha!' calling,
Ere the early dews be falling;
I shall never hear her song,
'Cusha! Cusha!' all along
Where the sunny Lindis floweth,
   Goeth, floweth;
From the meads where melick groweth,
When the water winding down,
Onward floweth to the town.

I shall never see her more
Where the reeds and rushes quiver,
   Shiver, quiver;
Stand beside the sobbing river,
Sobbing, throbbing, in its falling
To the sandy lonesome shore;
I shall never hear her calling,

'Leave your meadow grasses mellow,
    Mellow, mellow;
Quit your cowslips, cowslips yellow;
Come uppe Whitefoot, come uppe Lightfoot;
Quit your pipes of parsley hollow,
    Hollow, hollow;
Come uppe Lightfoot, rise and follow;
    Lightfoot, Whitefoot,
From your clovers lift the head;
Come uppe Jetty, follow, follow,
Jetty, to the milking shed.'

EDWARD FITZGERALD

## *Rubáiyát of Omar Khayyám of Naishápúr*

Awake! for Morning in the Bowl of Night
Has flung the Stone that puts the Stars to Flight:
    And Lo! the Hunter of the East has caught
The Sultán's Turret in a Noose of Light.

Dreaming when Dawn's Left Hand was in the Sky
I heard a Voice within the Tavern cry,
    'Awake, my Little ones, and fill the Cup
Before Life's Liquor in its Cup be dry.'

And, as the Cock crew, those who stood before
The Tavern shouted—'Open then the Door!
    'You know how little while we have to stay,
And, once departed, may return no more.'

Now the New Year reviving old Desires,
The thoughtful Soul to Solitude retires,
    Where the WHITE HAND OF MOSES on the Bough
Puts out, and Jesus from the Ground suspires.

Irám indeed is gone with all its Rose,
And Jamshýd's Sev'n-ring'd Cup where no one knows;
    But still the Vine her ancient Ruby yields,
And still a Garden by the Water blows.

And David's Lips are lock't; but in divine
High-piping Pehleví, with 'Wine! Wine! Wine!
    *Red* Wine!'—the Nightingale cries to the Rose
That yellow Cheek of hers to incarnadine.

Come, fill the Cup, and in the Fire of Spring
The Winter Garment of Repentance fling:
    The Bird of Time has but a little way
To fly—and Lo! the Bird is on the Wing.

And look—a thousand Blossoms with the Day
Woke—and a thousand scatter'd into Clay:
    And this first Summer Month that brings the Rose
Shall take Jamshýd and Kaikobád away.

But come with old Khayyám, and leave the Lot
Of Kaikobád and Kaikhosrú forgot:
    Let Rustum lay about him as he will,
Or Hátim Tai cry Supper—heed them not.

With me along some Strip of Herbage strown
That just divides the desert from the sown,
    Where name of Slave and Sultán scarce is known,
And pity Sultán Máhmúd on his Throne.

Here with a Loaf of Bread beneath the Bough,
A Flask of Wine, a Book of Verse—and Thou
    Beside me singing in the Wilderness—
And Wilderness is Paradise enow.

'How sweet is mortal Sovranty'—think some:
Others—'How blest the Paradise to come!'
    Ah, take the Cash in hand and waive the Rest;
Oh, the brave Music of a *distant* Drum!

Look to the Rose that blows about us—'Lo,
Laughing,' she says, 'into the World I blow:
    At once the silken Tassel of my Purse
Tear, and its Treasure on the Garden throw.'

The Worldly Hope men set their Hearts upon
Turns Ashes—or it prospers; and anon,
    Like Snow upon the Desert's dusty Face
Lighting a little Hour or two—is gone.

And those who husbanded the Golden Grain,
And those who flung it to the Winds like Rain,
    Alike to no such aureate Earth are turn'd
As, buried once, Men want dug up again.

Think, in this batter'd Caravanserai
Whose Doorways are alternate Night and Day,
    How Sultán after Sultán with his Pomp
Abode his Hour or two, and went his way.

They say the Lion and the Lizard keep
The Courts where Jamshýd gloried and drank deep;
     And Bahrám, that great Hunter—the Wild Ass
Stamps o'er his Head, and he lies fast asleep.

I sometimes think that never blows so red
The Rose as where some buried Caesar bled;
     That every Hyacinth the Garden wears
Dropt in its Lap from some once lovely Head.

And this delightful Herb whose tender Green
Fledges the River's Lip on which we lean—
     Ah, lean upon it lightly! for who knows
From what once lovely Lip it springs unseen!

Ah, my Belovèd, fill the Cup that clears
To-DAY of past Regrets and future Fears—
     *To-morrow?*— Why, To-morrow I may be
Myself with Yesterday's Sev'n Thousand Years.

Lo! some we loved, the loveliest and best
That Time and Fate of all their Vintage prest,
     Have drunk their Cup a Round or two before,
And one by one crept silently to Rest.

And we, that now make merry in the Room
They left, and Summer dresses in new Bloom,
     Ourselves must we beneath the Couch of Earth
Descend, ourselves to make a Couch—for whom?

Ah, make the most of what we yet may spend,
Before we too into the Dust descend;
     Dust into Dust, and under Dust, to lie,
Sans Wine, sans Song, sans Singer, and—sans End!

Alike for those who for To-DAY prepare,
And those that after a To-MORROW stare,
     A Muezzín from the Tower of Darkness cries
'Fools! your Reward is neither Here nor There!'

Why, all the Saints and Sages who discuss'd
Of the Two Worlds so learnedly, are thrust
     Like foolish Prophets forth; their Words to Scorn
Are scatter'd, and their Mouths are stopt with Dust.

Oh, come with old Khayyám, and leave the Wise
To talk; one thing is certain, that Life flies;
     One thing is certain, and the Rest is Lies;
The Flower that once has blown for ever dies.

Myself when young did eagerly frequent
Doctor and Saint, and heard great Argument
    About it and about: but evermore
Came out by the same Door as in I went.

With them the Seed of Wisdom did I sow,
And with my own hand labour'd it to grow:
    And this was all the Harvest that I reap'd—
'I came like Water, and like Wind I go.'

Into this Universe, and *why* not knowing,
Nor *whence*, like Water willy-nilly flowing:
    And out of it, as Wind along the Waste,
I know not *whither*, willy-nilly blowing.

What, without asking, hither hurried *whence?*
And, without asking, *whither* hurried hence!
    Another and another Cup to drown
The Memory of this Impertinence!

Up from Earth's Centre through the Seventh Gate
I rose, and on the Throne of Saturn sate,
    And many Knots unravel'd by the Road;
But not the Knot of Human Death and Fate.

There was a Door to which I found no Key:
There was a Veil past which I could not see:
    Some little Talk awhile of ME and THEE
There seem'd—and then no more of THEE and ME.

Then to the rolling Heav'n itself I cried,
Asking, 'What Lamp had Destiny to guide
    'Her little Children stumbling in the Dark?'
And—'A blind Understanding!' Heav'n replied.

Then to this earthen Bowl did I adjourn
My Lip the secret Well of Life to learn:
    And Lip to Lip it murmur'd— 'While you live
Drink!—for once dead you never shall return.'

I think the Vessel, that with fugitive
Articulation answer'd, once did live,
    And merry-make; and the cold Lip I kiss'd
How many Kisses might it take—and give!

For in the Market-place, one Dusk of Day,
I watch'd the Potter thumping his wet Clay:
    And with its all obliterated Tongue
It murmur'd—'Gently, Brother, gently, pray!'

Ah, fill the Cup:—what boots it to repeat
How Time is slipping underneath our Feet:
    Unborn TO-MORROW and dead YESTERDAY,
Why fret about them if TO-DAY be sweet!

One Moment in Annihilation's Waste,
One Moment, of the Well of Life to taste—
    The Stars are setting and the Caravan
Starts for the Dawn of Nothing—Oh, make haste!

How long, how long, in definite Pursuit
Of This and That Endeavour and dispute?
    Better be merry with the fruitful Grape
Than sadder after none, or bitter, Fruit.

You know, my Friends, how long since in my House
For a new Marriage I did make Carouse:
    Divorced old barren Reason from my Bed,
And took the Daughter of the Vine to Spouse.

For 'Is' and 'Is-NOT' though *with* Rule and Line,
And 'UP-AND-DOWN' *without*, I could define,
    I yet in all I only cared to know,
Was never deep in anything but—Wine.

And lately, by the Tavern Door agape,
Came stealing through the Dusk an Angel Shape
    Bearing a Vessel on his Shoulder; and
He bid me taste of it; and 'twas—the Grape!

The Grape that can with Logic absolute
The Two-and-Seventy jarring Sects confute:
    The subtle Alchemist that in a Trice
Life's leaden Metal into Gold transmute.

The mighty Mahmúd, the victorious Lord,
That all the misbelieving and black Horde
    Of Fears and Sorrows that infest the Soul
Scatters and slays with his enchanted Sword.

But leave the Wise to wrangle, and with me
The Quarrel of the Universe let be:
    And, in some corner of the Hubbub coucht,
Make Game of that which makes as much of Thee.

For in and out, above, about, below,
'Tis nothing but a Magic Shadow-show,
    Play'd in a Box whose Candle is the Sun,
Round which we Phantom Figures come and go.

And if the Wine you drink, the Lip you press,
End in the Nothing all Things end in—Yes—
  Then fancy while Thou art, Thou art but what
Thou shalt be—Nothing—Thou shalt not be less.

While the Rose blows along the River Brink,
With old Khayyám the Ruby Vintage drink:
  And when the Angel with his darker Draught
Draws up to Thee—take that, and do not shrink.

'Tis all a Chequer-board of Nights and Days
Where Destiny with Men for Pieces plays:
  Hither and thither moves, and mates, and slays,
And one by one back in the Closet lays.

The Ball no Question makes of Ayes and Noes,
But Right or Left as strikes the Player goes;
  And He that toss'd Thee down into the Field,
*He* knows about it all—HE knows—HE knows!

The Moving Finger writes; and, having writ,
Moves on: nor all thy Piety nor Wit
  Shall lure it back to cancel half a Line,
Nor all thy Tears wash out a Word of it.

And that inverted Bowl we call The Sky,
Whereunder crawling coop't we live and die,
  Lift not thy hands to *It* for help—for It
Rolls impotently on as Thou or I.

With Earth's first Clay They did the last Man's knead,
And then of the Last Harvest sow'd the Seed:
  Yea, the first Morning of Creation wrote
What the Last Dawn of Reckoning shall read.

I tell Thee this—When, starting from the Goal,
Over the shoulders of the flaming Foal
  Of Heav'n Parwín and Mushtarí they flung,
In my predestin'd Plot of Dust and Soul

The Vine had struck a Fibre; which about
If clings my Being—let the Súfi flout;
  Of my Base Metal may be filed a Key,
That shall unlock the Door he howls without.

And this I know: whether the one True Light,
Kindle to Love, or Wrath consume me quite,
  One glimpse of It within the Tavern caught
Better than in the Temple lost outright.

Oh, Thou, who did'st with Pitfall and with Gin
Beset the Road I was to wander in,
  Thou wilt not with Predestination round
Enmesh me, and impute my Fall to Sin?

Oh, Thou, who Man of baser Earth didst make,
And who with Eden didst devise the Snake;
  For all the Sin wherewith the Face of Man
Is blacken'd, Man's Forgiveness give—and take!

     ·  ·  ·  ·  ·  ·

### Kúza—Náma

Listen again. One Evening at the Close
Of Ramazán, ere the better Moon arose,
  In that old Potter's Shop I stood alone
With the clay Population round in Rows.

And, strange to tell, among the Earthen Lot
Some could articulate, while others not:
  And suddenly one more impatient cried—
'Who *is* the Potter, pray, and who the Pot?'

Then said another—'Surely not in vain
My substance from the common Earth was ta'en,
  That He who subtly wrought me into Shape
Should stamp me back to common Earth again.'

Another said—'Why, ne'er a peevish Boy,
Would break the Bowl from which he drank in Joy;
  Shall He that *made* the Vessel in pure Love
And Fancy, in an after Rage destroy!'

None answer'd this; but after Silence spake
A Vessel of a more ungainly Make:
  They sneer at me for leaning all awry;
What! did the Hand then of the Potter shake?'

Said one—'Folks of a surly Tapster tell,
And daub his Visage with the Smoke of Hell;
  They talk of some strict Testing of us—Pish!
He's a Good Fellow, and 'twill all be well.'

Then said another with a long-drawn Sigh,
'My Clay with long oblivion is gone dry:
  But, fill me with the old familiar Juice,
Methinks I might recover by and by!'

So while the Vessels one by one were speaking,
One spied the little Crescent all were seeking:
   And then they jogg'd each other, 'Brother, Brother!
Hark to the Porter's Shoulder-knot a-creaking!'

.  .  .  .  .

Ah, with the Grape my fading Life provide,
And wash my Body whence the Life has died,
   And in a Winding-sheet of Vine-leaf wrapt,
So bury me by some sweet Garden-side.

That ev'n my buried Ashes such a Snare
Of Perfume shall fling up into the Air,
   As not a True Believer passing by
But shall be overtaken unaware.

Indeed the Idols I have loved so long
Have done my Credit in Men's Eye much wrong:
   Have drown'd my Honour in a shallow Cup,
And sold my Reputation for a Song.

Indeed, indeed, Repentance oft before
I swore—but was I sober when I swore?
   And then and then came Spring, and Rose-in-hand
My thread-bare Penitence apieces tore.

And much as Wine has play'd the Infidel,
And robb'd me of my Robe of Honour—well,
   I often wonder what the Vintners buy
One half so precious as the Goods they sell.

Alas, that Spring should vanish with the Rose!
That Youth's sweet-scented Manuscript should close!
   The Nightingale that in the Branches sang,
Ah, whence, and whither flown again, who knows!

Ah Love! could thou and I with Fate conspire
To grasp this sorry Scheme of Things entire,
   Would not we shatter it to bits—and then
Re-mould it nearer to the Heart's Desire!

Ah, Moon of my Delight who know'st no wane,
The Moon of Heav'n is rising once again:
   How oft hereafter rising shall she look
Through this same Garden after me—in vain!

And when Thyself with shining Foot shall pass
Among the Guests Star-scatter'd on the Grass,
   And in thy joyous Errand reach the Spot
Where I made one—turn down an empty Glass!

TAMÁM SHUD


ROBERT BROWNING

## Fra Lippo Lippi

I am poor brother Lippo, by your leave!
You need not clap your torches to my face.
Zooks, what's to blame? you think you see a monk!
What, 'tis past midnight, and you go the rounds,
And here you catch me at an alley's end
Where sportive ladies leave their doors ajar?
The Carmine's my cloister: hunt it up,
Do,—harry out, if you must show your zeal,
Whatever rat, there, haps on his wrong hole,
And nip each softling of a wee white mouse,
*Weke, weke*, that's crept to keep him company!
Aha, you know your betters! Then, you'll take
Your hand away that's fiddling on my throat,
And please to know me likewise. Who am I?
Why, one, sir, who is lodging with a friend
Three streets off—he's a certain . . . how d'ye call?
Master—a . . . Cosimo of the Medici,
I' the house that caps the corner. Boh! you were best!
Remember and tell me, the day you're hanged,
How you affected such a gullet's-gripe!
But you, sir, it concerns you that your knaves
Pick up a manner nor discredit you:
Zooks, are we pilchards, that they sweep the streets
And count fair prize what comes into their net?
He's Judas to a tittle, that man is!
Just such a face! Why, sir, you make amends.
Lord, I'm not angry! Bid your hangdogs go
Drink out this quarter-florin to the health
Of the munificent House that harbours me
(And many more beside, lads! more beside!)
And all's come square again. I'd like his face—
His, elbowing on his comrade in the door

With the pike and lantern,—for the slave that holds
John Baptist's head a-dangle by the hair
With one hand ('Look you, now,' as who should say)
And his weapon in the other, yet unwiped!
It's not your chance to have a bit of chalk,
A wood-coal or the like? or you should see!
Yes, I'm the painter, since you style me so.
What, brother Lippo's doings, up and down,
You know them and they take you? like enough!
I saw the proper twinkle in your eye—
'Tell you, I liked your looks at very first.
Let's sit and set things straight now, hip to haunch.
Here's spring come, and the nights one makes up bands
To roam the town and sing out carnival,
And I've been three weeks shut within my mew,
A-painting for the great man, saints and saints
And saints again. I could not paint all night—
Ouf! I leaned out of window for fresh air.
There came a hurry of feet and little feet,
A sweep of lute-strings, laughs, and whifts of song,—
*Flower o' the broom,*
*Take away love, and our earth is a tomb!*
*Flower o' the quince,*
*I let Lisa go, and what good in life since?*
*Flower o' the thyme*— and so on. Round they went.
Scarce had they turned the corner when a titter
Like the skipping of rabbits by moonlight,—three slim shapes,
And a face that looked up . . . zooks, sir, flesh and blood,
That's all I'm made of! Into shreds it went,
Curtain and counterpane and coverlet,
All the bed-furniture—a dozen knots,
There was a ladder! Down I let myself,
Hands and feet, scrambling somehow, and so dropped,
And after them. I came up with the fun
Hard by Saint Laurence, hail fellow, well met,—
*Flower o' the rose,*
*If I've been merry, what matter who knows?*
And so as I was stealing back again
To get to bed and have a bit of sleep
Ere I rise up to-morrow and go work
On Jerome knocking at his poor old breast
With his great round stone to subdue the flesh,
You snap me of the sudden. Ah, I see!
Though your eye twinkles still, you shake your head—
Mine's shaved—a monk, you say—the sting's in that!

If Master Cosimo announced himself,
Mum's the word naturally; but a monk!
Come, what am I a beast for? tell us, now!
I was a baby when my mother died
And father died and left me in the street.
I starved there, God knows how, a year or two
On fig-skins, melon-parings, rinds and shucks,
Refuse and rubbish. One fine frosty day,
My stomach being empty as your hat,
The wind doubled me up and down I went.
Old Aunt Lapaccia trussed me with one hand,
(Its fellow was a stinger as I knew)
And so along the wall, over the bridge,
By the straight cut to the convent. Six words there,
While I stood munching my first bread that month:
'So, boy, you're minded,' quoth the good fat father
Wiping his own mouth, 'twas refection-time,—
'To quit this very miserable world?
Will you renounce' . . . 'the mouthful of bread?' thought I;
By no means! Brief, they made a monk of me;
I did renounce the world, its pride and greed,
Palace, farm, villa, shop and banking-house,
Trash, such as these poor devils of Medici
Have given their hearts to—all at eight years old.
Well, sir, I found in time, you may be sure,
'Twas not for nothing—the good bellyful,
The warm serge and the rope that goes all round,
And day-long blessed idleness beside!
'Let's see what the urchin's fit for'—that came next.
Not overmuch their way, I must confess.
Such a to-do! They tried me with their books:
Lord, they'd have taught me Latin in pure waste!
*Flower o' the clove,*
*All the Latin I construe is, 'amo' I love!*
But mind you, when a boy starves in the streets
Eight years together, as my fortune was,
Watching folk's faces to know who will fling
The bit of half-stripped grape-bunch he desires,
And who will curse or kick him for his pains,—
Which gentleman processional and fine,
Holding a candle to the Sacrament,
Will wink and let him lift a plate and catch
The droppings of the wax to sell again,
Or holla for the Eight and have him whipped,—
How say I?—nay, which dog bites, which lets drop
His bone from the heap of offal in the street,—

Why, soul and sense of him grow sharp alike,
He learns the look of things, and none the less
For admonition from the hunger-pinch.
I had a store of such remarks, be sure,
Which, after I found leisure, turned to use.
I drew men's faces on my copy-books,
Scrawled them within the antiphonary's marge,
Joined legs and arms to the long music-notes,
Found eyes and nose and chin for A's and B's,
And made a string of pictures of the world
Betwixt the ins and outs of verb and noun,
On the wall, the bench, the door. The monks looked black.
'Nay,' quoth the Prior, 'turn him out, d'ye say?
In no wise. Lose a crow and catch a lark.
What if at last we get our man of parts,
We Carmelites, like those Camaldolese
And Preaching Friars, to do our church up fine
And put the front on it that ought to be!'
And hereupon he bade me daub away.
Thank you! my head being crammed, the walls a blank,
Never was such prompt disemburdening.
First, every sort of monk, the black and white,
I drew them, fat and lean: then, folk at church,
From good old gossips waiting to confess
Their cribs of barrel-droppings, candle-ends,—
To the breathless fellow at the altar-foot,
Fresh from his murder, safe and sitting there
With the little children round him in a row
Of admiration, half for his beard and half
For that white anger of his victim's son
Shaking a fist at him with one fierce arm,
Signing himself with the other because of Christ
(Whose sad face on the cross sees only this
After the passion of a thousand years)
Till some poor girl, her apron o'er her head,
(Which the intense eyes looked through) came at eve
On tiptoe, said a word, dropped in a loaf,
Her pair of earrings and a bunch of flowers
(The brute took growling), prayed, and so was gone.
I painted all, then cried ' 'Tis ask and have;
Choose, for more's ready!'—laid the ladder flat,
And showed my covered bit of cloister-wall.
The monks closed in a circle and praised loud
Till checked, taught what to see and not to see,
Being simple bodies,—'That's the very man!
Look at the boy who stoops to pat the dog!

That woman's like the Prior's niece who comes
To care about his asthma: it's the life!'
But there my triumph's straw-fire flared and funked;
Their betters took their turn to see and say:
The Prior and the learned pulled a face
And stopped all that in no time. 'How? what's here?
Quite from the mark of painting, bless us all!
Faces, arms, legs and bodies like the true
As much as pea and pea! it's devil's-game!
Your business is not to catch men with show,
With homage to the perishable clay,
But lift them over it, ignore it all,
Make them forget there's such a thing as flesh.
Your business is to paint the souls of men—
Man's soul, and it's a fire, smoke . . . no, it's not . . .
It's vapour done up like a new-born babe—
(In that shape when you die it leaves your mouth)
It's . . . well, what matters talking, it's the soul!
Give us no more of body than shows soul!
Here's Giotto, with his Saint a-praising God,
That sets us praising,—why not stop with him?
Why put all thoughts of praise out of our head
With wonder at lines, colours, and what not?
Paint the soul, never mind the legs and arms!
Rub all out, try at it a second time.
Oh, that white smallish female with the breasts,
She's just my niece . . . Herodias, I would say,—
Who went and danced and got men's heads cut off!
Have it all out!' Now, is this sense, I ask?
A fine way to paint soul, by painting body
So ill, the eye can't stop there, must go further
And can't fare worse! Thus, yellow does for white
When what you put for yellow's simply black,
And any sort of meaning looks intense
When all beside itself means and looks nought.
Why can't a painter lift each foot in turn,
Left foot and right foot, go a double step,
Make his flesh liker and his soul more like,
Both in their order? Take the prettiest face,
The Prior's niece . . . patron-saint—is it so pretty
You can't discover if it means hope, fear,
Sorrow or joy? won't beauty go with these?
Suppose I've made her eyes all right and blue,
Can't I take breath and try to add life's flash,
And then add soul and heighten them threefold?
Or say there's beauty with no soul at all—

(I never saw it—put the case the same—)
If you get simple beauty and nought else,
You get about the best thing God invents:
That's somewhat: and you'll find the soul you have missed,
Within yourself, when you return him thanks.
'Rub all out!' Well, well, there's my life, in short,
And so the thing has gone on ever since.
I'm grown a man no doubt, I've broken bounds:
You should not take a fellow eight years old
And make him swear to never kiss the girls.
I'm my own master, paint now as I please—
Having a friend, you see, in the Corner-house!
Lord, it's fast holding by the rings in front—
Those great rings serve more purposes than just
To plant a flag in, or tie up a horse!
And yet the old schooling sticks, the old grave eyes
Are peeping o'er my shoulder as I work,
The heads shake still—'It's art's decline, my son!
You're not of the true painters, great and old;
Brother Angelico's the man, you'll find;
Brother Lorenzo stands his single peer:
Fag on at flesh, you'll never make the third!'
*Flower o' the pine,*
*You keep your mistr . . . manners, and I'll stick to mine!*
I'm not the third, then: bless us, they must know!
Don't you think they're the likeliest to know,
They with their Latin? So, I swallow my rage,
Clench my teeth, suck my lips in tight, and paint
To please them—sometimes do and sometimes don't;
For, doing most, there's pretty sure to come
A turn, some warm eve finds me at my saints—
A laugh, a cry, the business of the world—
(*Flower o' the peach,*
*Death for us all, and his own life for each!*)
And my whole soul revolves, the cup runs over,
The world and life's too big to pass for a dream,
And I do these wild things in sheer despite,
And play the fooleries you catch me at,
In pure rage! The old mill-horse, out at grass
After hard years, throws up his stiff heels so,
Although the miller does not preach to him
The only good of grass is to make chaff.
What would men have? Do they like grass or no—
May they or mayn't they? all I want's the thing
Settled for ever one way. As it is,
You tell too many lies and hurt yourself:

You don't like what you only like too much,
You do like what, if given you at your word
You find abundantly detestable.
For me, I think I speak as I was taught;
I always see the garden and God there
A-making man's wife: and, my lesson learned,
The value and significance of flesh,
I can't unlearn ten minutes afterwards,
   You understand me: I'm a beast, I know.
But see, now—why, I see as certainly
As that the morning-star's about to shine,
What will hap some day. We've a youngster here
Comes to our convent, studies what I do,
Slouches and stares and lets no atom drop:
His name is Guidi—he'll not mind the monks—
They call him Hulking Tom, he lets them talk—
He picks my practice up—he'll paint apace,
I hope so—though I never live so long,
I know what's sure to follow. You be judge!
You speak no Latin more than I, belike;
However, you're my man, you've seen the world
—The beauty and the wonder and the power,
The shapes of things, their colours, lights and shades,
Changes, surprises,—and God made it all!
—For what? Do you feel thankful, ay or no,
For this fair town's face, yonder river's line,
The mountain round it and the sky above,
Much more the figures of man, woman, child,
These are the frame to? What's it all about?
To be passed over, despised? or dwelt upon,
Wondered at? oh, this last of course!—you say.
But why not do as well as say,—paint these
Just as they are, careless what comes of it?
God's works—paint any one, and count it crime
To let a truth slip. Don't object, 'His works
Are here already; nature is complete:
Suppose you reproduce her—(which you can't)
There's no advantage! you must beat her, then.'
For, don't you mark? we're made so that we love
First when we see them painted, things we have passed
Perhaps a hundred times nor cared to see;
And so they are better, painted—better to us,
Which is the same thing. Art was given for that;
God uses us to help each other so,
Lending our minds out. Have you noticed, now,
Your cullion's hanging face? A bit of chalk,

And trust me but you should, though! How much more,
If I drew higher things with the same truth!
That were to take the Prior's pulpit-place,
Interpret God to all of you! Oh, oh,
It makes me mad to see what men shall do
And we in our graves! This world's no blot for us,
Nor blank; it means intensely, and means good:
To find its meaning is my meat and drink.
'Ay, but you don't so instigate to prayer!'
Strikes in the Prior: 'when your meaning's plain
It does not say to folk—remember matins,
Or, mind you fast next Friday!' Why, for this
What need of art at all? A skull and bones,
Two bits of stick nailed crosswise, or, what's best,
A bell to chime the hour with, does as well.
I painted a Saint Laurence six months since
At Prato, splashed the fresco in fine style:
'How looks my painting, now the scaffold's down?'
I ask a brother: 'Hugely,' he returns—
'Already not one phiz of your three slaves
Who turn the Deacon off his toasted side,
But's scratched and prodded to our heart's content,
The pious people have so eased their own
With coming to say prayers there in a rage:
We get on fast to see the bricks beneath.
Expect another job this time next year,
For pity and religion grow i' the crowd—
Your painting serves its purpose!' Hang the fools!

—That is—you'll not mistake an idle word
Spoke in a huff by a poor monk, God wot,
Tasting the air this spicy night which turns
The unaccustomed head like Chianti wine!
Oh, the church knows! don't misreport me, now!
It's natural a poor monk out of bounds
Should have his apt word to excuse himself:
And hearken how I plot to make amends.
I have bethought me: I shall paint a piece
. . . There's for you! Give me six months, then go, see
Something in Sant' Ambrogio's! Bless the nuns!
They want a cast o' my office. I shall paint
God in the midst, Madonna and her babe,
Ringed by a bowery flowery angel-brood,
Lilies and vestments and white faces, sweet
As puff on puff of grated orris-root
When ladies crowd to Church at midsummer.

And then i' the front, of course a saint or two—
Saint John, because he saves the Florentines,
Saint Ambrose, who puts down in black and white
The convent's friends and gives them a long day,
And Job, I must have him there past mistake,
The man of Uz (and Us without the z,
Painters who need his patience). Well, all these
Secured at their devotion, up shall come
Out of a corner when you least expect,
As one by a dark stair into a great light,
Music and talking, who but Lippo! I!—
Mazed, motionless and moonstruck—I'm the man!
Back I shrink—what is this I see and hear?
I, caught up with my monk's-things by mistake,
My old serge gown and rope that goes all round,
I, in this presence, this pure company!
Where's a hole, where's a corner for escape?
Then steps a sweet angelic slip of a thing
Forward, puts out a soft palm—'Not so fast!'
—Addresses the celestial presence, 'nay—
He made you and devised you, after all,
Though he's none of you! Could Saint John there draw—
His camel-hair make up a painting-brush?
We come to brother Lippo for all that,
*Iste perfecit opus!'* So, all smile—
I shuffle sideways with my blushing face
Under the cover of a hundred wings
Thrown like a spread of kirtles when you're gay
And play hot cockles, all the doors being shut,
Till, wholly unexpected, in there pops
The hothead husband! Thus I scuttle off
To some safe bench behind, not letting go
The palm of her, the little lily thing
That spoke the good word for me in the nick,
Like the Prior's niece . . . Saint Lucy, I would say.
And so all's saved for me, and for the church
A pretty picture gained. Go, six months hence!
Your hand, sir, and good-bye: no lights, no lights!
The street's hushed, and I know my own way back,
Don't fear me! There's the grey beginning. Zooks!

ARTHUR HUGH CLOUGH

## *The Latest Decalogue*

Thou shalt have one God only; who
Would be at the expense of two?
No graven images may be
Worshipped, except the currency:
Swear not at all; for, for thy curse
Thine enemy is none the worse:
At church on Sunday to attend
Will serve to keep the world thy friend:
Honour thy parents; that is, all
From whom advancement may befall;
Thou shalt not kill; but need'st not strive
Officiously to keep alive:
Do not adultery commit;
Advantage rarely comes of it:
Thou shalt not steal; an empty feat,
When it's so lucrative to cheat:
Bear not false witness; let the lie
Have time on its own wings to fly:
Thou shalt not covet, but tradition
Approves all forms of competition.

ROBERT STEPHEN HAWKER

## From *The Quest of the Sangraal*

.  .  .

'The land is lonely now: Anathema:
The link that bound it to the silent grasp
Of thrilling worlds is gathered up and gone:
The glory is departed; and the disk
So full of radiance from the touch of God!
This orb is darkened to the distant watch
Of Saturn and his reapers, when they pause,
Amid their sheaves, to count the nightly stars.

'All gone! but not for ever: on a day
There shall arise a king from Keltic loins,
Of mystic birth and name, tender and true;
His vassals shall be noble, to a man:
Knights strong in battle till the war is won:

Then while the land is hushed on Tamar side,
So that the warder upon Carradon
Shall hear at once the river and the sea—
That king shall call a Quest: a kindling cry:
"Ho! for the Sangraal! vanished vase of God!"

'Yea! and it shall be won! a chosen knight,
The ninth from Joseph in the line of blood,
Clean as a maid from guile and fleshly sin—
He with the shield of Sarras; and the lance,
Ruddy and moistened with a freshening stain,
As from a severed wound of yesterday—
He shall achieve the Graal: he alone!

'Thus wrote Bard Merlin on the Runic hide
Of a slain deer: rolled in an aumry chest.

'And now, fair Sirs, your voices: who will gird
His belt for travel in the perilous ways?
This thing must be fulfilled:—in vain our land
Of noble name, high deed, and famous men;
Vain the proud homage of our thrall, the sea,
If we be shorn of God:—ah! loathsome shame!
To hurl in battle for the pride of arms:
To ride in native tournay, foreign war:
To count the stars; to ponder pictured runes:—
And grasp great knowledge, as the demons do—
If we be shorn of God:—we must assay
The myth and meaning of this marvellous bowl:
It shall be sought and found:—'

                                Thus said the King.

Then rose a storm of voices; like the sea,
When Ocean, bounding, shouts with all his waves!
High-hearted men: the purpose and the theme,
Smote the fine chord that thrills the warrior's soul
With touch and impulse for a deed of fame.
Then spake Sir Gauvain, counsellor of the King—
A man of Pentecost for words that burn:—

'Sirs! we are soldiers of the rock and ring:
Our table-round is earth's most honoured stone;
Thereon two worlds of life and glory blend!
The boss upon the shield of many a land:
The midway link with light beyond the stars!

This is our fount of fame! let us arise,
And cleave the earth like rivers: like the streams
That win from Paradise their immortal name:
To the four winds of God! casting the lot.

'So shall we share the regions! and unfold
The shrouded mystery of those fields of air.

'Eastward! the source and spring of life and light!
Thence came, and thither went, the rush of worlds,
When the great cone of space was sown with stars!
There rolled the gateway of the double dawn,
When the mere God shone down a breathing man
There, up from Bethany, the Syrian Twelve
Watched their dear Master darken into day!
Thence, too, will gleam the Cross, the arisen wood:
Ah, shuddering sign one day of terrible doom!
Therefore the Orient is the home of God.

'The West! a Galilee: the shore of men!
The symbol and the scene of populous life:
Full Japhet journeyed thither, Noe's son,
The prophecy of increase in his loins.
Westward Lord Jesu looked His latest love,—
His yearning Cross along the peopled sea,
The innumerable nations in His soul:
Thus came that type and token of our kind,
The realm and region of the set of sun,
The wide, wide West: the imaged zone of man.

'The North! the lair of demons, where they coil,
And bound, and glide, and travel to and fro:
Their gulph, the underworld, this hollow orb,
Where vaulted columns curve beneath the hills
And shoulder us on their arches: there they throng;
The portal of their pit, the polar gate;
Their fiery dungeon mocked with northern snow:
Their doom and demon haunt a native land,
Where dreamy thunder mutters in the cloud,
Storm broods, and battle breathes, and baleful fires
Shed a fierce horror o'er the shuddering North!

'But thou! O South Wind, breathe thy fragrant sigh:
We follow on thy perfume, breath of heaven!
Myriads, in girded albs, for ever young,
Their stately semblance of embodied air,
Troop round the footstool of the Southern Cross—
That pentacle of stars: the very sign

That led the Wise Men towards the Awful Child,
Then came and stood to rule the peaceful sea!
So, too, Lord Jesu from His mighty tomb
Cast the dear shadow of His red right hand,
To soothe the happy South: the Angels' home!

'Then let us search the regions! one by one,
And pluck this Sangraal from its cloudy cave!'

So Merlin brought the arrows: graven lots,
Shrouded from sight within a quivered sheath,
For choice and guidance in the perilous path,
That so the travellers might divide the lands.
They met at Lauds, in good Saint Nectan's cell,
For fast, and vigil, and their knightly vow:
Then knelt, and prayed, and all received their God.

'Now for the silvery arrows, grasp and hold!'

Sir Lancelot drew the North: that fell domain,
Where fleshly man must brook the airy fiend—
His battle-foe, the demon: ghastly war!
Ho! stout Saint Michael shield them, knight and knave!

The South fell softly to Sir Perceval's hand:
Some shadowy Angel breathed a silent sign:
That so that blameless man, that courteous knight,
Might mount and mingle with the happy host
Of God's white army in their native land!
Yea, they shall woo and soothe him, like the dove.
But hark! the greeting!— 'Tristan for the West!'

Among the multitudes, his watchful way:
The billowy hordes beside the seething sea;
But will the glory gleam in loathsome lands?
Will the lost pearl shine out among the swine?
Woe, father Adam, to thy loins and thee.
Sir Galahad holds the Orient arrow's name:
His chosen hand unbars the gate of day!
There glows that heart, filled with his mother's blood,
That rules in every pulse, the world of man;
Link of the awful Three, with many a star.
O! blessèd East! 'mid visions such as thine,
'Twere well to grasp the Sangraal, and die.

Now feast and festival in Arthur's hall:
Hark! stern Dundagel softens into song!
They meet for solemn severance, knight and king:
Where gate and bulwark darken o'er the sea.

Strong men for meat, and warriors at the wine:
They wreak the wrath of hunger on the beeves,—
They rend rich morsels from the savoury deer,—
And quench the flagon like Brun-guillie dew!
Hear! how the minstrels prophesy in sound.
Shout the King's Waes-hael, and Drink-hael the Queen!

Then said Sir Kay, he of the arrowy tongue,
'Joseph and Pharaoh! how they build their bones!
Happier the boar were quick than dead to-day.'

The Queen! the Queen! how haughty on the dais!
The sunset tangled in her golden hair:
A dove amid the eagles: Gwennivar!
Aishah! what might is in that glorious eye!
See their tamed lion from Brocelian's glade,
Couched on the granite like a captive king:
A word—a gesture—or a mute caress—
How fiercely fond he droops his billowy mane,
And wooes, with tawny lip, his lady's hand!

The dawn is deep: the mountains yearn for day!
The hooting cairn is hushed: that fiendish noise,
Yelled from the utterance of the rending rock,
When the fierce dog of Cain barks from the moon.

The bird of judgment chants the doom of night:
The billows laugh a welcome to the day,
And Camlan ripples, seaward, with a smile.

'Down with the eastern bridge! the warriors ride,
And thou, Sir Herald, blazon as they pass!'
Foremost sad Lancelot, throned upon his steed,
His yellow banner, northward, lapping light:
The crest, a lily, with a broken stem,
The legend, *Stately once and ever fair*;
It hath a meaning, seek it not, O King!

A quaint embroidery Sir Perceval wore;
A turbaned Syrian, underneath a palm,
Wrestled for mastery with a stately foe,
Robed in a Levite's raiment, white as wool:
His touch o'erwhelmed the Hebrew, and his word,
*Whoso is strong with God shall conquer man*,
Coiled in rich tracery round the knightly shield.
Did Ysolt's delicate fingers weave the web,
That gleamed in silken radiance o'er her lord?

A molten rainbow, bent; that arch in heaven,
Which leads straightway to Paradise and God;
Beneath, came up a gloved and sigilled hand,
Amid this cunning needlework of words,
*When toil and tears have worn the westering day,*
*Behold the smile of fame! so brief: so bright.*

A vast Archangel floods Sir Galahad's shield:
Mid-breast, and lifted high, an Orient cruse,
Full filled, and running o'er with numynous light,
As though it held and shed the visible God;
Then shone this utterance as in graven fire,
*I thirst! O Jesu! let me drink and die!*

So forth they fare, King Arthur and his men;
Like stout quaternions of the Maccabee:
They halt, and form at craggy Carradon;
Fit scene for haughty hope and stern farewell.
Lo! the rude altar; and the rough-hewn rock:
The grim and ghastly semblance of the fiend:
His haunt and coil within that pillared home.
Hark, the wild echo! did the demon breathe,
That yell of vengeance from the conscious stone?

There the brown barrow curves its sullen breast,
Above the bones of some dead Gentile's soul:
All hushed—and calm—and cold—until anon
Gleams the old dawn—the well-remembered day—
Then may you hear, beneath that hollow cairn,
The clash of arms: the muffled shout of war;
Blent with the rustle of the kindling dead!
They stand—and hush their hearts to hear the King.

Then said he, like a prince of Tamar-land,
Around his soul, Dundagel and the sea—

'Ha! Sirs—ye seek a noble crest to-day,
To win and wear the starry Sangraal,
The link that binds to God a lonely land.
Would that my arm went with you, like my heart!
But the true shepherd must not shun the fold:
For in this flock are crouching grievous wolves,
And chief among them all, my own false kin.
Therefore I tarry by the cruel sea:
To hear at eve the treacherous mermaid's song—
And watch the wallowing monsters of the wave,—
'Mid all things fierce, and wild, and strange, alone!

'Ay! all beside can win companionship:
The churl may clip his mate beneath the thatch,
While his brown urchins nestle at his knees:
The soldier give and grasp a mutual palm,
Knit to his flesh in sinewy bonds of war:
The knight may seek at eve his castle-gate,
Mount the old stair, and lift the accustomed latch,
To find, for throbbing brow and weary limb,
That paradise of pillows, one true breast:
But he, the lofty ruler of the land,
Like yonder Tor, first greeted by the dawn,
And wooed the latest by the lingering day,
With happy homes and hearths beneath his breast,
Must soar and gleam in solitary snow!
The lonely one is, evermore, the King.
So now farewell, my lieges, fare ye well,
And God's sweet Mother be your benison!
Since by grey Merlin's gloss, this wondrous cup
Is, like the golden vase in Aaron's ark,
A fount of manha for a yearning world,
As full as it can hold of God and heaven:
Search the four winds until the balsam breathe,
Then grasp, and fold it in your very soul!

'I have no son, no daughter of my loins,
To breathe, 'mid future men, their father's name:
My blood will perish when these veins are dry.
Yet am I fain some deeds of mine should live—
I would not be forgotten in this land:
I yearn that men I know not, men unborn,
Should find, amid these fields, King Arthur's fame!
Here let them say, by proud Dundagel's walls—
They brought the Sangraal back by his command,
They touched these rugged rocks with hues of God:
So shall my name have worship, and my land!

'Ah! native Cornwall! throned upon the hills:
Thy moorland pathways worn by Angel feet,
Thy streams that march in music to the sea
'Mid Ocean's merry noise, his billowy laugh!
Ah me! a gloom falls heavy on my soul—
The birds that sung to me in youth are dead;
I think, in dreamy vigils of the night,
It may be God is angry with my land—
Too much athirst for fame: too fond of blood;
And all for earth, for shadows, and the dream
To glean an echo from the winds of song!

'But now, let hearts be high: the Archangel held
A tournay with the fiend on Abarim,
And good Saint Michael won his dragon-crest!

'Be this our cry! the battle is for God!
If bevies of foul fiends withstand your path—
Nay, if strong Angels hold the watch and ward,
Plunge in their midst, and shout, "a Sangraal!" '

He ceased; the warriors bent a knightly knee,
And touched with kiss and sign, Excalibur;
Then turned, and mounted for their perilous way!

That night Dundagel shuddered into storm—
The deep foundations shook beneath the sea:
Yet there they stood, beneath the murky moon,
Above the bastion, Merlin and the King.
Thrice waved the sage his staff, and thrice they saw
A peopled vision throng the rocky moor!

First fell a gloom, thick as a thousand nights—
A pall that hid whole armies; and beneath
Stormed the wild tide of war; until on high
Gleamed red the dragon, and the Keltic glaive
Smote the loose battle of the roving Dane!
Then yelled a fiercer fight: for brother blood
Rushed mingling; and twin dragons fought the field!

The grisly shadows of his faithful knights
Perplexed their lord: and in their midst, behold!
His own stern semblance waved a phantom-brand,
Drooped, and went down the war:—then cried the King,
'Ho! Arthur to the rescue!' and half drew
Excalibur—but sank, and fell entranced!

A touch aroused the monarch: and there stood
He, of the billowy beard and Awful eye,
The ashes of whole ages on his brow,
Merlin the bard: son of a demon-sire!
High, like Ben Amram at the thirsty rock,
He raised his prophet staff: that runic rod,
The stem of Igdrasil—the crutch of Raun—
And wrote strange words along the conscious air.

Forth gleamed the east, and yet it was not day:
A white and glowing horse outrode the dawn;
A youthful rider ruled the bounding rein,
And he, in semblance of Sir Galahad shone:

A vase he held on high; one molten gem,
Like massive ruby or the chrysolite:
Thence gushed the light in flakes; and flowing, fell
As though the pavement of the sky brake up,
And stars were shed to sojourn on the hills,
From grey Morwenna's stone to Michael's tor,
Until the rocky land was like a heaven.

Then saw they that the mighty quest was won:
The Sangraal swooned along the golden air:
The sea breathed balsam, like Gennesaret:
The streams were touched with supernatural light:
And fonts of Saxon rock, stood, full of God!
Altars arose, each like a kingly throne,
Where the royal chalice, with its lineal blood,
The glory of the presence, ruled and reigned.
This lasted long: until the white horse fled,
The fierce fangs of the libbard in his loins:
Whole ages glided in that blink of time,
While Merlin and the King, looked, wondering, on.

But see! once more the wizard-wand arise,
To cleave the air with signals, and a scene.

Troops of the demon-north, in yellow garb,
The sickly hue of vile Iscariot's hair,
Mingle with men, in unseen multitudes!
Unscared, they throng the valley and the hill;
That which held God was gone: Maran-atha:
The Awful shadows of the Sangraal, fled!
Yet giant-men arose, that seemed as gods—
Such might they gathered from the swarthy kind:
The myths were rendered up: and one by one,
The fire—the light—the air—were tamed and bound
Like votive vassals at their chariot-wheel!

The shrines were darkened and the chalice void:
Then learnt they war: yet not that noble wrath,
That brings the generous champion face to face
With equal shield, and with a measured brand,
To peril life for life, and do or die!
But the false valour of the lurking fiend—
To hurl a distant death from some deep den:
To wing with flame the metal of the mine:
And so they rend God's image, reck not who!

'Ah! haughty England! lady of the wave:'
Thus said pale Merlin to the listening King:

'What is thy glory in the world of stars?
To scorch and slay: to win demoniac fame,
In arts and arms; and then to flash and die!
Thou art the diamond of the demon-crown,
Smitten by Michael upon Abarim,
That fell; and glared, an island of the sea!
Ah! native England! wake thine ancient cry;
Ho! for the Sangraal! vanished vase of heaven,
That held, like Christ's own heart, an hin of blood!'

He ceased; and all around was dreamy night:
There stood Dundagel, throned: and the great sea,
Lay, a strong vassal at his master's gate,
And, like a drunken giant, sobbed in sleep!


ROBERT STEPHEN HAWKER

## The Cornish Emigrant's Song

Oh! the eastern winds are blowing;
  The breezes seem to say,
'We are going, we are going,
  To North Americay.

'There the merry bees are humming
  Around the poor man's hive;
Parson Kingdon is not coming
  To take away their tithe.

'There the yellow corn is growing
  Free as the king's highway;
So, we're going, we are going,
  To North Americay.

'Uncle Rab shall be churchwarden,
  And Dick shall be the squire,
And Jem, that lived at Norton,
  Shall be leader of the quire;

'And I will be the preacher,
  And preach three times a day
To every living creature
  In North Americay.'

RICHARD MONCKTON MILNES

## England and America, 1863

We only know that in the sultry weather,
Men toiled for us as in the steaming room,
And in our minds we hardly set together
The bondman's penance and the freeman's loom.

We never thought the jealous gods would store
For us ill deeds of time-forgotten graves,
Nor heeded that the May-Flower one day bore
A freight of pilgrims, and another slaves.

First on the bold upholders of the wrong,
And last on us, the heavy-laden years
Avenge the cruel triumphs of the strong—
Trampled affections, and derided tears.

Labour, degraded from her high behest,
Cries, 'Ye shall know I am the living breath,
And not the curse of Man. Ye shall have Rest—
The rest of Famine and the rest of Death.'

Oh, happy distant hours! that shall restore
Honour to work, and pleasure to repose,
Hasten your steps, just heard above the war
Of wildering passions and the crash of foes.

DORA GREENWELL

## The Saturday Review

'Learn to live, and live and learn.'
In the days when I used to go to school,
    Would always pass for an excellent rule;
But now it's grown a serious concern
The number of things I've had to *un*learn
Since first I began the page to turn
    Of *The Saturday Review*.
For once (I believe) I believed in truth
    And love, and the hundred foolish things
One sees in one's dreams and believes in one's youth—
    In Angels with curls, and in Angels with wings,

In Saints, and Heroes, and Shepherds too;
The pictures that David and Virgil drew
    So sweetly, I thought were taken
From very life, but now I find
A Shepherd is but an uncouth Hind,
Songless, soulless, from time out of mind,
    Who has cared for nothing but bacon.

And though to confess it may well seem strange,
    When I had them by scores and dozens
(I was young, to be sure, and all things change),
    I really *have* liked my cousins,
And schoolfellows too, and can bring to mind
Some uncles of mine who were truly kind,
    And aunts who were far from crusty;
And even my country neighbours too
Didn't seem by half such a tedious crew
    As now I find they must be.

And I used to think it might be kind,
    In the world's great marching order,
To help the poor stragglers left behind,
Halt and maimed, and broken and blind,
    On their way to a distant border;
Not to speak of the virtuous poor. I thought
    There was here and there a sinner
Might be mended a little, though not of the sort
    One would think of asking to dinner.
But now I find that no one believes
In Ragged Children, or Penitent Thieves,
Or Homeless Homes, but a few Old Maids
Who have tried and failed at all other trades,
And who take to these things for recreation
In their aimless life's dull Long Vacation.

And so as we're going along with the Priest
And Levite (the roads are more dry in the East)
    We need have no hesitation,
When the mud is lying about so thick,
To scatter a little and let it stick
To the coat of the Good Samaritan, used
To be spattered, battered, blackened, and bruised;
These sort of people don't mind in the least—
    Why, bless you, its *their* vocation!

Yet sometimes I've thought it a little strange,—
When good people get such very hard change,
    In return for their kindly halfpence,

When the few who are grieved for sorrows and sins
Are bowled to the earth like wooden pins,
When to care for the heathen, or pity the slave,
Sets a man down for fool or knave,
  With *The Saturday* in its sapience,—
Things that are mean and base and low
Are checked by never a word or blow;
The gaping crowds that go in hope
To see Blondin slip from the cruel rope
Tightened or slack, and come away
In trust of more luck another day,
  Meet never a line's reproving;
Heenan and Sayers may pound and thwack
Each other blue and yellow and black,
And only get a pat on the back
  From the power that keeps all moving.

And I sometimes think, if this same Review,
And the world a little longer too
Should last, will the violets come out blue?
Will the rose be red, and will lovers woo
In the foolish way that they used to do?
Will doves in the summer woodlands coo,
And the nightingales mourn without asking leave?
Will the lark have an instinct left to cleave
The sunny air with her song and her wing?—
Perhaps we may move to abolish spring;
And now that we've grown so hard to please,
We may think that we're bored by the grass and the trees;
The moon may be proved a piece of cheese,
  Or an operatic delusion.
Fathers and Mothers may have to go,
Brothers and sisters be voted slow,
Christmas a tax that one's forced to pay,
And Heaven itself but an out-of-the-way
Old-fashioned place that has had its day,
  That one wouldn't a residence choose in.

And though so easily learnt, and brief
  Is the form our new faith's put in,
When we've said, 'I believe in a Round of Beef,
  And live by a Leg of Mutton,'
We come to another region of facts,
That are met quite as well by the Gospel and *Acts*
  As by any teaching that's newer—
Life has its problems hard to clear,
And its knots too stiff to be cut by the sneer
  Of the sharpest, smartest Reviewer.

ROBERT LEIGHTON

## *The Bunch of Larks*

Portly he was, in carriage somewhat grand;
    Of gentleman he wore the accepted marks:
He thrid the busy street, and in his hand
    He bore a bunch of larks!

There be some things that may be carried—yes,
    A gentleman may carry larks—if dead;
Or any slaughtered game; not fish, still less
    The homely beef or bread.

I met him in the street, and turned about,
    And mused long after he had flaunted by.
A bunch of larks! and his intent, no doubt,
    To have them in a pie.

Yes, four-and-twenty larks baked in a pie!
    O, what a feast of melody is there!
The ringing chorus of a summer sky!
    A dish of warbling air!

How many dusty wanderers of the earth
    Have those stilled voices lifted from the dust!
And now to end their almost Heavenly mirth
    Beneath a gourmand's crust!

But as he picks their thin ambrosial throats,
    Will no accusing memories arise,
Of grassy glebes, and heaven-descending notes,
    And soul-engulfing skies?

'Give me,' cries he, 'the *substance* of the thing—
    Something that I can eat, or drink, or feel—
A poem for the money it will bring—
    Larks for a dainty meal.'

Well, he may have his substance, and I mine.
    Deep in my soul the throbbing lark-notes lie.
My substance lasts, and takes a life divine—
    His passes with the pie.

ROBERT BROUGH

## My Lord Tomnoddy

My Lord Tomnoddy's the son of an Earl,
His hair is straight, but his whiskers curl;
His Lordship's forehead is far from wide,
But there's plenty of room for the brains inside.
He writes his name with indifferent ease,
He's rather uncertain about the 'd's',—
But what does it matter, if three or one,
To the Earl of Fitzdotterel's eldest son?

My Lord Tomnoddy to college went,
Much time he lost, much money he spent;
Rules, and windows, and heads, he broke—
Authorities winked—young men will joke!
He never peeped inside of a book—
In two years' time a degree he took;
And the newspapers vaunted the honours won
By the Earl of Fitzdotterel's eldest son.

My Lord Tomnoddy came out in the world,
Waists were tightened, and ringlets curled.
Virgins languished, and matrons smiled—
'Tis true, his Lordship is rather wild;
In very queer places he spends his life;
There's talk of some children, by nobody's wife—
But we mustn't look close into what is done
By the Earl of Fitzdotterel's eldest son.

My Lord Tomnoddy must settle down—
There's a vacant seat in the family town!
('Tis time he should sow his eccentric oats)—
He hasn't the wit to apply for votes:
He cannot e'en learn his election speech,
Three phrases he speaks—a mistake in each!
And then breaks down—but the borough is won
For the Earl of Fitzdotterel's eldest son.

My Lord Tomnoddy prefers the Guards,
(The House is a bore) so!—it's on the cards!
My Lord's a Lieutenant at twenty-three,
A Captain at twenty-six is he—
He never drew sword, except on drill;
The tricks of parade he has learnt but ill—
A full-blown Colonel at thirty-one
Is the Earl of Fitzdotterel's eldest son!

My Lord Tomnoddy is thirty-four;
The Earl can last but a few years more.
My Lord in the Peers will take his place:
Her Majesty's councils his words will grace.
Office he'll hold, and patronage sway;
Fortunes and lives he will vote away—
And what are his qualifications?—ONE!
He's the Earl of Fitzdotterel's eldest son.


DORA GREENWELL

## When the Night and Morning Meet

In the dark and narrow street,
  Into a world of woe,
Where the tread of many feet
  Went trampling to and fro,
A child was born—speak low!
When the night and morning meet.

Full seventy summers back
  Was this, so long ago,
The feet that wore the track
  Are lying straight and low;
Yet hath there been no lack
  Of passers to and fro

Within the narrow street
  This childhood ever played;
Beyond the narrow street
  This manhood never strayed;
  This age sat still and prayed
Anear the trampling feet.

The tread of ceaseless feet
  Flowed through his life, unstirred
By waters' fall, or fleet
  Wind music, or the bird
Of morn; these sounds are sweet,
  But they were still unheard.

Within the narrow street
  I stood beside a bed,
  I held a dying head

When the night and morning meet;
And every word was sweet,
    Though few the words we said.

And as we talked, dawn drew
    To day, the world was fair
In fields afar, I knew;
    Yet spoke not to him there
Of how the grasses grew,
    Besprent with dewdrops rare.

We spoke not of the sun,
    Nor of this green earth fair;
This soul, whose day was done,
    Had never claimed its share
    In these, and yet its rare
Rich heritage had won.

From the dark and narrow street.
    Into a world of love
A child was born,—speak low,
Speak reverent, for we know
    Not how they speak above,
When the night and morning meet.

ROBERT F. MURRAY

## The Wasted Day

Another day let slip! Its hours have run,
Its golden hours, with prodigal excess,
All run to waste. A day of life the less;
Of many wasted days, alas, but one!

Through my west window streams the setting sun.
I kneel within my chamber, and confess
My sin and sorrow, filled with vain distress,
In place of honest joy for work well done.

At noon I passed some labourers in a field.
The sweat ran down upon each sunburnt face,
Which shone like copper in the ardent glow.
And one looked up, with envy unconcealed,
Beholding my cool cheeks and listless pace,
Yet he was happier, though he did not know.

CHARLES KINGSLEY

## A Farewell

My fairest child, I have no song to give you;
　　No lark could pipe in skies so dull and gray;
Yet if you will, one quiet hint I'll leave you,
　　　　For every day.

I'll tell you how to sing a clearer carol
　　Than lark who hails the dawn or breezy down;
To earn yourself a purer poet's laurel
　　　　Than Shakespeare's crown.

Be good, sweet maid, and let who can be clever;
　　Do lovely things, not dream them, all day long;
And so make Life, and Death, and that For Ever,
　　　　One grand sweet song.

DAVID GRAY

## My Epitaph

Below lies one whose name was traced in sand—
He died not knowing what it was to live:
Died while the first sweet consciousness of manhood
And maiden thought electrified his soul:
Faint beatings in the calyx of the rose.
Bewildered reader, pass without a sigh
In a proud sorrow! There is life with God,
In other kingdom of a sweeter air:
In Eden every flower is blown: Amen.

GEORGE ELIOT

O may I join the choir invisible
Of those immortal dead who live again
In minds made better by their presence: live
In pulses stirred to generosity,

In deeds of daring rectitude, in scorn
For miserable aims that end with self,
In thoughts sublime that pierce the night like stars,
And with their mild persistence urge man's search
To vaster issues.

So to live is heaven:
To make undying music in the world,
Breathing as beauteous order that controls
With growing sway the growing life of man.
So we inherit that sweet purity
For which we struggled, failed, and agonised
With widening retrospect that bred despair.
Rebellious flesh that would not be subdued,
A vicious parent shaming still its child
Poor anxious penitence, is quick dissolved;
Its discords, quenched by meeting harmonies,
Die in the large and charitable air.
And all our rarer, better, truer self,
That sobbed religiously in yearning song,
That watched to ease the burthen of the world,
Laboriously tracing what must be,
And what may yet be better—saw within

A worthier image for the sanctuary,
And shaped it forth before the multitude
Divinely human, raising worship so
To higher reverence more mixed with love—
That better self shall live till human Time
Shall fold its eyelids, and the human sky
Be gathered like a scroll within the tomb
Unread for ever.

This is life to come,
Which martyred men have made more glorious
For us who strive to follow. May I reach
That purest heaven, be to other souls
The cup of strength in some great agony,
Enkindle generous ardour, feed pure love,
Beget the smiles that have no cruelty—
Be the sweet presence of a good diffused,
And in diffusion ever more intense.
So shall I join the choir invisible
Whose music is the gladness of the world.

DIGBY MACKWORTH DOLBEN

## *Enough*

When all my words were said,
  When all my songs were sung,
  I thought to pass among
The unforgotten dead,

A Queen of ruth to reign
  With her, who gathereth tears
  From all the lands and years,
The Lesbian maid of pain;

That lovers, when they wove
  The double myrtle-wreath,
  Should sigh with mingled breath
Beneath the wings of Love:

'How piteous were her wrongs,
  Her words were falling dew,
  All pleasant verse she knew,
But not the Song of songs.'

Yet now, O Love, that you
  Have kissed my forehead, I
  Have sung indeed, can die,
And be forgotten too.

DIGBY MACKWORTH DOLBEN

## *A Sea Song*

In the days before the high tide
  Swept away the towers of sand
Built with so much care and labour
  By the children of the land,

Pale, upon the pallid beaches,
  Thirsting, on the thirsty sands,
Ever cried I to the Distance,
  Ever seaward spread my hands.

See, they come, they come, the ripples,
    Singing, singing fast and low,
Meet the longing of the sea-shores,
    Clasp them, kiss them once, and go.

'Stay, sweet Ocean, satisfying
    All desires into rest—'
Not a word the Ocean answered,
    Rolling sunward down the west.

Then I wept: 'Oh, who will give me
    To behold the stable sea,
On whose tideless shores for ever
    Sounds of many waters be?'

SEBASTIAN EVANS

## The Seven Fiddlers

A blue robe on their shoulder,
    And an ivory bow in hand,
Seven fiddlers came with their fiddles
    A-fiddling through the land,
And they fiddled a tune on their fiddles
    That none could understand.

For none who heard their fiddling
    Might keep his ten toes still,
E'en the cripple threw down his crutches,
    And danced against his will:
Young and old they all fell a-dancing,
    While the fiddlers fiddled their fill.

They fiddled down to the ferry—
    The ferry by Severn-side,
And they stepped aboard the ferry,
    None else to row or guide,
And deftly steered the pilot,
    And stoutly the oars they plied.

Then suddenly in mid-channel
    These fiddlers ceased to row,
And the pilot spake to his fellows
    In a tongue that none may know:
'Let us home to our fathers and brothers,
    And the maidens we love below.'

Then the fiddlers seized their fiddles,
   And sang to their fiddles a song:
'We are coming, coming, O brothers,
   To the home we have left so long,
For the world still loves the fiddler,
   And the fiddler's tune is strong.'

Then they stepped from out the ferry
   Into the Severn-sea,
Down into the depths of the waters
   Where the homes of the fiddlers be,
And the ferry-boat drifted slowly
   Forth to the ocean free!

But where those jolly fiddlers
   Walked down into the deep,
The ripples are never quiet,
   But for ever dance and leap,
Though the Severn-sea be silent,
   And the winds be all asleep.


GEORGE MACDONALD

## A Mammon-Marriage

The croak of a raven hoar!
   A dog's howl, kennel-tied!
Loud shuts the carriage-door:
   The two are away on their ghastly ride
To Death's salt shore!

Where are the love and the grace?
   The bridegroom is thirsty and cold!
The bride's skull sharpens her face!
   But the coachman is driving, jubilant, bold,
The devil's pace.

The horses shivered and shook
   Waiting gaunt and haggard
With sorry and evil look,
   But swift as a drunken wind they staggered
'Longst Lethe brook.

Long since, they ran no more;
 Heavily pulling they died
On the sand of the hopeless shore
 Where never swelled or sank a tide,
And the salt burns sore.

Flat their skeletons lie,
 White shadows on shining sand;
The crusted reins go high
 To the crumbling coachman's bony hand
On his knees awry.

Side by side, jarring no more,
 Day and night side by side,
Each by a doorless door,
 Motionless sit the bridegroom and bride
On the Dead Sea shore.

GEORGE MACDONALD

## The Sheep and the Goat

The thousand streets of London gray
 Repel all country sights;
But bar not winds upon their way,
Nor quench the scent of new-mown hay
 In depth of summer nights.

And here and there an open spot,
 Still bare to light and dark,
With grass receives the wanderer hot;
There trees are growing, houses not—
 They call the place a park.

Soft creatures, with ungentle guides,
 God's sheep from hill and plain,
Flow thitherward in fitful tides,
There weary lie on woolly sides,
 Or crop the grass amain.

And from dark alley, yard, and den,
 In ragged skirts and coats,
Come thither children of poor men,
Wild things, untaught of word or pen—
 The little human goats.

In Regent's Park, one cloudless day,
  An overdriven sheep,
Come a hard, long, and dusty way,
Throbbing with thirst and hotness lay,
  A panting woollen heap.

But help is nearer than we know
  For ills of every name:
Ragged enough to scare the crow,
But with a heart to pity woe,
  A quick-eyed urchin came.

Little he knew of field or fold,
  Yet knew what ailed; his cap
Was ready cup for water cold;
Though creased, and stained, and very old,
  'Twas not much torn, good hap!

Shaping the rim and crown he went,
  Till crown from rim was deep;
The water gushed from pore and rent,
Before he came one half was spent—
  The other saved the sheep.

O little goat, born, bred in ill,
  Unwashed, half-fed, unshorn,
Thou to the sheep from breezy hill
Wast bishop, pastor, what you will,
  In London dry and lorn!

And let priests say the thing they please,
  My faith, though poor and dim,
Thinks he will say who always sees,
In doing it to one of these
  Thou didst it unto him.


RICHARD GARNETT

## Fading-Leaf and Fallen-Leaf

Said Fading-leaf to Fallen-leaf:—
  'I toss alone on a forsaken tree,
It rocks and cracks with every gust that racks
  Its straining bulk; say, how is it with thee?'

Said Fallen-leaf to Fading-leaf:—
  'A heavy foot went by, an hour ago;
Crushed into clay I stain the way;
  The loud wind calls me, and I cannot go.'

Said Fading-leaf to Fallen-leaf:—
  'Death lessons Life, a ghost is ever wise;
Teach me a way to live till May
  Laughs fair with fragrant lips and loving eyes.'

Said Fallen-leaf to Fading-leaf:—
  'Hast loved fair eyes and lips of gentle breath?
Fade then and fall—thou hast had all
  That Life can give, ask somewhat now of Death.'


DORA GREENWELL

## A Picture


It was in autumn that I met
  Her whom I love; the sunflowers bold
Stood up like guards around her set,
And all the air with mignonette
  Was warm within the garden old;
  Beside her feet the marigold
Glowed star-like, and the sweet-pea sent
A sigh to follow as she went
Slowly adown the terrace;—there
I saw thee, oh my love! and thou wert fair.

She stood in the full noonday, unafraid,
  As one beloved of sunlight, for awhile
She leant upon the timeworn balustrade;
The white clematis wooed her, and the clove
  Hung all its burning heart upon her smile;
And on her cheek and in her eyes was love;
And on her lips that, like an opening rose,
Seemed parting some sweet secret to disclose,
The soul of all the summer lingered;—there
I saw thee, oh my love! and thou wert fair.

CHRISTINA ROSSETTI

## *Echo*

Come to me in the silence of the night;
 Come in the speaking silence of a dream:
Come with soft rounded cheeks and eyes as bright
 As sunlight on a stream;
  Come back in tears,
O memory, hope, love of finished years.

Oh dream how sweet, too sweet, too bitter sweet,
 Whose wakening should have been in Paradise,
Where souls brimfull of love abide and meet;
 Where thirsting longing eyes
  Watch the slow door
That opening, letting in, lets out no more.

Yet come to me in dreams, that I may live
 My very life again though cold in death:
Come back to me in dreams, that I may give
 Pulse for pulse, breath for breath:
  Speak low, lean low,
As long ago, my love, how long ago!

DANTE GABRIEL ROSSETTI

## *An Old Song Ended*

*'How should I your true love know*
 *From another one?'*
*'By his cockle-hat and staff*
 *And his sandal-shoon.'*

'And what signs have told you now
 That he hastens home?'
'Lo! the spring is nearly gone,
 He is nearly come.'

'For a token is there nought,
 Say, that he should bring?'
'He will bear a ring I gave
 And another ring.'

'How may I, when he shall ask,
   Tell him who lies there?'
'Nay, but leave my face unveiled
   And unbound my hair.'

'Can you say to me some word
   I shall say to him?'
'Say I'm looking in his eyes
   Though my eyes are dim.'


CHRISTINA ROSSETTI

## Maude Clare


Out of the church she followed them
   With a lofty step and mien:
His bride was like a village maid,
   Maude Clare was like a queen.

'Son Thomas,' his lady mother said,
   With smiles, almost with tears:
'May Nell and you but live as true
   As we have done for years;

'Your father thirty years ago
   Had just your tale to tell;
But he was not so pale as you,
   Nor I so pale as Nell.'

My lord was pale with inward strife,
   And Nell was pale with pride;
My lord gazed long on pale Maude Clare
   Or ever he kissed the bride.

'Lo, I have brought my gift, my lord,
   Have brought my gift,' she said:
'To bless the hearth, to bless the board,
   To bless the marriage-bed.

'Here's my half of the golden chain
   You wore about your neck,
That day we waded ankle-deep
   For lilies in the beck.

'Here's my half of the faded leaves
   We plucked from budding bough,

With feet amongst the lily leaves,—
   The lilies are budding now.'

He strove to match her scorn with scorn,
   He faltered in his place:
'Lady,' he said,—'Maude Clare,' he said,—
   'Maude Clare':—and hid his face.

She turned to Nell: 'My Lady Nell,
   I have a gift for you;
Though, were it fruit, the bloom were gone,
   Or, were it flowers, the dew.

'Take my share of a fickle heart,
   Mine of a paltry love:
Take it or leave it as you will,
   I wash my hands thereof.'

'And what you leave,' said Nell, 'I'll take,
   And what you spurn I'll wear;
For he's my lord for better and worse,
   And him I love, Maude Clare.

'Yea though you're taller by the head,
   More wise, and much more fair,
I'll love him till he loves me best—
   Me best of all, Maude Clare.'

CHRISTINA ROSSETTI

## A Dirge

Why were you born when the snow was falling?
You should have come to the cuckoo's calling,
Or when grapes are green in the cluster,
Or at least when lithe swallows muster
   For their far off flying
   From summer dying.

Why did you die when the lambs were cropping?
You should have died at the apples' dropping,
When the grasshopper comes to trouble,
And the wheat-fields are sodden stubble,
   And all winds go sighing
   For sweet things dying.

CHRISTINA ROSSETTI

# Up-Hill

Does the road wind up-hill all the way?
   Yes, to the very end.
Will the day's journey take the whole long day?
   From morn to night, my friend.

But is there for the night a resting-place?
   A roof for when the slow dark hours begin.
May not the darkness hide it from my face?
   You cannot miss that inn.

Shall I meet other wayfarers at night?
   Those who have gone before.
Then must I knock, or call when just in sight?
   They will not keep you standing at that door.

Shall I find comfort, travel-sore and weak?
   Of labour you shall find the sum.
Will there be beds for me and all who seek?
   Yea, beds for all who come.

DANTE GABRIEL ROSSETTI

# From *The House of Life*

### Sonnet III   Lovesight

When do I see thee most, belovèd one?
   When in the light the spirits of mine eyes
   Before thy face, their altar, solemnize
The worship of that Love through thee made known?
Or when in the dusk hours, (we two alone,)
   Close-kissed and eloquent of still replies
   Thy twilight-hidden glimmering visage lies,
And my soul only sees thy soul its own?

O love, my love! if I no more should see
Thyself, nor on the earth the shadow of thee,
   Nor image of thine eyes in any spring,—
How then should sound upon Life's darkening slope
The ground-whirl of the perished leaves of Hope,
   The wind of Death's imperishable wing?

### Sonnet V   Nuptial Sleep

At length their long kiss severed, with sweet smart:
　　And as the last slow sudden drops are shed
　　From sparkling eaves when all the storm has fled,
So singly flagged the pulses of each heart.
Their bosoms sundered, with the opening start
　　Of married flowers to either side outspread
　　From the knit stem; yet still their mouths, burnt red,
Fawned on each other where they lay apart.

Sleep sank them lower than the tide of dreams,
　　And their dreams watched them sink, and slid away.
Slowly their souls swam up again, through gleams
　　Of watered light and dull drowned waifs of day;
Till from some wonder of new woods and streams
　　He woke, and wondered more: for there she lay.

### Sonnet XXXIV   Barren Spring

Once more the changed year's turning wheel returns:
　　And as a girl sails balanced in the wind,
　　And now before and now again behind
Stoops as it swoops, with cheek that laughs and burns,—
So Spring comes merry towards me now, but earns
　　No answering smile from me, whose life is twined
　　With the dead boughs that winter still must bind,
And whom to-day the Spring no more concerns.

Behold, this crocus is a withering flame;
　　This snowdrop, snow; this apple-blossom's part
　　To breed the fruit that breeds the serpent's art.
Nay, for these Spring-flowers, turn thy face from them,
Nor gaze till on the year's last lily-stem
　　The white cup shrivels round the golden heart.

### Sonnet XLVI   A Superscription

Look in my face; my name is Might-have-been;
　　I am also called No-more, Too-late, Farewell;
　　Unto thine ear I hold the dead-sea shell
Cast up thy Life's foam-fretted feet between;
Unto thine eyes the glass where that is seen
　　Which had Life's form and Love's, but by my spell
　　Is now a shaken shadow intolerable,
Of ultimate things unuttered the frail screen.

Mark me, how still I am! But should there dart
  One moment through thy soul the soft surprise
  Of that winged Peace which lulls the breath of sighs,—
Then shalt thou see me smile, and turn apart
Thy visage to mine ambush at thy heart
  Sleepless with cold commemorative eyes.


ALGERNON CHARLES SWINBURNE

From *Atalanta in Calydon*

[1]
**Chorus**

When the hounds of spring are on winter's traces,
  The mother of months in meadow or plain
Fills the shadows and windy places
  With lisp of leaves and ripple of rain;
And the brown bright nightingale amorous
Is half assuaged for Itylus,
For the Thracian ships and the foreign faces,
  The tongueless vigil, and all the pain.

Come with bows bent and with emptying of quivers,
  Maiden most perfect, lady of light,
With a noise of winds and many rivers,
  With a clamour of waters, and with might;
Bind on thy sandals, O thou most fleet,
Over the splendour and speed of thy feet;
For the faint east quickens, the wan west shivers,
  Round the feet of the day and the feet of the night.

Where shall we find her, how shall we sing to her,
  Fold our hands round her knees, and cling?
O that man's heart were as fire and could spring to her,
  Fire, or the strength of the streams that spring!
For the stars and the winds are unto her
As raiment, as songs of the harp-player;
For the risen stars and the fallen cling to her,
  And the southwest-wind and the west-wind sing.

For winter's rains and ruins are over,
  And all the season of snows and sins;
The days dividing lover and lover,
  The light that loses, the night that wins;

And time remembered is grief forgotten,
And frosts are slain and flowers begotten,
And in green underwood and cover
   Blossom by blossom the spring begins.

The full streams feed on flower of rushes,
   Ripe grasses trammel a travelling foot,
The faint fresh flame of the young year flushes
   From leaf to flower and flower to fruit;
And fruit and leaf are as gold and fire,
And the oat is heard above the lyre,
And the hoofèd heel of a satyr crushes
   The chestnut-husk at the chestnut-root.

And Pan by noon and Bacchus by night,
   Fleeter of foot than the fleet-foot kid,
Follows with dancing and fills with delight
   The Maenad and the Bassarid;
And soft as lips that laugh and hide
The laughing leaves of the trees divide,
And screen from seeing and leave in sight
   The god pursuing, the maiden hid.

The ivy falls with the Bacchanal's hair
   Over her eyebrows hiding her eyes;
The wild vine slipping down leaves bare
   Her bright breast shortening into sighs;
The wild vine slips with the weight of its leaves,
But the berried ivy catches and cleaves
To the limbs that glitter, the feet that scare
   The wolf that follows, the fawn that flies.

## [2]
### Chorus

Before the beginning of years
   There came to the making of man
Time, with a gift of tears;
   Grief, with a glass that ran;
Pleasure, with pain for leaven;
   Summer, with flowers that fell;
Remembrance fallen from heaven,
   And madness risen from hell;
Strength without hands to smite;
   Love that endures for a breath:
Night, the shadow of light,
   And life, the shadow of death.

And the high gods took in hand
   Fire, and the falling of tears,
And a measure of sliding sand
   From under the feet of the years;
And froth and drift of the sea;
   And dust of the labouring earth;
And bodies of things to be
   In the houses of death and of birth;
And wrought with weeping and laughter,
   And fashioned with loathing and love.
With life before and after
   And death beneath and above,
For a day and a night and a morrow,
   That his strength might endure for a span
With travail and heavy sorrow,
   The holy spirit of man.

From the winds of the north and the south
   They gathered as unto strife;
They breathed upon his mouth,
   They filled his body with life;
Eyesight and speech they wrought
   For the veils of the soul therein,
A time for labour and thought,
   A time to serve and to sin;
They gave him light in his ways,
   And love, and a space for delight,
And beauty and length of days,
   And night, and sleep in the night.
His speech is a burning fire;
   With his lips he travaileth;
In his heart is a blind desire,
   In his eyes foreknowledge of death;
He weaves, and is clothed with derision;
   Sows, and he shall not reap;
His life is a watch or a vision
   Between a sleep and a sleep.

ALGERNON CHARLES SWINBURNE

## Hymn to Proserpine

*(After the Proclamation in Rome of
the Christian Faith)*

*Vicisti, Galilæe*

I have lived long enough, having seen one thing, that love hath an end;
Goddess and maiden and queen, be near me now and befriend.
Thou art more than the day or the morrow, the seasons that laugh or
    that weep;
For these give joy and sorrow; but thou, Proserpina, sleep.
Sweet is the treading of wine, and sweet the feet of the dove;
But a goodlier gift is thine than foam of the grapes or love.
Yea, is not even Apollo, with hair and harpstring of gold,
A bitter God to follow, a beautiful God to behold?
I am sick of singing: the bays burn deep and chafe: I am fain
To rest a little from praise and grievous pleasure and pain.
For the Gods we know not of, who give us our daily breath,
We know they are cruel as love or life, and lovely as death.
O Gods dethroned and deceased, cast forth, wiped out in a day!
From your wrath is the world released, redeemed from your chains, men say.
New Gods are crowned in the city; their flowers have broken your rods;
They are merciful, clothed with pity, the young compassionate Gods.
But for me their new device is barren, the days are bare;
Things long past over suffice, and men forgotten that were.
Time and the Gods are at strife; ye dwell in the midst thereof,
Draining a little life from the barren breasts of love.
I say to you, cease, take rest; yea, I say to you all, be at peace,
Till the bitter milk of her breast and the barren bosom shall cease.
Wilt thou yet take all, Galilean? but these thou shalt not take,
The laurel, the palms and the paean, the breasts of the nymphs in the brake;
Breasts more soft than a dove's, that tremble with tenderer breath;
And all the wings of the Loves, and all the joy before death;
All the feet of the hours that sound as a single lyre,
Dropped and deep in the flowers, with strings that flicker like fire.
More than these wilt thou give, things fairer than all these things?
Nay, for a little we live, and life hath mutable wings.
A little while and we die; shall life not thrive as it may?
For no man under the sky lives twice, outliving his day.
And grief is a grievous thing, and a man hath enough of his tears:
Why should he labour, and bring fresh grief to blacken his years?
Thou hast conquered, O pale Galilean; the world has grown grey from
    thy breath;

We have drunken of things Lethean, and fed on the fullness of death.
Laurel is green for a season, and love is sweet for a day;
But love grows bitter with treason, and laurel outlives not May.
Sleep, shall we sleep after all? for the world is not sweet in the end;
For the old faiths loosen and fall, the new years ruin and rend.
Fate is a sea without shore, and the soul is a rock that abides;
But her ears are vexed with the roar and her face with the foam of the tides
O lips that the live blood faints in, the leavings of racks and rods!
O ghastly glories of saints, dead limbs of gibbeted Gods!
Though all men abase them before you in spirit, and all knees bend,
I kneel not neither adore you, but standing, look to the end.
All delicate days and pleasant, all spirits and sorrows are cast
Far out with the foam of the present that sweeps to the surf of the past:
Where beyond the extreme sea-wall, and between the remote sea-gates,
Waste water washes, and tall ships founder, and deep death waits:
Where, mighty with deepening sides, clad about with the seas as with wings,
And impelled of invisible tides, and fulfilled of unspeakable things,
White-eyed and poisonous-finned, shark-toothed and serpentine-curled,
Rolls, under the whitening wind of the future, the wave of the world.
The depths stand naked in sunder behind it, the storms flee away;
In the hollow before it the thunder is taken and snared as a prey;
In its sides is the north-wind bound; and its salt is of all men's tears;
With light of ruin, and sound of changes, and pulse of years:
With travail of day after day, and with trouble of hour upon hour;
And bitter as blood is the spray; and the crests are as fangs that devour;
And its vapour and storm of its steam as the sighing of spirits to be;
And its noise as the noise in a dream; and its depth as the roots of the sea:
And the height of its heads as the height of the utmost stars of the air:
And the ends of the earth at the might thereof tremble, and time is made bare.
Will ye bridle the deep sea with reins, will ye chasten the high sea with rods?
Will ye take her to chain her with chains, who is older than all ye Gods?
All ye as a wind shall go by, as a fire shall ye pass and be past;
Ye are Gods, and behold, ye shall die, and the waves be upon you at last.
In the darkness of time, in the deeps of the years, in the changes of things,
Ye shall sleep as a slain man sleeps, and the world shall forget you for kings.
Though the feet of thine high priests tread where thy lords and our forefathers
    trod,
Though these that were Gods are dead, and thou being dead art a God,
Though before thee the throned Cytherean be fallen, and hidden her head,
Yet thy kingdom shall pass, Galilean, thy dead shall go down to thee dead.
Of the maiden thy mother men sing as a goddess with grace clad around;
Thou art throned where another was king; where another was queen she
    is crowned.
Yea, once we had sight of another: but now she is queen, say these.
Not as thine, not as thine was our mother, a blossom of flowering seas,
Clothed round with the world's desire as with raiment, and fair as the foam,

And fleeter than kindled fire, and a goddess, and mother of Rome.
For thine came pale and a maiden, and sister to sorrow; but ours,
Her deep hair heavily laden with odour and colour of flowers,
White rose of the rose-white water, a silver splendour, a flame,
Bent down unto us that besought her, and earth grew sweet with her name.
For thine came weeping, a slave among slaves, and rejected; but she
Came flushed from the full-flushed wave, and imperial, her foot on the sea.
And the wonderful waters knew her, the winds and the viewless ways,
And the roses grew rosier, and bluer the sea-blue stream of the bays.
Ye are fallen, our lords, by what token? we wist that ye should not fall.
Ye were all so fair that are broken; and one more fair than ye all.
But I turn to her still, having seen she shall surely abide in the end;
Goddess and maiden and queen, be near me now and befriend.
O daughter of earth, of my mother, her crown and blossom of birth,
I am also, I also, thy brother; I go as I came unto earth.
In the night where thine eyes are as moons are in heaven, the night where
    thou art,
Where the silence is more than all tunes, where sleep overflows from the heart,
Where the poppies are sweet as the rose in our world, and the red rose is white,
And the wind falls faint as it blows with the fume of the flowers of the night,
And the murmur of spirits that sleep in the shadow of Gods from afar
Grows dim in thine ears and deep as the deep dim soul of a star,
In the sweet low light of thy face, under heavens untrod by the sun,
Let my soul with their souls find place, and forget what is done and undone.
Thou art more than the Gods who number the days of our temporal breath;
For these give labour and slumber; but thou, Proserpina, death.
Therefore now at thy feet I abide for a season in silence. I know
I shall die as my fathers died, and sleep as they sleep; even so.
For the glass of the years is brittle wherein we gaze for a span;
A little soul for a little bears up this corpse which is man.
So long I endure, no longer; and laugh not again, neither weep.
For there is no God found stronger than death; and death is a sleep.

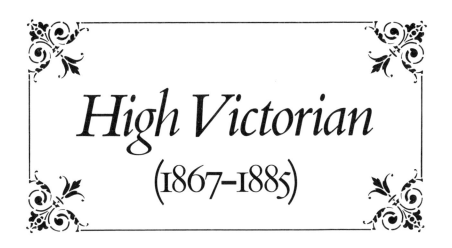

# High Victorian
## (1867–1885)

WILLIAM MORRIS

## The Haystack in the Floods

Had she come all the way for this,
To part at last without a kiss?
Yea, had she borne the dirt and rain
That her own eyes might see him slain
Beside the haystack in the floods?

Along the dripping leafless woods,
The stirrup touching either shoe,
She rode astride as troopers do;
With kirtle kilted to her knee,
To which the mud splashed wretchedly;
And the wet dripped from every tree
Upon her head and heavy hair,
And on her eyelids broad and fair;
The tears and rain ran down her face.
By fits and starts they rode apace,
And very often was his place
Far off from her; he had to ride
Ahead, to see what might betide
When the roads crossed; and sometimes, when
There rose a murmuring from his men,
Had to turn back with promises;
Ah me! she had but little ease;
And often for pure doubt and dread
She sobbed, made giddy in the head
By the swift riding; while, for cold,
Her slender fingers scarce could hold
The wet reins; yea, and scarcely, too,
She felt the foot within her shoe
Against the stirrup: all for this,
To part at last without a kiss
Beside the haystack in the floods.

For when they neared that old soaked hay,
They saw across the only way
That Judas, Godmar, and the three
Red running lions dismally
Grinned from his pennon, under which,
In one straight line along the ditch,
They counted thirty heads.

So then,
While Robert turned round to his men,
She saw at once the wretched end,
And, stooping down, tried hard to rend
Her coif the wrong way from her head,
And hid her eyes; while Robert said:
'Nay, love, 'tis scarcely two to one,
At Poictiers where we made them run
So fast—why, sweet my love, good cheer.
The Gascon frontier is so near,
Nought after this.'

But, 'O,' she said,
'My God! my God! I have to tread
The long way back without you; then
The court at Paris; those six men;
The gratings of the Chatelet;
The swift Seine on some rainy day
Like this, and people standing by,
And laughing, while my weak hands try
To recollect how strong men swim.
All this, or else a life with him,
For which I should be damned at last,
Would God that this next hour were past!'

He answered not, but cried his cry,
'St George for Marny!' cheerily;
And laid his hand upon her rein.
Alas! no man of all his train
Gave back that cheery cry again;
And, while for rage his thumb beat fast
Upon his sword-hilt, some one cast
About his neck a kerchief long,
And bound him.

Then they went along
To Godmar; who said: 'Now, Jehane,
Your lover's life is on the wane
So fast, that, if this very hour
You yield not as my paramour,
He will not see the rain leave off—
Nay, keep your tongue from gibe and scoff,
Sir Robert, or I slay you now.'

She laid her hand upon her brow,
Then gazed upon the palm, as though
She thought her forehead bled, and—'No'

She said, and turned her head away,
As there were nothing else to say,
And everything were settled: red
Grew Godmar's face from chin to head:
'Jehane, on yonder hill there stands
My castle, guarding well my lands:
What hinders me from taking you,
And doing that I list to do
To your fair wilful body, while
Your knight lies dead?'

               A wicked smile
Wrinkled her face, her lips grew thin,
A long way out she thrust her chin:
'You know that I should strangle you
While you were sleeping; or bite through
Your throat, by God's help—ah!' she said,
'Lord Jesus, pity your poor maid!
For in such wise they hem me in,
I cannot choose but sin and sin,
Whatever happens: yet I think
They could not make me eat or drink,
And so should I just reach my rest.'
'Nay, if you do not my behest,
O Jehane! though I love you well,'
Said Godmar, 'would I fail to tell
All that I know.' 'Foul lies,' she said.
'Eh? lies my Jehane? by God's head,
At Paris folks would deem them true!
Do you know, Jehane, they cry for you,
"Jehane the brown! Jehane the brown!
Give us Jehane to burn or drown!"—
Eh—gag me Robert!—sweet my friend,
This were indeed a piteous end
For those long fingers, and long feet,
And long neck, and smooth shoulders sweet;
An end that few men would forget
That saw it—So, an hour yet:
Consider, Jehane, which to take
Of life or death!'

             So, scarce awake,
Dismounting, did she leave that place,
And totter some yards: with her face
Turned upward to the sky she lay,
Her head on a wet heap of hay,

And fell asleep: and while she slept,
And did not dream, the minutes crept
Round to the twelve again; but she,
Being waked at last, sighed quietly,
And strangely childlike came, and said:
'I will not.' Straightway Godmar's head,
As though it hung on strong wires, turned
Most sharply round, and his face burned.

For Robert—both his eyes were dry,
He could not weep, but gloomily
He seemed to watch the rain; yea, too,
His lips were firm; he tried once more
To touch her lips; she reached out, sore
And vain desire so tortured them,
The poor grey lips, and now the hem
Of his sleeve brushed them.

                  With a start
Up Godmar rose, thrust them apart;
From Robert's throat he loosed the bands
Of silk and mail; with empty hands
Held out, she stood and gazed, and saw,
The long bright blade without a flaw
Glide out from Godmar's sheath, his hand
In Robert's hair; she saw him bend
Back Robert's head; she saw him send
The thin steel down; the blow told well,
Right backward the knight Robert fell,
And moaned as dogs do, being half dead,
Unwitting, as I deem: so then
Godmar turned grinning to his men,
Who ran, some five or six, and beat
His head to pieces at their feet.

Then Godmar turned again and said:
'So, Jehane, the first fitte is read!
Take note, my lady, that your way
Lies backward to the Chatelet!'
She shook her head and gazed awhile
At her cold hands with a rueful smile,
As though this thing had made her mad.

This was the parting that they had
Beside the haystack in the floods.

WILLIAM MORRIS

## From *The Earthly Paradise*

### The Earthly Paradise

Of Heaven or Hell I have no power to sing,
I cannot ease the burden of your fears;
Or make quick-coming death a little thing,
Or bring again the pleasure of past years,
Nor for my words shall ye forget your tears,
Or hope again for aught that I can say,
The idle singer of an empty day.

But rather, when aweary of your mirth,
From full hearts still unsatisfied ye sigh,
And, feeling kindly unto all the earth,
Grudge every minute as it passes by,
Made the more mindful that the sweet days die—
Remember me a little then I pray,
The idle singer of an empty day.

The heavy trouble, the bewildering care
That weighs us down who live and earn our bread,
These idle verses have no power to bear;
So let me sing of names remembered,
Because they, living not, can ne'er be dead,
Or long time take their memory quite away
From us poor singers of an empty day.

Dreamer of dreams, born out of my due time,
Why should I strive to set the crooked straight?
Let it suffice me that my murmuring rhyme
Beats with light wing against the ivory gate,
Telling a tale not too importunate
To those who in the sleepy region stay,
Lulled by the singer of an empty day.

Folk say, a wizard to a northern king
At Christmas-tide such wondrous things did show,
That through one window men beheld the spring,
And through another saw the summer glow,
And through a third the fruited vines a-row,
While still, unheard, but in its wonted way,
Piped the drear wind of that December day.

So with this Earthly Paradise it is,
If ye will read aright, and pardon me,
Who strive to build a shadowy isle of bliss
Midmost the beating of the steely sea,
Where tossed about all hearts of men must be;
Whose ravening monsters mighty men shall slay,
Not the poor singer of an empty day.

### From **Prologue: The Wanderers**

Forget six counties overhung with smoke,
Forget the snorting steam and piston stroke,
Forget the spreading of the hideous town;
Think rather of the pack-horse on the down,
And dream of London, small, and white, and clean,
The clear Thames bordered by its gardens green:
Think, that below bridge the green lapping waves
Smite some few keels that bear Levantine staves,
Cut from the yew wood on the burnt-up hill,
And pointed jars that Greek hands toiled to fill,
And treasured scanty spice from some far sea,
Florence gold cloth, and Ypres napery,
And cloth of Bruges, and hogsheads of Guienne;
While nigh the thronged wharf Geoffrey Chaucer's pen
Moves over bills of lading—mid such times
Shall dwell the hollow puppets of my rhymes.

### The Outlanders

Outlanders, whence come ye last?
    *The snow in the street and the wind on the door.*
Through what green seas and great have ye passed?
    *Minstrels and maids, stand forth on the floor.*

From far away, O masters mine,
    *The snow in the street and the wind on the door.*
We come to bear you goodly wine,
    *Minstrels and maids, stand forth on the floor.*

From far away we come to you,
    *The snow in the street and the wind on the door.*
To tell of great tidings strange and true.
    *Minstrels and maids, stand forth on the floor.*

News, news of the Trinity,
    *The snow in the street and the wind on the door.*
And Mary and Joseph from over the sea!
    *Minstrels and maids, stand forth on the floor.*

For as we wandered far and wide,
  *The snow in the street and the wind on the door.*
What hap do ye deem there should us betide!
  *Minstrels and maids, stand forth on the floor.*

Under a bent when the night was deep,
  *The snow in the street and the wind on the door.*
There lay three shepherds tending their sheep.
  *Minstrels and maids, stand forth on the floor.*

'O ye shepherds, what have ye seen,
  *The snow in the street and the wind on the door.*
To slay your sorrow, and heal your teen?'
  *Minstrels and maids, stand forth on the floor.*

'In an ox-stall this night we saw
  *The snow in the street and the wind on the door.*
A babe and a maid without a flaw.
  *Minstrels and maids, stand forth on the floor.*

'There was an old man there beside,
  *The snow in the street and the wind on the door.*
His hair was white and his hood was wide.
  *Minstrels and maids, stand forth on the floor.*

'And as we gazed this thing upon,
  *The snow in the street and the wind on the door.*
Those twain knelt down to the Little One.
  *Minstrels and maids, stand forth on the floor.*

'And a marvellous song we straight did hear,
  *The snow in the street and the wind on the door.*
That slew our sorrow and healed our care.'
  *Minstrels and maids, stand forth on the floor.*

News of a fair and a marvellous thing,
  *The snow in the street and the wind on the door.*
Nowell, nowell, nowell, we sing!
  *Minstrels and maids, stand forth on the floor.*

WILLIAM MORRIS

## Two Red Roses across the Moon

There was a lady lived in a hall,
Large in the eyes, and slim and tall;
And ever she sung from noon to noon,
*Two red roses across the moon.*

There was a knight came riding by
In early spring, when the roads were dry;
And he heard that lady sing at the noon,
*Two red roses across the moon.*

Yet none the more he stopped at all,
But he rode a-gallop past the hall;
And left that lady singing at noon,
*Two red roses across the moon.*

Because, forsooth, the battle was set,
And the scarlet and blue had got to be met,
He rode on the spur till the next warm noon:—
*Two red roses across the moon.*

But the battle was scattered from hill to hill,
From the windmill to the watermill;
And he said to himself, as it neared the noon,
*Two red roses across the moon.*

You scarce could see for the scarlet and blue,
A golden helm or a golden shoe;
So he cried, as the fight grew thick at the noon,
*Two red roses across the moon!*

Verily then the gold bore through
The huddled spears of the scarlet and blue;
And they cried, as they cut them down at the noon,
*Two red roses across the moon!*

I trow he stopped when he rode again
By the hall, though draggled sore with the rain;
And his lips were pinched to kiss at the noon
*Two red roses across the moon.*

Under the may she stooped to the crown,
All was gold, there was nothing of brown;
And the horns blew up in the hall at noon,
*Two red roses across the moon.*

HUGH CONWAY

## *Falkland at Newbury, 1643*

Now which is wrong or right? Too glib we talk
Of 'crop-eared knaves, malignants'—prate too fast
Of 'round-head rebels'. Those who bid, to-day,
Defiance sullen to our haughty ranks
War not for pleasure, plunder, nor the fame
Sweet to a soldier. Nay, their hearts are moved
By some strange sense of wrong; the when or how
Perchance misunderstood, yet roused and strung
Till awe-struck homage and the right divine
Of kings are swept away before the blast
Of mighty anger, stirring to the depths
A people stern at Liberty assailed.

'The king can do no wrong!' Have I not seen
Fair treaties cancelled, regal oaths recalled;
The danger past that dragged from royal lips
The lulling words—and then, once more the need,
The promise made—and broken? Ay, until
My heart grew sick, and through a cloud of doubt
This thought would glimmer—'They are just, these men,
And I should stand beside them, plead their cause,
And, if the bitter end at last must come,
Fall with them fighting.'
                              Then around me closed
The iron bands of old tradition—rank
And order, knightly vows and fealty,
And, stronger yet, the love I bear my lord
As fellow-man, not king. Again, I shrank
From calling traitor Essex friend, or with
The shifty Fairfax linking in my lot
And name. Sure, if their cause be right,
The tools it needs to shape it to its ends
Are chosen strangely.
                              Yet, I dreamt last night,
One came to me with starry eyes and clear,
Reading the very doubts that swayed my soul,—
A goddess, belted, armed. She grasped a sword—
No slender blade, with handle gilt and gemmed,
Meet for a courtier's side,—the steel she shook
Was keen and stout as one might wish to hold
When blows are thickly dealt, and ready hands
Must guard the head. Outstretching it, she said,

'Take this, and strike for England.'
                          Then I asked,
'Which England?'—Oh, the regal scorn that curled
Her lip, as clear and cold the answer came:
'There is but one—the people's. Take and strike!'
And, wavering, I reached, and then again
Withdrew, and whispering the while, 'The king
Can do no wrong'; and her proud face I saw
Grow stern and sad, and I awoke.
                        Ah! now
The battle opens, and amid those ranks
Sombre and sullen, waits, maybe, a point
Meant for a foe, yet bearing to a friend
A soldier's death to end a statesman's doubts.

### THOMAS HARDY

### *'When I set out for Lyonnesse'*

When I set out for Lyonnesse,
    A hundred miles away,
    The rime was on the spray,
And starlight lit my lonesomeness
When I set out for Lyonnesse
    A hundred miles away.

What would bechance at Lyonnesse
    While I should sojourn there
    No prophet durst declare,
Nor did the wisest wizard guess
What would bechance at Lyonnesse
    While I should sojourn there.

When I came back from Lyonnesse
    With magic in my eyes,
    All marked with mute surmise
My radiance rare and fathomless,
When I came back from Lyonnesse
    With magic in my eyes!

EDMUND GOSSE

## *Lying in the Grass*

Between two golden tufts of summer grass,
I see the world through hot air as through glass,
And by my face sweet lights and colours pass.

Before me, dark against the fading sky,
I watch three mowers mowing, as I lie:
With brawny arms they sweep in harmony.

Brown English faces by the sun burnt red,
Rich glowing colour on bare throat and head,
My heart would leap to watch them, were I dead!

And in my strong young living as I lie,
I seem to move with them in harmony—
A fourth is mowing, and that fourth am I.

The music of the scythes that glide and leap,
The young men whistling as their great arms sweep,
And all the perfume and sweet sense of sleep,

The weary butterflies that droop their wings,
The dreamy nightingale that hardly sings,
And all the lassitude of happy things,

Is mingling with the warm and pulsing blood,
That gushes through my veins a languid flood,
And feeds my spirit as the sap a bud.

Behind the mowers, on the amber air,
A dark-green beech-wood rises, still and fair,
A white path winding up it like a stair.

And see that girl, with pitcher on her head,
A clean white apron on her gown of red,—
Her even-song of love is but half-said:

She waits the youngest mower. Now he goes;
Her cheeks are redder than a wild blush-rose:
They climb up where the deepest shadows close.

But though they pass, and vanish, I am there.
I watch his rough hands meet beneath her hair,
Their broken speech sounds sweet to me like prayer.

Ah! now the rosy children come to play,
And romp and struggle with the new-mown hay;
Their clear high voices sound from far away.

They know so little why the world is sad,
They dig themselves warm graves and yet are glad;
Their muffled screams and laughter make me mad!

I long to go and play among them there;
Unseen, like wind, to take them by the hair.
And gently make their rosy cheeks more fair.

The happy children! full of frank surprise,
And sudden whims and innocent ecstasies;
What godhead sparkles from their liquid eyes!

No wonder round those urns of mingled clays
That Tuscan potters fashioned in old days,
And coloured like the torrid earth ablaze,

We find the little gods and loves portrayed,
Through ancient forests wandering undismayed,
And fluting hymns of pleasure unafraid.

They knew, as I do now, what keen delight
A strong man feels to watch the tender flight
Of little children playing in his sight;

What pure sweet pleasure, and what sacred love,
Comes drifting down upon us from above,
In watching how their limbs and features move.

I do not hunger for a well-stored mind,
I only wish to live my life, and find
My heart in unison with all mankind.

My life is like the single dewy star
That trembles on the horizon's primrose-bar,—
A microcosm where all things living are.

And if, among the noiseless grasses, Death
Should come behind and take away my breath,
I should not rise as one who sorroweth;

For I should pass; but all the world would be
Full of desire and young delight and glee,
And why should men be sad through loss of me?

The light is flying; in the silver-blue
The young moon shines from her bright window through:
The mowers are all gone, and I go too.

PHILIP BOURKE MARSTON

## The Old Churchyard of Bonchurch

*(This old churchyard has been for many years slipping*
*toward the sea, which it is expected will ultimately engulf it.)*

The churchyard leans to the sea with its dead,—
It leans to the sea with its dead so long,
Do they hear, I wonder, the first bird's song,
When the winter's anger is all but fled;
The high, sweet voice of the west wind,
The fall of the warm, soft rain,
When the second month of the year
Puts heart in the earth again?

Do they hear, through the glad April weather,
The green grasses waving above them?
Do they think there are none left to love them,
They have lain for so long there, together?
Do they hear the note of the cuckoo,
The cry of gulls on the wing,
The laughter of winds and waters,
The feet of the dancing Spring?

Do they feel the old land slipping seaward,—
The old land, with its hills and its graves,—
As they gradually slide to the waves,
With the wind blowing on them from leeward?
Do they know of the change that awaits them,—
The sepulchre vast and strange?
Do they long for the days to go over,
And bring that miraculous change?

Or love they their night with no moonlight,
With no starlight, no dawn to its gloom?
Do they sigh: ''Neath the snow, or the bloom
Of the wild things that wave from our night,
We are warm, through winter and summer;
We hear the winds rave, and we say,—
"The storm-wind blows over our heads,
But we, here, are out of its way" '?

Do they mumble low, one to another,
With a sense that the waters that thunder
Shall ingather them all, draw them under,—
'Ah, how long to our moving, my brother?

How long shall we quietly rest here,
In graves of darkness and ease?
The waves, even now, may be on us,
To draw us down under the seas!'

Do they think 'twill be cold when the waters
That they love not, that neither can love them
Shall eternally thunder above them?
Have they dread of the sea's shining daughters,
That people the bright sea-regions
And play with the young sea-kings?
Have they dread of their cold embraces,
And dread of all strange sea-things?

But their dread or their joy,—it is bootless:
They shall pass from the breast of their mother;
They shall lie low, dead brother by brother,
In a place that is radiant and fruitless;
And the folk that sail over their heads
In violent weather
Shall come down to them, haply, and all
They shall lie there, together.


PHILIP BOURKE MARSTON

## Speechless

*Upon the Marriage of Two Deaf and Dumb Persons*


Their lips upon each other's lips are laid;
Strong moans of joy, wild laughter, and short cries
Seem uttered in the passion of their eyes.
He sees her body fair and fallen head,
And she the face whereon her soul is fed;
And by the way her white breasts sink and rise,
He knows she must be shaken by sweet sighs;
But all delight of sound for them is dead.
They dance a strange, weird measure, who know not
The tune to which their dancing feet are led;
Their breath in kissing is made doubly hot
With flame of pent-up speech; strange light is shed
About their spirits, as they mix and meet
In passion-lighted silence, 'tranced and sweet.

THOMAS HARDY

## Hap

If but some vengeful god would call to me
From up the sky, and laugh: 'Thou suffering thing,
Know that thy sorrow is my ecstasy,
That thy love's loss is my hate's profiting!'

Then would I bear it, clench myself, and die,
Steeled by the sense of ire unmerited;
Half-eased in that a Powerfuller than I
Had willed and meted me the tears I shed.

But not so. How arrives it joy lies slain,
And why unblooms the best hope ever sown?
—Crass Casualty obstructs the sun and rain,
And dicing Time for gladness casts a moan. . . .
These purblind Doomsters had as readily strown
Blisses about my pilgrimage as pain.

THOMAS HARDY

## Neutral Tones

We stood by a pond that winter day,
And the sun was white, as though chidden of God,
And a few leaves lay on the starving sod; ˙
    —They had fallen from an ash, and were gray.

Your eyes on me were as eyes that rove
Over tedious riddles of years ago;
And some words played between us to and fro
    On which lost the more by our love.

The smile on your mouth was the deadest thing
Alive enough to have strength to die;
And a grin of bitterness swept thereby
    Like an ominous bird a-wing. . .

Since then, keen lessons that love deceives,
And wrings with wrong, have shaped to me
Your face, and the God-curst sun, and a tree,
    And a pond edged with grayish leaves.

JAMES THOMSON ('B.V.')

## From *The City of Dreadful Night*

I

The City is of Night; perchance of Death,
    But certainly of Night; for never there
Can come the lucid morning's fragrant breath
    After the dewy dawning's cold grey air;
The moon and stars may shine with scorn or pity;
The sun has never visited that city,
    For it dissolveth in the daylight fair.

Dissolveth like a dream of night away;
    Though present in distempered gloom of thought
And deadly weariness of heart all day.
    But when a dream night after night is brought
Throughout a week, and such weeks few or many
Recur each year for several years, can any
    Discern that dream from real life in aught?

For life is but a dream whose shapes return,
    Some frequently, some seldom, some by night
And some by day, some night and day: we learn,
    The while all change and many vanish quite,
In their recurrence with recurrent changes
A certain seeming order; where this ranges
    We count things real; such is memory's might.

A river girds the city west and south,
    The main north channel of a broad lagoon,
Regurging with the salt tides from the mouth;
    Waste marshes shine and glister to the moon
For leagues, then moorland black, then stony ridges;
Great piers and causeways, many noble bridges,
    Connect the town and islet suburbs strewn.

Upon an easy slope it lies at large,
    And scarcely overlaps the long curved crest
Which swells out two leagues from the river marge.
    A trackless wilderness rolls north and west,
Savannahs, savage woods, enormous mountains,
Bleak uplands, black ravines with torrent fountains;
    And eastwards rolls the shipless sea's unrest.

The city is not ruinous, although
  Great ruins of an unremembered past,
With others of a few short years ago
  More sad, are found within its precincts vast.
The street-lamps always burn; but scarce a casement
In house or palace front from roof to basement
  Doth glow or gleam athwart the mirk air cast.

The street-lamps burn amidst the baleful glooms,
  Amidst the soundless solitudes immense
Of rangèd mansions dark and still as tombs.
  The silence which benumbs or strains the sense
Fulfils with awe the soul's despair unweeping:
Myriads of habitants are ever sleeping,
  Or dead, or fled from nameless pestilence!

Yet as in some necropolis you find
  Perchance one mourner to a thousand dead,
So there; worn faces that look deaf and blind
  Like tragic masks of stone. With weary tread,
Each wrapt in his own doom, they wander, wander,
Or sit foredone and desolately ponder
  Through sleepless hours with heavy drooping head.

Mature men chiefly, few in age or youth,
  A woman rarely, now and then a child:
A child! If here the heart turns sick with ruth
  To see a little one from birth defiled,
Or lame or blind, as preordained to languish
Through youthless life, think how it bleeds with anguish
  To meet one erring in that homeless wild.

They often murmur to themselves, they speak
  To one another seldom, for their woe
Broods maddening inwardly and scorns to wreak
  Itself abroad; and if at whiles it grow
To frenzy which must rave, none heeds the clamour,
Unless there waits some victim of like glamour,
  To rave in turn, who lends attentive show.

The City is of Night, but not of Sleep;
  There sweet sleep is not for the weary brain;
The pitiless hours like years and ages creep,
  A night seems termless hell. This dreadful strain
Of thought and consciousness which never ceases,
Or which some moments' stupor but increases,
  This, worse than woe, makes wretches there insane.

They leave all hope behind who enter there:
   One certitude while sane they cannot leave,
One anodyne for torture and despair;
   The certitude of Death, which no reprieve
Can put off long; and which, divinely tender,
But waits the outstretched hand to promptly render
   That draught whose slumber nothing can bereave.


### III

Although lamps burn along the silent streets,
   Even when moonlight silvers empty squares
The dark holds countless lanes and close retreats;
   But when the night its sphereless mantle wears
The open spaces yawn with gloom abysmal,
The sombre mansions loom immense and dismal,
   The lanes are black as subterranean lairs.

And soon the eye a strange new vision learns:
   The night remains for it as dark and dense,
Yet clearly in this darkness it discerns
   As in the daylight with its natural sense;
Perceives a shade in shadow not obscurely,
Pursues a stir of black in blackness surely,
   Sees spectres also in the gloom intense.

The ear, too, with the silence vast and deep
   Becomes familiar though unreconciled;
Hears breathings as of hidden life asleep,
   And muffled throbs as of pent passions wild,
Far murmurs, speech of pity or derision;
But all more dubious than the things of vision,
   So that it knows not when it is beguiled.

No time abates the first despair and awe,
   But wonder ceases soon; the weirdest thing
Is felt least strange beneath the lawless law
   Where Death-in-Life is the eternal king;
Crushed impotent beneath this reign of terror,
Dazed with such mysteries of woe and error,
   The soul is too outworn for wondering.


### XI

What men are they who haunt these fatal glooms,
   And fill their living mouths with dust of death,
And make their habitations in the tombs,
   And breathe eternal sighs with mortal breath,

And pierce life's pleasant veil of various error
To reach that void of darkness and old terror
    Wherein expire the lamps of hope and faith?

They have much wisdom yet they are not wise,
    They have much goodness yet they do not well,
(The fools we know have their own Paradise,
    The wicked also have their proper Hell);
They have much strength but still their doom is stronger,
Much patience but their time endureth longer,
    Much valour but life mocks it with some spell.

They are most rational and yet insane:
    An outward madness not to be controlled;
A perfect reason in the central brain,
    Which has no power, but sitteth wan and cold,
And sees the madness, and foresees as plainly
The ruin in its path, and trieth vainly
    To cheat itself refusing to behold.

And some are great in rank and wealth and power,
    And some renowned for genius and for worth;
And some are poor and mean, who brood and cower
    And shrink from notice, and accept all dearth
Of body, heart and soul, and leave to others
All boons of life: yet these and those are brothers,
    The saddest and the weariest men on earth.


## XIX

The mighty river flowing dark and deep,
    With ebb and flood from the remote sea-tides
Vague-sounding through the City's sleepless sleep,
    Is named the River of the Suicides;
For night by night some lorn wretch overweary,
And shuddering from the future yet more dreary,
    Within its cold secure oblivion hides.

One plunges from a bridge's parapet,
    As by some blind and sudden frenzy hurled;
Another wades in slow with purpose set
    Until the waters are above him furled;
Another in a boat with dreamlike motion
Glides drifting down into the desert ocean,
    To starve or sink from out the desert world.

They perish from their suffering surely thus,
   For none beholding them attempts to save,
The while each thinks how soon, solicitous,
   He may seek refuge in the self-same wave;
Some hour when tired of ever-vain endurance
Impatience will forerun the sweet assurance
   Of perfect peace eventual in the grave.

When this poor tragic-farce has palled us long,
   Why actors and spectators do we stay?—
To fill our so-short *rôles* out right or wrong;
   To see what shifts are yet in the dull play
For our illusion; to refrain from grieving
Dear foolish friends by our untimely leaving:
   But those asleep at home, how blest are they!

Yet it is but for one night after all:
   What matters one brief night of dreary pain?
When after it the weary eyelids fall
   Upon the weary eyes and wasted brain;
And all sad scenes and thoughts and feelings vanish
In that sweet sleep no power can ever banish,
   That one best sleep which never wakes again.

WATHEN MARK WILKS CALL

## Summer Days

In summer, when the days were long,
We walked, two friends, in field and wood,
Our heart was light, our step was strong,
And life lay round us, fair as good,
In summer, when the days were long.

We strayed from morn till evening came,
We gathered flowers, and wove us crowns,
We walked mid poppies red as flame,
Or sat upon the yellow downs,
And always wished our life the same.

In summer, when the days were long,
We leapt the hedgerow, crossed the brook;
And still her voice flowed forth in song,
Or else she read some graceful book,
In summer, when the days were long.

And then we sat beneath the trees,
With shadows lessening in the noon;
And in the sunlight and the breeze,
We revelled, many a glorious June,
While larks were singing o'er the leas.

In summer, when the days were long,
We plucked wild strawberries, ripe and red,
Or feasted, with no grace but song,
On golden nectar, snow-white bread,
In summer, when the days were long.

We loved, and yet we knew it not,
For loving seemed like breathing then,
We found a heaven in every spot,
Saw angels, too, in all good men,
And dreamt of gods in grove and grot.

In summer, when the days are long,
Alone I wander, muse alone;
I see her not, but that old song,
Under the fragrant wind is blown,
In summer, when the days are long.

Alone I wander in the wood,
But one fair spirit hears my sighs;
And half I see the crimson hood,
The radiant hair, the calm glad eyes,
That charmed me in life's summer mood.

In summer, when the days are long,
I love her as I loved of old;
My heart is light, my step is strong,
For love brings back those hours of gold,
In summer, when the days are long.


EDWARD DOWDEN

## In the Cathedral Close

In the Dean's porch a nest of clay
    With five small tenants may be seen,
Five solemn faces, each as wise
    As if its owner were a Dean;

Five downy fledglings in a row,
    Packed close, as in the antique pew
The school-girls are whose foreheads clear
    At the *Venite* shine on you.

Day after day the swallows sit
    With scarce a stir, with scarce a sound,
But dreaming and digesting much
    They grow thus wise and soft and round.

They watch the Canons come to dine,
    And hear the mullion-bars across,
Over the fragrant fruit and wine
    Deep talk of rood-screen and reredos.

Her hands with field-flowers drenched, a child
    Leaps past in wind-blown dress and hair,
The swallows turn their heads askew—
    Five judges deem that she is fair.

Prelusive touches sound within,
    Straightway they recognise the sign,
And, blandly nodding, they approve
    The minuet of Rubinstein.

They mark the cousins' schoolboy talk,
    (Male birds flown wide from minster bell),
And blink at each broad term of art,
    Binominal or bicycle.

Ah! downy young ones, soft and warm,
    Doth such a stillness mask from sight
Such swiftness? can such peace conceal
    Passion and ecstasy of flight?

Yet somewhere 'mid your Eastern suns,
    Under a white Greek architrave
At morn, or when the shaft of fire
    Lies large upon the Indian wave,

A sense of something dear gone by
    Will stir, strange longings thrill the heart
For a small world embowered and close,
    Of which ye some time were a part.

The dew-drenched flowers, the child's glad eyes
    Your joy unhuman shall control,
And in your wings a light and wind
    Shall move from the Maestro's soul.

FRANCIS TURNER PALGRAVE

## The Linnet in November

Late singer of a sunless day,
   I know not if with pain
Or pleasure more, I hear thy lay
   Renew its vernal strain.

As gleams of youth, when youth is o'er,
   And bare the summer bowers,
Thy song brings back the years of yore,
   And unreturning hours.

So was it once! So yet again
   It never more will be!
Yet sing; and lend us in thy strain
   A moment's youth with thee.

FRANCIS TURNER PALGRAVE

## Eutopia

There is a garden where lilies
   And roses are side by side;
And all day between them in silence
   The silken butterflies glide.

I may not enter the garden,
   Though I know the road thereto;
And morn by morn to the gateway
   I see the children go.

They bring back light on their faces;
   But they cannot bring back to me
What the lilies say to the roses,
   Or the songs of the butterflies be.

## C. S. CALVERLEY

### *The Palace*

They come, they come, with fife and drum,
  And gleaming pikes and glancing banners:
Though the eyes flash, the lips are dumb;
  To talk in rank would not be manners.
Onward they stride, as Britons can;
The ladies following in the Van.

Who, who be these that tramp in threes
  Through sumptuous Piccadilly, through
The roaring Strand, and stand at ease
  At last 'neath shadowy Waterloo?
Some gallant Guild, I ween, are they,
Taking their annual holiday.

To catch the destined train—to pay
  Their willing fares, and plunge within it—
Is, as in old Romaunt they say,
  With them the work of half-a-minute.
Then off they're whirled, with songs and shouting,
To cedared Sydenham for their outing.

I marked them light, with faces bright
  As pansies or a new coined florin,
And up the sunless stair take flight,
  Close-packed as rabbits in a warren.
Honour the Brave, who in that stress
Still trod not upon Beauty's dress!

Kerchief in hand I saw them stand;
  In every kerchief lurked a lunch;
When they unfurled them, it was grand
  To watch bronzed men and maidens crunch
The sounding celery-stick, or ram
The knife into the blushing ham.

Dashed the bold fork through pies of pork;
  O'er hard-boiled eggs the saltspoon shook;
Leapt from its lair the playful cork:
  Yet some there were, to whom the brook
Seemed sweetest beverage, and for meat
They chose the red root of the beet.

Then many a song, some rather long,
    Came quivering up from girlish throats;
And one young man he came out strong,
    And gave 'The Wolf' without his notes.
While they who knew not song or ballad
Still munched, approvingly, their salad.

But ah! what bard could sing how hard,
    The artless banquet o'er, they ran
Down the soft slope with daisies starred
    And kingcups! onward, maid with man,
They flew, to scale the breezy swing,
Or court frank kisses in the ring.

Such are the sylvan scenes that thrill
    This heart! The lawns, the happy shade,
Where matrons, whom the sunbeams grill,
    Stir with slow spoon their lemonade;
And maidens flirt (no extra charge)
In comfort at the fountain's marge!

Others may praise the 'grand displays'
    Where 'fiery arch', 'cascade', and 'comet',
Set the whole garden in a 'blaze'!
    Far, at such times, may I be from it;
Though then the public may be 'lost
In wonder' at a trifling cost.

Fanned by the breeze, to puff at ease
    My faithful pipe is all I crave:
And if folks rave about the 'trees
    Lit up by fireworks', let them rave.
Your monster fêtes, I like not these;
Though they bring grist to the lessees.

WILLIAM SCHWENK GILBERT

## *The Aesthete*

If you're anxious for to shine in the high aesthetic line, as a man of culture rare,
You must get up all the germs of the transcendental terms, and plant them
    everywhere.
You must lie upon the daisies and discourse in novel phrases of your
    complicated state of mind
(The meaning doesn't matter if it's only idle chatter of a transcendental kind).

And every one will say,
As you walk your mystic way,
'If this young man expresses himself in terms too deep for *me*,
Why, what a very singularly deep young man this deep young man must be!'


Be eloquent in praise of the very dull old days which have long since
passed away,
And convince 'em, if you can, that the reign of good QUEEN ANNE
was Culture's palmiest day.
Of course you will pooh-pooh whatever's fresh and new, and declare it's
crude and mean,
And that Art stopped short in the cultivated court of the EMPRESS JOSEPHINE.
And every one will say,
As you walk your mystic way,
'If that's not good enough for him which is good enough for *me*,
Why, what a very cultivated kind of youth this kind of youth must be!'

Then a sentimental passion of a vegetable fashion must excite your languid
spleen,
An attachment *à la* Plato for a bashful young potato, or a not-too-French
French bean.
Though the Philistines may jostle, you will rank as an apostle in the high
aesthetic band,
If you walk down Piccadilly with a poppy or a lily in your mediaeval hand.
And every one will say,
As you walk your flowery way,
'If he's content with a vegetable love which would certainly not suit *me*,
Why, what a most particularly pure young man this pure young man must be!'


EDWARD JAMES MORTIMER COLLINS

## The Positivists

Life and the Universe show Spontaneity;
Down with ridiculous notions of Deity!
    Churches and creeds are all lost in the mists;
    Truth must be sought with the Positivists.

Wise are their teachers beyond all comparison,
Comte, Huxley, Tyndall, Mill, Morley, and Harrison;
    Who will adventure to enter the lists,
    With such a squadron of Positivists?

Social arrangements are awful miscarriages;
Cause of all crime is our system of marriages;
   Poets with sonnets, and lovers with trysts,
   Kindle the ire of the Positivists.

Husbands and wives should be all one community,
Exquisite freedom with absolute unity;
   Wedding rings worse are than manacled wrists,—
   Such is the creed of the Positivists.

There was an APE in the days that were earlier;
Centuries passed and his hair became curlier;
   Centuries more gave a thumb to his wrist,—
   Then he was MAN—and a Positivist.

If you are pious, (mild form of insanity,)
Bow down and worship the mass of humanity,
   Other religions are buried in mists;
   We're our own gods, say the Positivists.


LEWIS CARROLL

## *Jabberwocky*

  'Twas brillig, and the slithy toves
    Did gyre and gimble in the wabe:
  All mimsy were the borogoves,
    And the mome raths outgrabe.

  'Beware the Jabberwock, my son!
    The jaws that bite, the claws that catch!
  Beware the Jubjub bird, and shun
    The frumious Bandersnatch!'

  He took his vorpal sword in hand:
    Long time the manxome foe he sought—
  So rested he by the Tumtum tree,
    And stood awhile in thought.

  And, as in uffish thought he stood,
    The Jabberwock, with eyes of flame,
  Came whiffling through the tulgey wood,
    And burbled as it came!

One, two! One, two! And through and through
  The vorpal blade went snicker-snack!
He left it dead, and with its head
  He went galumphing back.

'And hast thou slain the Jabberwock?
  Come to my arms, my beamish boy!
O frabjous day! Callooh! Callay!'
  He chortled in his joy.

'Twas brillig, and the slithy toves
  Did gyre and gimble in the wabe:
All mimsy were the borogoves,
  And the mome raths outgrabe.

AUSTIN DOBSON

## Incognita

Just for a space that I met her—
  Just for a day in the train!
It began when she feared it would wet her,
  That tiniest spurtle of rain:
So we tucked a great rug in the sashes,
  And carefully padded the pane;
And I sorrow in sackcloth and ashes,
  Longing to do it again!

Then it grew when she begged me to reach her
  A dressing-case under the seat;
She was 'really so tiny a creature,
  That she needed a stool for her feet!'
Which was promptly arranged to her order
  With a care that was even minute,
And a glimpse—of an open-worked border,
  And a glance—of the fairyest boot.

Then it drooped, and revived at some hovels—
  'Were they houses for men or for pigs?'
Then it shifted to muscular novels,
  With a little digression on prigs:
She thought 'Wives and Daughters' '*so* jolly';
  'Had I read it?' She knew when I had,
Like the rest, I should dote upon 'Molly';
  And 'poor Mrs Gaskell—how sad!'

'Like Browning?' 'But so-so.' His proof lay
    Too deep for her frivolous mood,
That preferred your mere metrical *soufflé*
    To the stronger poetical food;
Yet at times he was good—'as a tonic';
    Was Tennyson writing just now?
And was this new poet Byronic,
    And clever, and naughty, or how?

Then we trifled with concerts and croquet,
    Then she daintily dusted her face;
Then she sprinkled herself with 'Ess Bouquet',
    Fished out from the foregoing case;
And we chattered of Gassier and Grisi,
    And voted Aunt Sally a bore;
Discussed if the tight rope were easy,
    Or Chopin much harder than Spohr.

And oh! the odd things that she quoted,
    With the prettiest possible look,
And the price of two buns that she noted
    In the prettiest possible book;
While her talk like a musical rillet
    Flashed on with the hours that flew,
And the carriage, her smile seemed to fill it
    With just enough summer—for Two.

Till at last in her corner, peeping
    From a nest of rugs and of furs,
With the white shut eyelids sleeping
    On those dangerous looks of hers,
She seemed like a snowdrop breaking,
    Not wholly alive nor dead,
But with one blind impulse making
    To the sounds of the spring overhead;

And I watched in the lamplight's swerving
    The shade of the down-dropped lid,
And the lip-line's delicate curving,
    Where a slumbering smile lay hid,
Till I longed that, rather than sever,
    The train should shriek into space,
And carry us onward—for ever—
    Me and that beautiful face.

But she suddenly woke in a fidget,
　With fears she was 'nearly at home',
And talk of a certain Aunt Bridget,
　Whom I mentally wished—well at Rome;
Got out at the very next station,
　Looking back with a merry *Bon Soir*,
Adding, too, to my utter vexation,
　A surplus, unkind *Au Revoir*.

So left me to muse on her graces,
　To doze and to muse, till I dreamed
That we sailed through the sunniest places
　In a glorified galley, it seemed;
But the cabin was made of a carriage,
　And the ocean was Eau-de-Cologne,
And we split on a rock labelled MARRIAGE,
　And I woke,—as cold as a stone.

And that's how I lost her—a jewel,
　*Incognita*—one in a crowd,
Not prudent enough to be cruel,
　Not worldly enough to be proud.
It was just a shut lid and its lashes,
　Just a few hours in a train,
And I sorrow in sackcloth and ashes,
　Longing to see her again.


WILLIAM HURRELL MALLOCK

*Brussels and Oxford*


How first we met do you still remember?
　Do you still remember our last adieu?
You were all to me, that sweet September:
　Oh, what, I wonder, was I to you?

But I will not ask. I will leave in haze
　My thoughts of you, and your thoughts of me;
And will rest content that those sweet fleet days
　Are still my tenderest memory.

I often dream how we went together
　Mid glimmering leaves and glittering lights,
And watched the twilight Belgian weather
　Dying into the starriest nights;

And over our heads the throbbing million
　　Of bright fires beat, like my heart, on high;
And the music clashed from the lit pavilion,
　　And we were together, you and I.

But a hollow memory now suffices
　　For what, last summer, was real and true;
Since here I am by the misty Isis,
　　And under the fogs of London you.

But what if you, like a swift magician,
　　Were to change the failing, flowerless year—
Were to make that true that is now a vision,
　　And to bring back summer and Brussels here?

For Fanny, I know, that if you come hither
　　You will bring with you the time of flowers,
And a breath of the tender Belgian weather,
　　To Oxford's grey autumnal towers.

And in frost and fog though the late year dies,
　　Yet the hours again will be warm and fair,
If they meet once more in your dark, deep eyes,
　　And are meshed again in your golden hair.


LORD DE TABLEY

## The Pilgrim Cranes

The pilgrim cranes are moving to their south,
The clouds are herded pale and rolling slow.
One flower is withered in the warm wind's mouth,
Whereby the gentle waters always flow.

The cloud-fire wanes beyond the lighted trees.
The sudden glory leaves the mountain dome.
Sleep into night, old anguish mine, and cease
To listen for a step that will not come.

LORD DE TABLEY

## Sonnet

Record is nothing, and the hero great
Without it; the vitality of fame
Is more than monument or fading state
That leaves us but the echo of a name.
Rumour, imperial mistress of the time,
Is slandered where she feigns no specious lies,
Caters no reticence of cringing rhyme,
To blow her dust-cloud full on unborn eyes—
The glory of the shows of gilded shields,
Wild music, fluttering blazons,—and 'tis all.
Lonely the dead men stare on battlefields,—
Can glory reach them now though clarions call?
Some shadow of their onset's broken gleam
May yet outlast the pageant and the dream.

EDWARD LEAR

## The Dong with a Luminous Nose

When awful darkness and silence reign
Over the great Gromboolian plain,
    Through the long, long wintry nights;—
When the angry breakers roar
As they beat on the rocky shore;—
    When Storm-clouds brood on the towering heights
Of the Hills of the Chankly Bore:—

Then, through the vast and gloomy dark,
There moves what seems a fiery spark,
    A lonely spark with silvery rays
    Piercing the coal-black night,—
    A Meteor strange and bright:—
Hither and thither the vision strays,
    A single lurid light.

Slowly it wanders,—pauses,—creeps,—
Anon it sparkles,—flashes and leaps;
And ever as onward it gleaming goes
A light on the Bong-tree stems it throws.

And those who watch at that midnight hour
From Hall or Terrace, or lofty Tower,
Cry, as the wild light passes along,—
   'The Dong!—the Dong!
  The wandering Dong through the forest goes!
   The Dong! the Dong!
  The Dong with a luminous Nose!'

   Long years ago
  The Dong was happy and gay,
Till he fell in love with a Jumbly Girl
  Who came to those shores one day,
For the Jumblies came in a sieve, they did,—
Landing at eve near the Zemmery Fidd
  Where the Oblong Oysters grow,
  And the rocks are smooth and gray.
And all the woods and the valleys rang
With the Chorus they daily and nightly sang,—
   *'Far and few, far and few,*
   *Are the lands where the Jumblies live;*
   *Their heads are green, and their hands are blue*
   *And they went to sea in a sieve.'*

Happily, happily passed those days!
   While the cheerful Jumblies staid;
  They danced in circlets all night long,
  To the plaintive pipe of the lively Dong,
   In moonlight, shine, or shade.
For day and night he was always there
By the side of the Jumbly Girl so fair,
With her sky-blue hands, and her sea-green hair,
Till the morning came of that hateful day
When the Jumblies sailed in their sieve away,
And the Dong was left on the cruel shore
Gazing—gazing for evermore,—
Ever keeping his weary eyes on
That pea-green sail on the far horizon,—
Singing the Jumbly Chorus still
As he sate all day on the grassy hill,—
   *'Far and few, far. and few,*
   *Are the lands where the Jumblies live;*
   *Their heads are green, and their hands are blue,*
   *And they went to sea in a sieve.'*

But when the sun was low in the West,
  The Dong arose and said;—
—'What little sense I once possessed
  Has quite gone out of my head!'—

And since that day he wanders still
By lake and forest, marsh and hill,
Singing—'O somewhere, in valley or plain
Might I find my Jumbly Girl again!
For ever I'll seek by lake and shore
Till I find my Jumbly Girl once more!'

Playing a pipe with silvery squeaks,
Since then his Jumbly Girl he seeks,
And because by night he could not see,
He gathered the bark of the Twangum Tree
   On the flowery plain that grows,
    And he wove him a wondrous Nose,—
A Nose as strange as a Nose could be!
Of vast proportions and painted red,
And tied with cords to the back of his head.
      —In a hollow rounded space it ended
      With a luminous Lamp within suspended,
        All fenced about
        With a bandage stout
        To prevent the wind from blowing it out;
      And with holes all round to send the light,
      In gleaming rays on the dismal night.

And now each night, and all night long,
Over those plains still roams the Dong;
And above the wail of the Chimp and Snipe
You may hear the squeak of his plaintive pipe
While ever he seeks, but seeks in vain
To meet with his Jumbly Girl again;
Lonely and wild—all night he goes,—
The Dong with a luminous Nose!
And all who watch at the midnight hour,
From Hall or Terrace, or lofty Tower,
Cry, as they trace the Meteor bright,
Moving along through the dreary night,—
    'This is the hour when forth he goes,
    The Dong with a luminous Nose!
    Yonder—over the plain he goes;
        He goes!
        He goes;
    The Dong with a luminous Nose!'

GRANT ALLEN

## *A Ballade of Evolution*

In the mud of the Cambrian main
  Did our earliest ancestor dive:
From a shapeless albuminous grain
  We mortals our being derive.
He could split himself up into five,
  Or roll himself round like a ball;
For the fittest will always survive,
  While the weakliest go to the wall.

As an active ascidian again
  Fresh forms he began to contrive,
Till he grew to a fish with a brain
  And brought forth a mammal alive.
With his rivals he next had to strive
  To woo him a mate and a thrall;
So the handsomest managed to wive,
  While the ugliest went to the wall.

At length as an ape he was fain
  The nuts of the forest to rive,
Till he took to the low-lying plain,
  And proceeded his fellows to knive.
Thus did cannibal man first arrive
  One another to swallow and maul:
And the strongest continued to thrive,
  While the weakliest went to the wall.

### *Envoy*

Prince, in our civilized hive,
  Now money's the measure of all;
And the wealthy in coaches can drive
  While the needier go to the wall.

COVENTRY PATMORE

## From *The Unknown Eros*

### The Toys

My little Son, who looked from thoughtful eyes
And moved and spoke in quiet grown-up wise,
Having my law the seventh time disobeyed,
I struck him, and dismissed
With hard words and unkissed,
His Mother, who was patient, being dead.
Then, fearing lest his grief should hinder sleep,
I visited his bed,
But found him slumbering deep,
With darkened eyelids, and their lashes yet
From his late sobbing wet.
And I, with moan,
Kissing away his tears, left others of my own;
For, on a table drawn beside his head,
He had put, within his reach,
A box of counters and a red-veined stone,
A piece of glass abraded by the beach
And six or seven shells,
A bottle with bluebells
And two French copper coins, ranged there with careful art,
To comfort his sad heart.

So when that night I prayed
To God, I wept, and said:
Ah, when at last we lie with trancèd breath,
Not vexing Thee in death,
And Thou rememberest of what toys
We made our joys,
How weakly understood,
Thy great commanded good,
Then, fatherly not less
Than I whom Thou hast moulded from the clay
Thou'lt leave Thy wrath, and say,
'I will be sorry for their childishness.'

COVENTRY PATMORE

## *Night and Sleep*

How strange at night to wake
  And watch, while others sleep,
Till sight and hearing ache
  For objects that may keep
The awful inner sense
  Unroused, lest it should mark
The life that haunts the emptiness
  And horror of the dark!

How strange at night the bay
  Of dogs, how wild the note
Of cocks that scream for day,
  In homesteads far remote;
How strange and wild to hear
  The old and crumbling tower,
Amid the darkness, suddenly
  Take tongue and speak the hour!

Albeit the love-sick brain
  Affects the dreary moon,
Ill things alone refrain
  From life's nocturnal swoon:
Men melancholy mad,
  Beasts ravenous and sly,
The robber, and the murderer,
  Remorse, with lidless eye.

The nightingale is gay,
  For she can vanquish night;
Dreaming, she sings of day
  Notes that make darkness bright;
But when the refluent gloom
  Saddens the gaps of song,
Men charge on her the dolefulness,
  And call her crazed with wrong.

COVENTRY PATMORE

## The Year

The crocus, while the days are dark,
　　Unfolds its saffron sheen;
At April's touch, the crudest bark
　　Discovers gems of green.

Then sleep the seasons, full of might;
　　While slowly swells the pod
And rounds the peach, and in the night
　　The mushroom bursts the sod.

The Winter falls; the frozen rut
　　Is bound with silver bars;
The snow-drift heaps against the hut,
　　And night is pierced with stars.

COVENTRY PATMORE

## A London Fête

All night fell hammers, shock on shock;
With echoes Newgate's granite clanged:
The scaffold built, at eight o'clock
They brought the man out to be hanged.
Then came from all the people there
A single cry, that shook the air;
Mothers held up their babes to see,
Who spread their hands, and crowed for glee;
Here a girl from her vesture tore
A rag to wave with, and joined the roar;
There a man, with yelling tired,
Stopped, and the culprit's crime inquired;
A sot, below the doomed man dumb,
Bawled his health in the world to come;
These blasphemed and fought for places;
Those, half-crushed, cast frantic faces,
To windows, where, in freedom sweet,
Others enjoyed the wicked treat.
At last, the show's black crisis pended;
Struggles for better standings ended;
The rabble's lips no longer cursed,
But stood agape with horrid thirst;

Thousands of breasts beat horrid hope;
Thousands of eyeballs, lit with hell,
Burnt one way all, to see the rope
Unslacken as the platform fell.
The rope flew tight; and then the roar
Burst forth afresh; less loud, but more
Confused and affrighting than before.
A few harsh tongues for ever led
The common din, the chaos of noises,
But ear could not catch what they said.
As when the realm of the damned rejoices
At winning a soul to its will,
That clatter and clangour of hateful voices
Sickened and stunned the air, until
The dangling corpse hung straight and still.
The show complete, the pleasure past,
The solid masses loosened fast:
A thief slunk off, with ample spoil,
To ply elsewhere his daily toil;
A baby strung its doll to a stick;
A mother praised the pretty trick;
Two children caught and hanged a cat;
Two friends walked on, in lively chat;
And two, who had disputed places,
Went forth to fight, with murderous faces.

GEORGE MEREDITH

## Lucifer in Starlight

On a starred night Prince Lucifer uprose.
Tired of his dark dominion swung the fiend
Above the rolling ball in cloud part screened,
Where sinners hugged their spectre of repose.
Poor prey to his hot fit of pride were those.
And now upon his western wing he leaned,
Now his huge bulk o'er Afric's sands careened,
Now the black planet shadowed Arctic snows.
Soaring through wider zones that pricked his scars
With memory of the old revolt from Awe,
He reached a middle height, and at the stars,
Which are the brain of heaven, he looked, and sank.
Around the ancient track marched, rank on rank,
The army of unalterable law.

GEORGE MEREDITH

## *Love in the Valley*

Under yonder beech-tree single on the green-sward,
  Couched with her arms behind her golden head,
Knees and tresses folded to slip and ripple idly,
  Lies my young love sleeping in the shade.
Had I the heart to slide an arm beneath her,
  Press her parting lips as her waist I gather slow,
Waking in amazement she could not but embrace me:
  Then would she hold me and never let me go?

Shy as the squirrel and wayward as the swallow,
  Swift as the swallow along the river's light
Circleting the surface to meet his mirrored winglets,
  Fleeter she seems in her stay than in her flight.
Shy as the squirrel that leaps among the pine-tops,
  Wayward as the swallow overhead at set of sun,
She whom I love is hard to catch and conquer,
  Hard, but O the glory of the winning were she won!

When her mother tends her before the laughing mirror,
  Tying up her laces, looping up her hair,
Often she thinks, were this wild thing wedded,
  More love should I have, and much less care.
When her mother tends her before the lighted mirror,
  Loosening her laces, combing down her curls,
Often she thinks, were this wild thing wedded,
  I should miss but one for many boys and girls.

Heartless she is as the shadow in the meadows
  Flying to the hills on a blue and breezy noon.
No, she is athirst and drinking up her wonder:
  Earth to her is young as the slip of the new moon.
Deals she an unkindness, 'tis but her rapid measure,
  Even as in a dance; and her smile can heal no less:
Like the swinging May-cloud that pelts the flowers with hailstones
  Off a sunny border, she was made to bruise and bless.

Lovely are the curves of the white owl sweeping
  Wavy in the dusk lit by one large star.
Lone on the fir-branch, his rattle-note unvaried,
  Brooding o'er the gloom, spins the brown eve-jar.
Darker grows the valley, more and more forgetting:
  So were it with me if forgetting could be willed.
Tell the grassy hollow that holds the bubbling well-spring
  Tell it to forget the source that keeps it filled.

Stepping down the hill with her fair companions,
   Arm in arm, all against the raying West,
Boldly she sings, to the merry tune she marches,
   Brave in her shape, and sweeter unpossessed.
Sweeter, for she is what my heart first awaking
   Whispered the world was; morning light is she.
Love that so desires would fain keep her changeless;
   Fain would fling the net, and fain have her free.

Happy happy time, when the white star hovers
   Low over dim fields fresh with bloomy dew,
Near the face of dawn, that draws athwart the darkness,
   Threading it with colour, like yewberries the yew.
Thicker crowd the shades as the grave East deepens
   Glowing, and with crimson a long cloud swells.
Maiden still the morn is; and strange she is, and secret;
   Strange her eyes; her cheeks are cold as cold sea-shells.

Sunrays, leaning on our southern hills and lighting
   Wild cloud-mountains that drag the hills along,
Oft ends the day of your shifting brilliant laughter
   Chill as a dull face frowning on a song.
Ay, but shows the South-West a ripple-feathered bosom
   Blown to silver while the clouds are shaken and ascend
Scaling the mid-heavens as they stream, there comes a sunset
   Rich, deep like love in beauty without end.

When at dawn she sighs, and like an infant to the window
   Turns grave eyes craving light, released from dreams,
Beautiful she looks, like a white water-lily
   Bursting out of bud in havens of the streams.
When from bed she rises clothed from neck to ankle
   In her long nightgown sweet as boughs of May,
Beautiful she looks, like a tall garden lily
   Pure from the night, and splendid for the day.

Mother of the dews, dark eye-lashed twilight,
   Low-lidded twilight, o'er the valley's brim,
Rounding on thy breast sings the dew-delighted skylark,
   Clear as though the dewdrops had their voice in him.
Hidden where the rose-flush drinks the rayless planet,
   Fountain-full he pours the spraying fountain-showers.
Let me hear her laughter, I would have her ever
   Cool as dew in twilight, the lark above the flowers.

All the girls are out with their baskets for the primrose;
   Up lanes, woods through, they troop in joyful bands.

My sweet leads: she knows not why, but now she loiters,
  Eyes the bent anemones, and hangs her hands.
Such a look will tell that the violets are peeping,
  Coming the rose: and unaware a cry
Springs in her bosom for odours and for colour,
  Covert and the nightingale; she knows not why.

Kerchiefed head and chin she darts between her tulips,
  Streaming like a willow grey in arrowy rain:
Some bend beaten cheek to gravel, and their angel
  She will be; she lifts them, and on she speeds again.
Black the driving raincloud breasts the iron gateway:
  She is forth to cheer a neighbour lacking mirth.
So when sky and grass met rolling dumb for thunder
  Saw I once a white dove, sole light of earth.

Prim little scholars are the flowers of her garden,
  Trained to stand in rows, and asking if they please.
I might love them well but for loving more the wild ones:
  O my wild ones! they tell me more than these.
You, my wild one, you tell of honied field-rose,
  Violet, blushing eglantine in life; and even as they,
They by the wayside are earnest of your goodness,
  You are of life's on the banks that line the way.

Peering at her chamber the white crowns the red rose,
  Jasmine winds the porch with stars two and three.
Parted is the window; she sleeps; the starry jasmine
  Breathes a falling breath that carries thoughts of me.
Sweeter unpossessed, have I said of her my sweetest?
  Not while she sleeps: while she sleeps the jasmine breathes,
Luring her to love; she sleeps; the starry jasmine
  Bears me to her pillow under white rose-wreaths.

Yellow with birdfoot-trefoil are the grass-glades;
  Yellow with cinquefoil of the dew-grey leaf;
Yellow with stonecrop; the moss-mounds are yellow;
  Blue-necked the wheat sways, yellowing to the sheaf.
Green-yellow bursts from the copse the laughing yaffle;
  Sharp as a sickle is the edge of shade and shine:
Earth in her heart laughs looking at the heavens,
  Thinking of the harvest: I look and think of mine.

This I may know: her dressing and undressing
  Such a change of light shows as when the skies in sport
Shift from cloud to moonlight; or edging over thunder
  Slips a ray of sun; or sweeping into port
White sails furl; or on the ocean borders
  White sails lean along the waves leaping green.

Visions of her shower before me, but from eyesight
   Guarded she would be like the sun were she seen.

Front door and back of the mossed old farmhouse
   Open with the morn, and in a breezy link
Freshly sparkles garden to stripe-shadowed orchard,
   Green across a rill where on sand the minnows wink.
Busy in the grass the early sun of summer
   Swarms, and the blackbird's mellow fluting notes
Call my darling up with round and roguish challenge:
   Quaintest, richest carol of all the singing throats!

Cool was the woodside; cool as her white dairy
   Keeping sweet the cream-pan; and there the boys from school,
Cricketing below, rushed brown and red with sunshine;
   O the dark translucence of the deep-eyed cool!
Spying from the farm, herself she fetched a pitcher
   Full of milk, and tilted for each in turn the beak.
Then a little fellow, mouth up and on tiptoe,
   Said, 'I will kiss you': she laughed and leaned her cheek.

Doves of the fir-wood walling high our red roof
   Through the long noon coo, crooning through the coo.
Loose droop the leaves, and down the sleepy roadway
   Sometimes pipes a chaffinch; loose droops the blue.
Cows flap a slow tail knee-deep in the river,
   Breathless, given up to sun and gnat and fly.
Nowhere is she seen; and if I see her nowhere,
   Lightning may come, straight rains and tiger sky.

O the golden sheaf, the rustling treasure-armful!
   O the nutbrown tresses nodding interlaced!
O the treasure-tresses one another over
   Nodding! O the girdle slack about the waist!
Slain are the poppies that shot their random scarlet
   Quick amid the wheatears: wound about the waist,
Gathered, see these brides of Earth one blush of ripeness!
   O the nutbrown tresses nodding interlaced!

Large and smoky red the sun's cold disk drops,
   Clipped by naked hills, on violet shaded snow:
Eastward large and still lights up a bower of moonrise,
   Whence at her leisure steps the moon aglow.
Nightlong on black print-branches our beech-tree
   Gazes in this whiteness: nightlong could I.
Here may life on death or death on life be painted.
   Let me clasp her soul to know she cannot die!

Gossips count her faults; they scour a narrow chamber
   Where there is no window, read not heaven or her.
'When she was a tiny,' one aged woman quavers,
   Plucks at my heart and leads me by the ear.
Faults she had once as she learnt to run and tumbled:
   Faults of feature some see, beauty not complete.
Yet, good gossips, beauty that makes holy
   Earth and air, may have faults from head to feet.

Hither she comes; she comes to me; she lingers,
   Deepens her brown eyebrows, while in new surprise
High rise the lashes in wonder of a stranger;
   Yet am I the light and living of her eyes.
Something friends have told her fills her heart to brimming,
   Nets her in her blushes, and wounds her, and tames.—
Sure of her haven, O like a dove alighting,
   Arms up, she dropped: our souls were in our names.

Soon will she lie like a white-frost sunrise.
   Yellow oats and brown wheat, barley pale as rye,
Long since your sheaves have yielded to the thresher,
   Felt the girdle loosened, seen the tresses fly.
Soon will she lie like a blood-red sunset.
   Swift with the to-morrow, green-winged Spring!
Sing from the South-West, bring her back the truants,
   Nightingale and swallow, song and dipping wing.

Soft new beech-leaves, up to beamy April
   Spreading bough on bough a primrose mountain, you,
Lucid in the moon, raise lilies to the skyfields,
   Youngest green transfused in silver shining through:
Fairer than the lily, than the wild white cherry:
   Fair as in image my seraph love appears
Borne to me by dreams when dawn is at my eyelids:
   Fair as in the flesh she swims to me on tears.

Could I find a place to be alone with heaven,
   I would speak my heart out: heaven is my need.
Every woodland tree is flushing like the dogwood,
   Flashing like the whitebeam, swaying like the reed.
Flushing like the dogwood crimson in October;
   Streaming like the flag-reed South-West blown;
Flashing as in gusts the sudden-lighted whitebeam:
   All seem to know what is for heaven alone.

JOHN ELLERTON

The day Thou gavest, Lord, is ended,
 The darkness falls at Thy behest;
To Thee our morning hymns ascended,
 Thy praise shall sanctify our rest.

We thank Thee that Thy Church unsleeping,
 While earth rolls onward into light,
Through all the world her watch is keeping,
 And rests not now by day or night.

As o'er each continent and island
 The dawn leads on another day,
The voice of prayer is never silent,
 Nor dies the strain of praise away.

The sun that bids us rest is waking
 Our brethren 'neath the western sky,
And hour by hour fresh lips are making
 Thy wondrous doings heard on high.

So be it, Lord; Thy throne shall never,
 Like earth's proud empires, pass away;
Thy kingdom stands, and grows for ever,
 Till all Thy creatures own Thy sway.

GERARD MANLEY HOPKINS

## God's Grandeur

The world is charged with the grandeur of God.
 It will flame out, like shining from shook foil;
 It gathers to a greatness, like the ooze of oil
Crushed. Why do men then now not reck his rod?
Generations have trod, have trod, have trod;
 And all is seared with trade; bleared, smeared with toil;
 And wears man's smudge and shares man's smell: the soil
Is bare now, nor can foot feel, being shod.

And for all this, nature is never spent;
   There lives the dearest freshness deep down things;
And though the last lights off the black West went
   Oh, morning, at the brown brink eastward, springs—
Because the Holy Ghost over the bent
   World broods with warm breast and with ah! bright wings.

GERARD MANLEY HOPKINS

## Spring

Nothing is so beautiful as spring—
   When weeds, in wheels, shoot long and lovely and lush;
   Thrush's eggs look little low heavens, and thrush
Through the echoing timber does so rinse and wring
The ear, it strikes like lightnings to hear him sing;
   The glassy peartree leaves and blooms, they brush
   The descending blue; that blue is all in a rush
With richness; the racing lambs too have fair their fling.

What is all this juice and all this joy?
   A strain of the earth's sweet being in the beginning
In Eden garden. – Have, get, before it cloy,
   Before it cloud, Christ, lord, and sour with sinning,
Innocent mind and Mayday in girl and boy,
   Most, O maid's child, thy choice and worthy the winning.

GERARD MANLEY HOPKINS

## The Windhover:
### To Christ Our Lord

I caught this morning morning's minion, king-
   dom of daylight's dauphin, dapple-dawn-drawn Falcon, in his riding
   Of the rolling level underneath him steady air, and striding
High there, how he rung upon the rein of a wimpling wing
In his ecstasy! then off, off forth on swing,
   As a skate's heel sweeps smooth on a bow-bend: the hurl and gliding
   Rebuffed the big wind. My heart in hiding
Stirred for a bird—the achieve of, the mastery of the thing!

Brute beauty and valour and act, oh, air, pride, plume here
 Buckle! AND the fire that breaks from thee then, a billion
Times told lovelier, more dangerous, O my chevalier!

No wonder of it: shéer plód makes plough down sillion
Shine, and blue-bleak embers, ah my dear,
 Fall, gall themselves, and gash gold-vermilion.


GERARD MANLEY HOPKINS

## Pied Beauty

Glory be to God for dappled things—
 For skies of couple-colour as a brinded cow;
  For rose-moles all in stipple upon trout that swim;
Fresh-firecoal chestnut-falls; finches' wings:
 Landscape plotted and pieced—fold, fallow, and plough;
  And áll trádes, their gear and tackle and trim.

All things counter, original, spare, strange;
 Whatever is fickle, freckled (who knows how?)
  With swift, slow; sweet, sour; adazzle, dim;
He fathers-forth whose beauty is past change:
          Praise him.


GERARD MANLEY HOPKINS

## Binsey Poplars
### felled 1879

My aspens dear, whose airy cages quelled,
Quelled or quenched in leaves the leaping sun,
All felled, felled, are all felled;
 Of a fresh and following folded rank
      Not spared, not one
      That dandled a sandalled
   Shadow that swam or sank
On meadow and river and wind-wandering weed-winding bank.

O if we but knew what we do
       When we delve or hew—
    Hack and rack the growing green!
       Since country is so tender
To touch, her being só slender,
That, like this sleek and seeing ball
But a prick will make no eye at all,
Where we, even where we mean

       To mend her we end her,
         When we hew or delve:
After-comers cannot guess the beauty been.
   Ten or twelve, only ten or twelve
       Strokes of havoc únselve
         The sweet especial scene,
       Rural scene, a rural scene,
       Sweet especial rural scene.


GERARD MANLEY HOPKINS

## Felix Randal

Felix Randal the farrier, O he is dead then? my duty all ended,
Who have watched his mould of man, big-boned and hardy-handsome
Pining, pining, till time when reason rambled in it and some
Fatal four disorders, fleshed there, all contended?

Sickness broke him. Impatient he cursed at first, but mended
Being anointed and all; though a heavenlier heart began some
Months earlier, since I had our sweet reprieve and ransom
Tendered to him. Ah well, God rest him all road ever he offended!

This seeing the sick endears them to us, us too it endears.
My tongue had taught thee comfort, touch had quenched thy tears,
Thy tears that touched my heart, child, Felix, poor Felix Randal;

How far from then forethought of, all thy more boisterous years,
When thou at the random grim forge, powerful amidst peers,
Didst fettle for the great grey drayhorse his bright and battering sandal!

GERARD MANLEY HOPKINS

As kingfishers catch fire, dragonflies dráw fláme;
As tumbled over rim in roundy wells
Stones ring; like each tucked string tells, each hung bell's
Bow swung finds tongue to fling out broad its name;
Each mortal thing does one thing and the same:
Deals out that being indoors each one dwells;
Selves—goes itself; *myself* it speaks and spells,
Crying *Whát I dó is me: for that I came.*

I say móre: the just man justices;
Kéeps gráce: thát keeps all his goings graces;
Acts in God's eye what in God's eye he is—
Chríst—for Christ plays in ten thousand places,
Lovely in limbs, and lovely in eyes not his
To the Father through the features of men's faces.

GERARD MANLEY HOPKINS

No worst, there is none. Pitched past pitch of grief,
More pangs will, schooled at forepangs, wilder wring.
Comforter, where, where is your comforting?
Mary, mother of us, where is your relief?
My cries heave, herds-long; huddle in a main, a chief
Woe, wórld-sorrow; on an áge-old anvil wince and sing—
Then lull, then leave off. Fury had shrieked 'No ling-
    ering! Let me be fell: force I must be brief'.

O the mind, mind has mountains; cliffs of fall
Frightful, sheer, no-man-fathomed. Hold them cheap
May who ne'er hung there. Nor does long our small
Durance deal with that steep or deep. Here! creep,
Wretch, under a comfort serves in a whirlwind: all
Life death does end and each day dies with sleep.

GERARD MANLEY HOPKINS

*Justus quidem tu es, Domine, si disputem tecum: verumtamen*
*justa loquar ad te: Quare via impiorum prosperatur? &c.*

Thou art indeed just, Lord, if I contend
With thee; but, sir, so what I plead is just.
Why do sinners' ways prosper? and why must
Disappointment all I endeavour end?
　Wert thou my enemy, O thou my friend,
How wouldst thou worse, I wonder, than thou dost
Defeat, thwart me? Oh, the sots and thralls of lust
Do in spare hours more thrive than I that spend,
Sir, life upon thy cause. See, banks and brakes
Now, leavèd how thick! lacèd they are again
With fretty chervil, look, and fresh wind shakes
Them; birds build—but not I build; no, but strain,
Time's eunuch, and not breed one work that wakes.
Mine, O thou lord of life, send my roots rain.

ROBERT BRIDGES

## Elegy

The wood is bare: a river-mist is steeping
　The trees that winter's chill of life bereaves:
Only their stiffened boughs break silence, weeping
　　Over their fallen leaves;

That lie upon the dank earth brown and rotten,
　Miry and matted in the soaking wet:
Forgotten with the spring, that is forgotten
　　By them that can forget.

Yet it was here we walked when ferns were springing,
　And through the mossy bank shot bud and blade:—
Here found in summer, when the birds were singing,
　　A green and pleasant shade.

'Twas here we loved in sunnier days and greener;
　And now, in this disconsolate decay,
I come to see her where I most have seen her,
　　And touch the happier day.

For on this path, at every turn and corner,
  The fancy of her figure on me falls:
Yet walks she with the slow step of a mourner,
    Nor hears my voice that calls.

So through my heart there winds a track of feeling,
  A path of memory, that is all her own:
Whereto her phantom beauty ever stealing
    Haunts the sad spot alone.

About her steps the trunks are bare, the branches
  Drip heavy tears upon her downcast head;
And bleed from unseen wounds that no sun staunches,
    For the year's sun is dead.

And dead leaves wrap the fruits that summer planted:
  And birds that love the South have taken wing.
The wanderer, loitering o'er the scene enchanted,
    Weeps, and despairs of spring.


ALFRED, LORD TENNYSON

*Frater Ave atque Vale*


Row us out from Desenzano, to your Sirmione row!
So they rowed, and there we landed—'O venusta Sirmio!'
There to me through all the groves of olive in the summer glow,
There beneath the Roman ruin where the purple flowers grow,
Came that 'Ave atque Vale' of the Poet's hopeless woe,
Tenderest of Roman poets nineteen-hundred years ago,
'Frater Ave atque Vale'—as we wandered to and fro
Gazing at the Lydian laughter of the Garda Lake below
Sweet Catullus's all-but-island, olive-silvery Sirmio!

OSCAR WILDE

## *Magdalen Walks*

The little white clouds are racing over the sky,
  And the fields are strewn with the gold of the flower of March,
  The daffodil breaks under foot, and the tasselled larch
Sways and swings as the thrush goes hurrying by.

A delicate odour is borne on the wings of the morning breeze,
  The odour of deep wet grass, and of brown new-furrowed earth,
  The birds are singing for joy of the Spring's glad birth,
Hopping from branch to branch on the rocking trees.

And all the woods are alive with the murmur and sound of spring,
  And the rose-bud breaks into pink on the climbing briar,
  And the crocus-bed is a quivering moon of fire
Girdled round with the belt of an amethyst ring.

And the plane to the pine-tree is whispering some tale of love
  Till it rustles with laughter and tosses its mantle of green,
  And the gloom of the wych-elm's hollow is lit with the iris sheen
Of the burnished rainbow throat and the silver breast of a dove.

See! the lark starts up from his bed in the meadow there,
  Breaking the gossamer threads and the nets of dew,
  And flashing adown the river, a flame of blue!
The kingfisher flies like an arrow, and wounds the air.

And the sense of my life is sweet! though I know that the end is nigh:
  For the ruin and rain of winter will shortly come,
  The lily will lose its gold, and the chestnut-bloom
In billows of red and white on the grass will lie.

And even the light of the sun will fade at the last,
  And the leaves will fall, and the birds will hasten away,
  And I will be left in the snow of a flowerless day
To think on the glories of Spring, and the joys of a youth long past.

Yet be silent, my heart! do not count it a profitless thing
  To have seen the splendour of the sun, and of grass, and of flower!
  To have lived and loved! for I hold that to love for an hour
Is better for man and for woman than cycles of blossoming Spring.

OSCAR WILDE

## *Les Silhouettes*

The sea is flecked with bars of grey,
The dull dead wind is out of tune,
And like a withered leaf the moon
Is blown across the stormy bay.

Etched clear upon the pallid sand
Lies the black boat: a sailor boy
Clambers aboard in careless joy
With laughing face and gleaming hand.

And overhead the curlews cry,
Where through the dusky upland grass
The young brown-throated reapers pass,
Like silhouettes against the sky.

OSCAR WILDE

## *By the Arno*

The oleander on the wall
Grows crimson in the dawning light,
Though the grey shadows of the night
Lie yet on Florence like a pall.

The dew is bright upon the hill,
And bright the blossoms overhead,
But ah! the grasshoppers have fled,
The little Attic song is still.

Only the leaves are gently stirred
By the soft breathing of the gale,
And in the almond-scented vale
The lonely nightingale is heard.

The day will make thee silent soon,
O nightingale sing on for love!
While yet upon the shadowy grove
Splinter the arrows of the moon.

Before across the silent lawn
In sea-green vest the morning steals,
And to love's frightened eyes reveals
The long white fingers of the dawn

Fast climbing up the eastern sky
To grasp and slay the shuddering night,
All careless of my heart's delight,
Or if the nightingale should die.

OSCAR WILDE

## My Voice

Within this restless, hurried, modern world
    We took our hearts' full pleasure—You and I,
And now the white sails of our ship are furled,
    And spent the lading of our argosy.

Wherefore my cheeks before their time are wan,
    For very weeping is my gladness fled,
Sorrow has paled my young mouth's vermilion,
    And Ruin draws the curtains of my bed.

But all this crowded life has been to thee
    No more than lyre, or lute, or subtle spell
Of viols, or the music of the sea
    That sleeps, a mimic echo, in the shell.

OSCAR WILDE

## The Harlot's House

We caught the tread of dancing feet,
We loitered down the moonlit street,
And stopped beneath the harlot's house.

Inside, above the din and fray,
We heard the loud musicians play
The 'Treues Liebes Herz' of Strauss.

Like strange mechanical grotesques,
Making fantastic arabesques,
The shadows raced across the blind.

We watched the ghostly dancers spin
To sound of horn and violin,
Like black leaves wheeling in the wind.

Like wire-pulled automatons,
Slim silhouetted skeletons
Went sidling through the slow quadrille.

They took each other by the hand,
And danced a stately saraband;
Their laughter echoed thin and shrill.

Sometimes a clockwork puppet pressed
A phantom lover to her breast,
Sometimes they seemed to try to sing.

Sometimes a horrible marionette
Came out, and smoked its cigarette
Upon the steps like a live thing.

Then turning to my love, I said,
'The dead are dancing with the dead,
The dust is whirling with the dust.'

But she—she heard the violin,
And left my side, and entered in:
Love passed into the house of lust.

Then suddenly the tune went false,
The dancers wearied of the waltz,
The shadows ceased to wheel and whirl.

And down the long and silent street,
The dawn, with silver-sandalled feet,
Crept like a frightened girl.

THOMAS ASHE

## Corpse-Bearing

I remember, they sent
   Some one to me, who said,
'You were his friend while he lived:
   Be so now he is dead.'

So I went next day to the house;
   And a woman nodded to me,
As I sat alone in thought:—
   Said, 'Sir, would you like to see

'The poor dead body upstairs,
   Before we rivet the lid?'
But I said, 'I would rather not:
   For the look would never be hid

'From my sight, day after day,
   From my soul, year after year.
Enough to look on the pall:
   Enough to follow the bier.'

So the mourners gathered at last;
   And the poor dead body was put
In a hearse with mournful plumes,
   And the door of the hearse was shut.

And when the mourners were all
   In the coaches, ready to start,
The sorrowing parent came
   To me, and whispered apart.

He smiled as well as he could;
   And the import of what he said
Was, that I should bear at the feet,
   And his son would bear at the head.

He was ever my friend;
   And I was happy to be
Of ever so small use still
   To one who had so loved me.

But, what a weight, O God!
   Was that one coffin to bear!
Like a coffin of lead!
   And I carry it everywhere

About, wherever I go!
   If I lift the slightest thing,
That requires an effort to lift,
   The effort at once will bring

The whole weight into my hands,
   And I carry the corpse at the feet;
And feel as if it would drop,
   And slip out of its winding-sheet.

I have made a vow in my heart,
   Whatever the friends may say,
Never to carry a corpse
   Again, to my dying day.


EDWARD ROBERT BULWER LYTTON

## Tears
### (From 'Glenaveril')

There be three hundred different ways and more
   Of speaking, but of weeping only one;
And that one way, the wide world o'er and o'er,
   Is known by all, though it is taught by none.
No man is master of this ancient lore,
   And no man pupil. Every simpleton
Can weep as well as every sage. The man
Does it no better than the infant can.

The first thing all men learn is how to speak,
   Yet understand they not each other's speech;
But tears are neither Latin, nor yet Greek,
   Nor prose, nor verse. The language that they teach
Is universal. Cleopatra's cheek
   They decked with pearls no richer than from each
Of earth's innumerable mourners fall
Unstudied, yet correctly classical.

Tears are the oldest and the commonest
   Of all things upon earth; and yet how new
The tale each time told by them! How unblessed
   Were life's hard way without their heavenly dew!

Joy borrows them from grief: faith trembles lest
　She lose them: even Hope herself smiles through
The rainbow they make round her as they fall:
And Death, that cannot weep, sets weeping all.


ROBERT LOUIS STEVENSON


O dull, cold northern sky,
　O brawling sabbath bells,
　O feebly twittering Autumn bird that tells
The year is like to die!

O still, spoiled trees, O city ways,
　O sun desired in vain,
　O dread presentiment of coming rain
That clogs the sullen days!

Thee, heart of mine, I greet.
　In what hard mountain pass
　Striv'st thou? In what importunate morass
Sink now thy weary feet?

Thou run'st a hopeless race
　To win despair. No crown
　Awaits success; but leaden gods look down
On thee, with evil face.

And those that would befriend
　And cherish thy defeat,
　With angry welcome shall turn sour the sweet
Home-coming of the end.

Yea, those that offer praise
　To idleness, shall yet
　Insult thee, coming glorious in the sweat
Of honourable ways.

ROBERT LOUIS STEVENSON

Swallows travel to and fro,
And the great winds come and go,
And the steady breezes blow,
  Bearing perfume, bearing love.
Breezes hasten, swallows fly,
Towered clouds forever ply,
And at noonday you and I
  See the same sun shine above.

Dew and rain fall everywhere,
Harvests ripen, flowers are fair,
And the whole round earth is bare
  To the moonshine and the sun;
And the live air, fanned with wings,
Bright with breeze and sunshine, brings
Into contact distant things,
  And makes all the countries one.

Let us wander where we will,
Something kindred greets us still;
Something seen on vale or hill
  Falls familiar on the heart;
So, at scent or sound or sight,
Severed souls by day and night
Tremble with the same delight—
  Tremble, half the world apart.


ROBERT LOUIS STEVENSON

## Christmas at Sea

The sheets were frozen hard, and they cut the naked hand;
The decks were like a slide, where a seaman scarce could stand;
The wind was a nor'wester, blowing squally off the sea;
And cliffs and spouting breakers were the only things a-lee.

They heard the surf a-roaring before the break of day;
But 'twas only with the peep of light we saw how ill we lay.
We tumbled every hand on deck instanter, with a shout,
And we gave her the maintops'l, and stood by to go about.

All day we tacked and tacked between the South Head and the North;
All day we hauled the frozen sheets, and got no further forth;
All day as cold as charity, in bitter pain and dread,
For very life and nature we tacked from head to head.

We gave the South a wider berth, for there the tide-race roared;
But every tack we made we brought the North Head close aboard:
So's we saw the cliffs and houses, and the breakers running high,
And the coastguard in his garden, with his glass against his eye.

The frost was on the village roofs as white as ocean foam;
The good red fires were burning bright in every 'longshore home;
The windows sparkled clear, and the chimneys volleyed out;
And I vow we sniffed the victuals as the vessel went about.

The bells upon the church were rung with a mighty jovial cheer;
For it's just that I should tell you how (of all days in the year)
This day of our adversity was blessèd Christmas morn,
And the house above the coastguard's was the house where I was born.

O well I saw the pleasant room, the pleasant faces there,
My mother's silver spectacles, my father's silver hair;
And well I saw the firelight, like a flight of homely elves,
Go dancing round the china-plates that stand upon the shelves.

And well I knew the talk they had, the talk that was of me,
Of the shadow on the household and the son that went to sea;
And O the wicked fool I seemed, in every kind of way,
To be here and hauling frozen ropes on blessèd Christmas Day.

They lit the high sea-light, and the dark began to fall.
'All hands to loose topgallant sails,' I heard the captain call.
'By the Lord, she'll never stand it,' our first mate, Jackson, cried.
. . . 'It's the one way or the other, Mr Jackson,' he replied.

She staggered to her bearings, but the sails were new and good,
And the ship smelt up to windward just as though she understood.
As the winter's day was ending, in the entry of the night,
We cleared the weary headland, and passed below the light.

And they heaved a mighty breath, every soul on board but me,
As they saw her nose again pointing handsome out to sea;
But all that I could think of, in the darkness and the cold,
Was just that I was leaving home and my folks were growing old.

ALFRED, LORD TENNYSON

## The Revenge
### A Ballad of the Fleet

At Flores in the Azores Sir Richard Grenville lay,
And a pinnace, like a fluttered bird, came flying from far away:
'Spanish ships of war at sea! we have sighted fifty-three!'
Then sware Lord Thomas Howard: ''Fore God I am no coward;
But I cannot meet them here, for my ships are out of gear,
And the half my men are sick. I must fly, but follow quick.
We are six ships of the line; can we fight with fifty-three?'

Then spake Sir Richard Grenville: 'I know you are no coward;
You fly them for a moment to fight with them again.
But I've ninety men and more that are lying sick ashore.
I should count myself the coward if I left them, my Lord Howard,
To these Inquisition dogs and the devildoms of Spain.'

So Lord Howard past away with five ships of war that day,
Till he melted like a cloud in the silent summer heaven;
But Sir Richard bore in hand all his sick men from the land
Very carefully and slow,
Men of Bideford in Devon,
And we laid them on the ballast down below;
For we brought them all aboard,
And they blest him in their pain, that they were not left to Spain,
To the thumbscrew and the stake, for the glory of the Lord.

He had only a hundred seamen to work the ship and to fight,
And he sailed away from Flores till the Spaniard came in sight,
With his huge sea-castles heaving upon the weather bow.
'Shall we fight or shall we fly?
Good Sir Richard, tell us now,
For to fight is but to die!
There'll be little of us left by the time this sun be set.'
And Sir Richard said again: 'We be all good English men.
Let us bang these dogs of Seville, the children of the devil,
For I never turned my back upon Don or devil yet.'

Sir Richard spoke and he laughed, and we roared a hurrah, and so
The little Revenge ran on sheer into the heart of the foe,
With her hundred fighters on deck, and her ninety sick below;
For half of their fleet to the right and half to the left were seen,
And the little Revenge ran on through the long sea-lane between.

Thousands of their soldiers looked down from their decks and laughed,
Thousands of their seamen made mock at the mad little craft
Running on and on, till delayed
By their mountain-like San Philip that, of fifteen hundred tons,
And up-shadowing high above us with her yawning tiers of guns,
Took the breath from our sails, and we stayed.

And while now the great San Philip hung above us like a cloud
Whence the thunderbolt will fall
Long and loud,
Four galleons drew away
From the Spanish fleet that day,
And two upon the larboard and two upon the starboard lay,
And the battle-thunder broke from them all.

But anon the great San Philip, she bethought herself and went
Having that within her womb that had left her ill content;
And the rest they came aboard us, and they fought us hand to hand,
For a dozen times they came with their pikes and musqueteers,
And a dozen times we shook 'em off as a dog that shakes his ears
When he leaps from the water to the land.

And the sun went down, and the stars came out far over the summer sea,
But never a moment ceased the fight of the one and the fifty-three.
Ship after ship, the whole night long, their high-built galleons came,
Ship and ship, the whole night long, with her battle-thunder and flame;
Ship after ship, the whole night long, drew back with her dead and her shame.
For some were sunk and many were shattered, and so could fight us no more—
God of battles, was ever a battle like this in the world before?

For he said 'Fight on! fight on!'
Though his vessel was all but a wreck;
And it chanced that, when half of the short summer night was gone,
With a grisly wound to be dressed he had left the deck,
But a bullet struck him that was dressing it suddenly dead,
And himself he was wounded again in the side and the head,
And he said 'Fight on! fight on!'

And the night went down, and the sun smiled out far over the summer sea,
And the Spanish fleet with broken sides lay round us all in a ring;
But they dared not touch us again, for they feared that we still could sting,
So they watched what the end would be.
And we had not fought them in vain,
But in perilous plight were we,
Seeing forty of our poor hundred were slain,
And half of the rest of us maimed for life
In the crash of the cannonades and the desperate strife;

And the sick men down in the hold were most of them stark and cold,
And the pikes were all broken or bent, and the powder was all of it spent;
And the masts and the rigging were lying over the side;
But Sir Richard cried in his English pride,
'We have fought such a fight for a day and a night
As may never be fought again!
We have won great glory, my men!
And a day less or more
At sea or ashore,
We die—does it matter when?
Sink me the ship, Master Gunner—sink her, split her in twain!
Fall into the hands of God, not into the hands of Spain!'

And the gunner said 'Ay, ay,' but the seamen made reply:
'We have children, we have wives,
And the Lord hath spared our lives.
We will make the Spaniard promise, if we yield, to let us go;
We shall live to fight again and to strike another blow.'
And the lion there lay dying, and they yielded to the foe.

And the stately Spanish men to their flagship bore him then,
Where they laid him by the mast, old Sir Richard caught at last,
And they praised him to his face with their courtly foreign grace;
But he rose upon their decks, and he cried:
'I have fought for Queen and Faith like a valiant man and true;
I have only done my duty as a man is bound to do:
With a joyful spirit I Sir Richard Grenville die!'
And he fell upon their decks, and he died.

And they stared at the dead that had been so valiant and true,
And had holden the power and glory of Spain so cheap
That he dared her with one little ship and his English few;
Was he devil or man? He was devil for aught they knew,
But they sank his body with honour down into the deep,
And they manned the Revenge with a swarthier alien crew,
And away she sailed with her loss and longed for her own;
When a wind from the lands they had ruined awoke from sleep,
And the water began to heave and the weather to moan,
And or ever that evening ended a great gale blew,
And a wave like the wave that is raised by an earthquake grew,
Till it smote on their hulls and their sails and their masts and their flags,
And the whole sea plunged and fell on the shot-shattered navy of Spain,
And the little Revenge herself went down by the island crags
To be lost evermore in the main.

ROBERT LOUIS STEVENSON

## From *The Light-Keeper*

The brilliant kernel of the night,
The flaming lightroom circles me:
I sit within a blaze of light
Held high above the dusky sea.
Far off the surf doth break and roar
Along bleak miles of moonlit shore,
Where through the tides the tumbling wave
Falls in an avalanche of foam
And drives its churnèd waters home
Up many an undercliff and cave.

The clear bell chimes: the clockworks strain,
The turning lenses flash and pass,
Frame turning within glittering frame
With frosty gleam of moving glass:
Unseen by me, each dusky hour
The sea-waves welter up the tower
Or in the ebb subside again;
And ever and anon all night,
Drawn from afar by charm of light,
A sea bird beats against the pane.

And lastly when dawn ends the night
And belts the semi-orb of sea,
The tall, pale pharos in the light
Looks white and spectral as may be.
The early ebb is out: the green
Straight belt of seaweed now is seen,
That round the basement of the tower
Marks out the interspace of tide;
And watching men are heavy-eyed,
And sleepless lips are dry and sour.

The night is over like a dream:
The sea-birds cry and dip themselves:
And in the early sunlight, steam
The newly bared and dripping shelves,
Around whose verge the glassy wave
With lisping wash is heard to lave;
While, on the white tower lifted high,
The circling lenses flash and pass
With yellow light in faded glass
And sickly shine against the sky.

ROBERT LOUIS STEVENSON

## Requiem

Under the wide and starry sky,
Dig the grave and let me lie.
Glad did I live and gladly die,
    And I laid me down with a will.

This be the verse you grave for me:
*Here he lies where he longed to be;*
*Home is the sailor, home from sea,*
    *And the hunter home from the hill.*

THOMAS ASHE

## A Vision of Children

I dreamed I saw a little brook
    Run rippling down the Strand;
With cherry-trees and apple-trees
    Abloom on either hand:
The sparrows gathered from the squares,
    Upon the branches green;
The pigeons flocked from Palace-Yard,
    Afresh their wings to preen;
And children down St Martin's Lane,
    And out of Westminster,
Came trooping, many a thousand strong,
    With a bewildered air.

They hugged each other round the neck,
    And tittered for delight,
To see the yellow daffodils,
    And see the daisies white;
They rolled upon the grassy slopes,
    And drank the water clear,
While 'buses the Embankment took,
    Ashamed to pass anear;
And sandwich-men stood still aghast,
    And costermongers smiled;
And a policeman on his beat
    Passed, weeping like a child.

THOMAS ASHE

## The City Clerk

'Tis strange how my head runs on! 'tis a puzzle to understand
Such fancies stirring in me, for a whiff of hay in the Strand!

I see the old farmhouse, and garden wall, and the bees;
I see the mowers stretched, with their bottles, under the trees;

I hear the little brook aripple down in the dell;
I hear the old-folk croon—'Our son, he is doing well!'

O yes, I am doing well; but I'd be again, for a day,
A simple farmer's lad, among the girls in the hay.

C. S. CALVERLEY

## Peace

### A Study

He stood, a worn-out City clerk—
    Who'd toiled, and seen no holiday,
For forty years from dawn to dark—
    Alone beside Caermarthen Bay.

He felt the salt spray on his lips;
    Heard children's voices on the sands;
Up the sun's path he saw the ships
    Sail on and on to other lands;

And laughed aloud. Each sight and sound
    To him was joy too deep for tears;
He sat him on the beach, and bound
    A blue bandana round his ears,

And thought how, posted near his door,
    His own green door on Camden Hill,
Two bands at least, most likely more,
    Were mingling at their own sweet will

Verdi with Vance. And at the thought
    He laughed again, and softly drew
That Morning Herald that he'd bought
    Forth from his breast, and read it through.

OSCAR WILDE

## *Symphony in Yellow*

An omnibus across the bridge
    Crawls like a yellow butterfly,
    And, here and there, a passer-by
Shows like a little restless midge.

Big barges full of yellow hay
    Are moved against the shadowy wharf,
    And, like a yellow silken scarf,
The thick fog hangs along the quay.

The yellow leaves begin to fade
    And flutter from the Temple elms,
    And at my feet the pale green Thames
Lies like a rod of rippled jade.

ROBERT BRIDGES

## *London Snow*

When men were all asleep the snow came flying,
In large white flakes falling on the city brown,
Stealthily and perpetually settling and loosely lying,
    Hushing the latest traffic of the drowsy town;
Deadening, muffling, stifling its murmurs failing;
Lazily and incessantly floating down and down:
    Silently sifting and veiling road, roof and railing;
Hiding difference, making unevenness even,
Into angles and crevices softly drifting and sailing.
    All night it fell, and when full inches seven
It lay in the depth of its uncompacted lightness,
The clouds blew off from a high and frosty heaven;
    And all woke earlier for the unaccustomed brightness
Of the winter dawning, the strange unheavenly glare:
The eye marvelled—marvelled at the dazzling whiteness;
    The ear hearkened to the stillness of the solemn air;
No sound of wheel rumbling nor of foot falling,
And the busy morning cries came thin and spare.
    Then boys I heard, as they went to school, calling,
They gathered up the crystal manna to freeze
Their tongues with tasting, their hands with snowballing;

Or rioted in a drift, plunging up to the knees;
Or peering up from under the white-mossed wonder,
'O look at the trees!' they cried, 'O look at the trees!'
   With lessened load a few carts creak and blunder,
Following along the white deserted way,
A country company long dispersed asunder:
   When now already the sun, in pale display
Standing by Paul's high dome, spread forth below
His sparkling beams, and awoke the stir of the day.
   For now doors open, and war is waged with the snow;
And trains of sombre men, past tale of number,
Tread long brown paths, as toward their toil they go:
   But even for them awhile no cares encumber
Their minds diverted; the daily word is unspoken,
The daily thoughts of labour and sorrow slumber
At the sight of the beauty that greets them, for the charm
   they have broken.


THOMAS ASHE

*A Word to the West End*


The dead leaves, one-time fair,
Whirl weirdly in the Square,
   And in them, fancy I,
Drift banned souls, that have missed
Chance of the heavenly tryst
   Of the fair year fled by.

You have loved glare of the gas,
And dancing girls, and as
   A new-found paradise
Have pasteboard trees and groves,
And footlight-litten loves,
   Dazed your admiring eyes.

And you have made night day,
And, as your feet tripped gay
   In dizzy dance, laughed free;
While kith and kin, 'neath dim
Bridge lamplight, slumbered grim,
   Or drifted out to sea.

OSCAR WILDE

## Impression du Matin

The Thames nocturne of blue and gold
   Changed to a Harmony in grey:
   A barge with ochre-coloured hay
Dropped from the wharf: and chill and cold

The yellow fog came creeping down
   The bridges, till the houses' walls
   Seemed changed to shadows and St Paul's
Loomed like a bubble o'er the town.

Then suddenly arose the clang
   Of waking life; the streets were stirred
   With country waggons: and a bird
Flew to the glistening roofs and sang.

But one pale woman all alone,
   The daylight kissing her wan hair,
   Loitered beneath the gas lamps' flare,
With lips of flame and heart of stone.

OSCAR WILDE

## Requiescat

   Tread lightly, she is near
     Under the snow,
   Speak gently, she can hear
     The daisies grow.

   All her bright golden hair
     Tarnished with rust,
   She that was young and fair
     Fallen to dust.

   Lily-like, white as snow,
     She hardly knew
   She was a woman, so
     Sweetly she grew.

Coffin-board, heavy stone,
  Lie on her breast,
I vex my heart alone,
  She is at rest.

Peace, Peace, she cannot hear
  Lyre or sonnet,
All my life's buried here,
  Heap earth upon it.


ROBERT LOUIS STEVENSON

## The Celestial Surgeon

If I have faltered more or less
In my great task of happiness;
If I have moved among my race
And shown no glorious morning face;
If beams from happy human eyes
Have moved me not; if morning skies,
Books, and my food, and summer rain
Knocked on my sullen heart in vain:
Lord, thy most pointed pleasure take
And stab my spirit broad awake;
Or, Lord, if too obdurate I,
Choose thou, before that spirit die,
A piercing pain, a killing sin,
And to my dead heart run them in!


ROBERT LOUIS STEVENSON

I will make you brooches and toys for your delight
Of bird-song at morning and star-shine at night.
I will make a palace fit for you and me
Of green days in forests and blue days at sea.

I will make my kitchen, and you shall keep your room,
Where white flows the river and bright blows the broom,
And you shall wash your linen and keep your body white
In rainfall at morning and dewfall at night.

And this shall be for music when no one else is near,
The fine song for singing, the rare song to hear!
That only I remember, that only you admire,
Of the broad road that stretches and the roadside fire.


JEAN INGELOW

## Echo and the Ferry


Ay, Oliver! I was but seven, and he was eleven;
He looked at me pouting and rosy. I blushed where I stood.
They had told us to play in the orchard (and I only seven!
A small guest at the farm); but he said 'Oh, a girl was no good!'
So he whistled and went, he went over the stile to the wood.
It was sad, it was sorrowful! Only a girl—only seven!
At home in the dark London smoke I had not found it out.
The pear-trees looked on in their white, and blue birds flashed about,
And they too were angry as Oliver. Were they eleven?
I thought so. Yes, every one else was eleven—eleven!

So Oliver went, but the cowslips were tall at my feet,
And all the white orchard with fast-falling blossom was littered;
And under and over the branches those little birds twittered,
While hanging head downwards they scolded because I was seven.
A pity. A very great pity. One should be eleven.
But soon I was happy, the smell of the world was so sweet,
And I saw a round hole in an apple-tree rosy and old.

Then I knew! for I peeped, and I felt it was right they should scold!
Eggs small and eggs many. For gladness I broke into laughter;
And then some one else—oh, how softly!—came after, came after
With laughter—with laughter came after.
And no one was near us to utter that sweet mocking call,
That soon very tired sank low with a mystical fall.
But this was the country—perhaps it was close under heaven;
Oh, nothing so likely; the voice might have come from it even.
I knew about heaven. But this was the country, of this
Light, blossom, and piping, and flashing of wings not at all.
Not at all. No. But one little bird was an easy forgiver:
She peeped, she drew near as I moved from her domicile small,
Then flashed down her hole like a dart—like a dart from the quiver.
And I waded atween the long grasses and felt it was bliss.

—So this was the country; clear dazzle of azure and shiver
And whisper of leaves, and a humming all over the tall
White branches, a humming of bees. And I came to the wall—
A little low wall—and looked over, and there was the river,
The lane that led on to the village, and then the sweet river
Clear shining and slow, she had far far to go from her snow;
But each rush gleamed a sword in the sunlight to guard her long flow,
And she murmured, methought, with a speech very soft—very low.
'The ways will be long, but the days will be long,' quoth the river,
'To me a long liver, long, long!' quoth the river—the river.

I dreamed of the country that night, of the orchard, the sky,
The voice that had mocked coming after and over and under.
But at last—in a day or two namely—Eleven and I
Were very fast friends, and to him I confided the wonder.
He said that was Echo. 'Was Echo a wise kind of bee
That had learned how to laugh: could it laugh in one's ear and then fly
And laugh again yonder?' 'No; Echo'—he whispered it low—
'Was a woman, they said, but a woman whom no one could see
And no one could find; and he did not believe it, not he,
But he could not get near for the river that held us asunder.
Yet I that had money—a shilling, a whole silver shilling—

We might cross if I thought I would spend it.' 'Oh yes, I was willing'—
And we ran hand in hand, we ran down to the ferry, the ferry,
And we heard how she mocked at the folk with a voice clear and merry
When they called for the ferry; but oh! she was very—was very
Swift-footed. She spoke and was gone; and when Oliver cried,
'Hie over! hie over! you man of the ferry—the ferry!'
By the still water's side she was heard far and wide—she replied
And she mocked in her voice sweet and merry, 'You man of the ferry,
You man of—you man of the ferry!'

'Hie over!' he shouted. The ferryman came at his calling,
Across the clear reed-bordered river he ferried us fast;—
Such a chase! Hand in hand, foot to foot, we ran on; it surpassed
All measure her doubling—so close, then so far away falling,
Then gone, and no more. Oh! to see her but once unaware,
And the mouth that had mocked, but we might not (yet sure she was there!),
Nor behold her wild eyes and her mystical countenance fair.

We sought in the wood, and we found the wood-wren in her stead;
In the field, and we found but the cuckoo that talked overhead;
By the brook, and we found the reed-sparrow deep-nested, in brown—
Not Echo, fair Echo! for Echo, sweet Echo! was flown.

So we came to the place where the dead people wait till God call.
The church was among them, grey moss over roof, over wall,
Very silent, so low. And we stood on a green grassy mound
And looked in at a window, for Echo, perhaps, in her round
Might have come in to hide there. But no; every oak-carven seat
Was empty. We saw the great Bible—old, old, very old,
And the parson's great Prayer-book beside it; we heard the slow beat
Of the pendulum swing in the tower; we saw the clear gold
Of a sunbeam float down the aisle and then waver and play
On the low chancel step and the railing, and Oliver said,
'Look, Katie! look, Katie! when Lettice came here to be wed
She stood where that sunbeam drops down, and all white was her gown;
And she stepped upon flowers they strewed for her.' Then quoth
    small Seven:
'Shall I wear a white gown and have flowers to walk upon ever?'

All doubtful: 'It takes a long time to grow up,' quoth Eleven;
'You're so little, you know, and the church is so old, it can never
Last on till you're tall.' And in whispers—because it was old
And holy, and fraught with strange meaning, half felt, but not told,
Full of old parsons' prayers, who were dead, of old days, of old folk,
Neither heard nor beheld, but about us, in whispers we spoke.
Then we went from it softly and ran hand in hand to the strand,
While bleating of flocks and birds piping made sweeter the land.
And Echo came back e'en as Oliver drew to the ferry,
'O Katie!' 'Oh Katie!' 'Come on, then!' 'Come on, then!' 'For, see,
The round sun, all red, lying low by the tree'— 'by the tree.'
'By the tree.' Ay, she mocked him again, with her voice sweet and merry:
'Hie over!' 'Hie over!' 'You man of the ferry'—'the ferry.'
     'You man of the ferry—
    You man of—you man of—the ferry.'
Ay, here—it was here that we woke her, the Echo of old;
All life of that day seems an echo, and many times told.
Shall I cross by the ferry to-morrow, and come in my white
To that little low church? and will Oliver meet me anon?
Will it all seem an echo from childhood passed over—passed on?
Will the grave parson bless us? Hark, hark! in the dim failing light
I hear her! As then the child's voice clear and high, sweet and merry
Now she mocks the man's tone with 'Hie over! Hie over the ferry!'
And Katie. 'And Katie.' 'Art out with the glow-worms to-night,
My Katie?' 'My Katie!' For gladness I break into laughter
And tears. Then it all comes again as from far-away years;
Again, some one else—oh, how softly! with laughter comes after,
    Comes after—with laughter comes after.

ROBERT LOUIS STEVENSON

## From *A Child's Garden of Verses*

### VIII   Armies in the Fire

The lamps now glitter down the street;
Faintly sound the falling feet;
And the blue even slowly falls
About the garden trees and walls.

Now in the falling of the gloom
The red fire paints the empty room:
And warmly on the roof it looks,
And flickers on the backs of books.

Armies march by tower and spire
Of cities blazing, in the fire;
Till as I gaze with staring eyes,
The armies fade, the lustre dies.

Then once again the glow returns;
Again the phantom city burns;
And down the red-hot valley, lo!
The phantom armies marching go!

Blinking embers, tell me true
Where are those armies marching to,
And what the burning city is
That crumbles in your furnaces!

### XXVII   Good and Bad Children

Children, you are very little,
And your bones are very brittle;
If you would grow great and stately,
You must try to walk sedately.

You must still be bright and quiet,
And content with simple diet;
And remain, through all bewildering,
Innocent and honest children.

Happy hearts and happy faces,
Happy play in grassy places—
That was how, in ancient ages,
Children grew to kings and sages.

But the unkind and the unruly,
And the sort who eat unduly,
They must never hope for glory—
Theirs is quite a different story!

Cruel children, crying babies,
All grow up as geese and gabies,
Hated, as their age increases,
By their nephews and their nieces.


### XXX  The Lamplighter

My tea is nearly ready and the sun has left the sky;
It's time to take the window to see Leerie going by;
For every night at teatime and before you take your seat,
With lantern and with ladder he comes posting up the street.

Now Tom would be a driver and Maria go to sea,
And my papa's a banker and as rich as he can be;
But I, when I am stronger and can choose what I'm to do,
O Leerie, I'll go round at night and light the lamps with you!

For we are very lucky, with a lamp before the door,
And Leerie stops to light it as he lights so many more;
And O! before you hurry by with ladder and with light,
O Leerie, see a little child and nod to him to-night!


### XXXVIII  Winter-Time

Late lies the wintry sun a-bed,
A frosty, fiery sleepy-head;
Blinks but an hour or two; and then,
A blood-red orange, sets again.

Before the stars have left the skies,
At morning in the dark I rise;
And shivering in my nakedness,
By the cold candle, bathe and dress.

Close by the jolly fire I sit
To warm my frozen bones a bit;
Or with a reindeer-sled, explore
The colder countries round the door.

When to go out, my nurse doth wrap
Me in my comforter and cap:
The cold wind burns my face, and blows
Its frosty pepper up my nose.

Black are my steps on silver sod;
Thick blows my frosty breath abroad;
And tree and house, and hill and lake,
Are frosted like a wedding-cake.

JOSEPH SKIPSEY

## Mother Wept

Mother wept, and father sighed;
  With delight a-glow
Cried the lad, 'To-morrow,' cried.
  'To the pit I go.'

Up and down the place he sped,—
  Greeted old and young,
Far and wide the tidings spread,—
  Clapped his hands and sung.

Came his cronies some to gaze
  Wrapped in wonder; some
Free with counsel; some with praise;
  Some with envy dumb.

'May he,' many a gossip cried,
  'Be from peril kept;'
Father hid his face and sighed,
  Mother turned and wept.

JOSEPH SKIPSEY

## Hey Robin
### (The first two lines are old)

Hey Robin, jolly Robin,
  Tell me how thy lady doth?
Is she laughing, is she sobbing,
  Is she gay, or grave, or both?

Is she like the finch, so merry,
  Lilting in her father's hall?
Or the crow with cry a very
  Plague to each, a plague to all.

Is she like the violet breathing
  Blessings on her native place?
Or the cruel nettle scathing
  All who dare approach her grace?

Is she like the dew-drop sparkling
  When the morn peeps o'er the land?
Or the cloud in mid-air darkling,
  When a fearful storm's at hand?

Tut, to count the freaks of woman,
  Count the pebbles of the seas;
Rob, thy lady's not uncommon,
  Be or do she what she please!


ROBERT LOUIS STEVENSON

## To S. R. Crockett

### On Receiving a Dedication

Blows the wind today, and the sun and the rain are flying,
  Blows the wind on the moors today and now,
Where about the graves of the martyrs the whaups are crying,
  My heart remembers how!

Grey recumbent tombs of the dead in desert places,
  Standing-stones on the vacant wine-red moor,
Hills of sheep, and the howes of the silent vanished races,
  And winds, austere and pure:

Be it granted me to behold you again in dying,
  Hills of home! and to hear again the call;
Hear about the graves of the martyrs the peewees crying,
  And hear no more at all.

WILLIAM JAMES LINTON

## *Epicurean*

In Childhood's unsuspicious hours
The fairies crowned my head with flowers.

Youth came: I lay at Beauty's feet;
She smiled and said my song was sweet.

Then Age: and, Love no longer mine,
My brows I shaded with the vine.

With flowers and love and wine and song,
O Death! life hath not been too long.


WILLIAM JAMES LINTON

## *Spring and Autumn*

'Thou wilt forget me.' 'Love has no such word.'
The soft Spring wind is whispering to the trees,
Among lime-blossoms have the hovering bees
    Those whispers heard?

'Or thou wilt change.' 'Love changeth not:' he said.
The purple heather cloys the air with scent
Of honey. O'er the moors her lover went,
    Nor turned his head.


ANDREW LANG

## *Tired of Towns*

'When we spoke to her of the New Jerusalem, she said she would rather
  go to a country place in Heaven.'—*Letters from the Black Country*

I'm weary of towns, it seems a'most a pity
  We didn't stop down i' the country and clem,
And you say that I'm bound for another city,
  For the streets o' the New Jerusalem.

And the streets are never like Sheffield, here,
  Nor the smoke don't cling like a smut to *them*;
But the water o' life flows cool and clear
  Through the streets o' the New Jerusalem.

And the houses, you say, are of jasper cut,
  And the gates are gaudy wi' gold and gem;
But there's times I could wish as the gates was shut—
  The gates o' the New Jerusalem.

For I come from a country that's over-built
  Wi' streets that stifle, and walls that hem,
And the gorse on a common's worth all the gilt
  And the gold of your New Jerusalem.

And I hope that they'll bring me, in Paradise,
  To green lanes leafy wi' bough and stem—
To a country place in the land o' the skies
  And not to the New Jerusalem.


ANDREW LANG

*Twilight on Tweed*


Three crests against the saffron sky,
  Beyond the purple plain,
The kind remembered melody
  Of Tweed once more again.

Wan water from the border hills,
  Dear voice from the old years,
Thy distant music lulls and stills,
  And moves to quiet tears.

Like a loved ghost thy fabled flood
  Fleets through the dusky land;
Where Scott, come home to die, has stood,
  My feet returning stand.

A mist of memory broods and floats,
  The Border waters flow;
The air is full of ballad notes,
  Borne out of long ago.

Old songs that sung themselves to me,
  Sweet through a boy's day-dream,
While trout below the blossomed tree
  Flashed in the golden stream.

.   .   .   .   .   .

Twilight, and Tweed, and Eildon Hill,
  Fair and too fair you be;
You tell me that the voice is still
  That should have welcomed me.

# Fin de Siècle

## (1885–1901)

W. E. HENLEY

Madam Life's a piece in bloom
  Death goes dogging everywhere:
She's the tenant of the room,
  He's the ruffian on the stair.

You shall see her as a friend,
  You shall bilk him once and twice;
But he'll trap you in the end,
  And he'll stick you for her price.

With his kneebones at your chest,
  And his knuckles in your throat,
You would reason—plead—protest!
  Clutching at her petticoat;

But she's heard it all before,
  Well she knows you've had your fun,
Gingerly she gains the door,
  And your little job is done.

W. E. HENLEY

On the way to Kew,
  By the river old and gray,
Where in the Long Ago
We laughed and loitered so,
I met a ghost to-day,
A ghost that told of you—
A ghost of low replies
And sweet, inscrutable eyes
Coming up from Richmond
As you used to do.

By the river old and gray,
The enchanted Long Ago
Murmured and smiled anew.
On the way to Kew,
March had the laugh of May,
The bare boughs looked aglow,

And old, immortal words
Sang in my breast like birds,
Coming up from Richmond
As I used with you.

With the life of Long Ago
Lived my thought of you.
By the river old and gray
Flowing his appointed way
As I watched I knew
What is so good to know—
Not in vain, not in vain,
Shall I look for you again
Coming up from Richmond
On the way to Kew.


WILLIAM CORY

## Heraclitus

They told me, Heraclitus, they told me you were dead,
They brought me bitter news to hear and bitter tears to shed.
I wept, as I remembered, how often you and I
Had tired the sun with talking and sent him down the sky.

And now that thou art lying, my dear old Carian guest,
A handful of grey ashes, long long ago at rest,
Still are thy pleasant voices, thy nightingales, awake;
For Death, he taketh all away, but them he cannot take.


WILLIAM CORY

## A Poor French Sailor's Scottish Sweetheart

I cannot forget my jo,
    I bid him be mine in sleep:
But battle and woe have changed him so,
    There's nothing to do but weep.

My mother rebukes me yet,
  And I never was meek before;
His jacket is wet, his lip cold set,
  He'll trouble our home no more.

Oh breaker of reeds that bend!
  Oh quencher of tow that smokes!
I'd rather descend to my sailor friend
  Than prosper with lofty folks.

I'm lying beside the gowan,
  My jo in the English bay;
I'm Annie Rowan, his Annie Rowan,
  He called me his *bien aimée*.

I'll hearken to all you quote,
  Though I'd rather be deaf and free;
The little he wrote in the sinking boat
  Is Bible and charm for me.

ALFRED, LORD TENNYSON

## Crossing the Bar

Sunset and evening star,
  And one clear call for me!
And may there be no moaning of the bar,
  When I put out to sea,

But such a tide as moving seems asleep,
  Too full for sound and foam,
When that which drew from out the boundless deep
  Turns again home.

Twilight and evening bell,
  And after that the dark!
And may there be no sadness of farewell,
  When I embark;

For though from out our bourne of Time and Place
  The flood may bear me far,
I hope to see my Pilot face to face
  When I have crossed the bar.

THOMAS HARDY

## Thoughts of Phena

### At News of Her Death

Not a line of her writing have I,
　　Not a thread of her hair,
No mark of her late time as dame in her dwelling, whereby
　　I may picture her there;
　And in vain do I urge my unsight
　　To conceive my lost prize
At her close, whom I knew when her dreams were upbrimming with light,
　　And with laughter her eyes.

What scenes spread around her last days,
　　Sad, shining, or dim?
Did her gifts and compassions enray and enarch her sweet ways
　　With an aureate nimb?
　Or did life-light decline from her years,
　　And mischances control
Her full day-star; unease, or regret, or forebodings, or fears
　　Disennoble her soul?

Thus I do but the phantom retain
　　Of the maiden of yore
As my relic; yet haply the best of her—fined in my brain
　　It may be the more
　That no line of her writing have I,
　　Nor a thread of her hair,
No mark of her late time as dame in her dwelling, whereby
　　I may picture her there.

LIONEL JOHNSON

## The Troopship

At early morning, clear and cold,
Still in her English harbour lay
The long, white ship: while winter gold
Shone pale upon her outward way.

Slowly she moved, slowly she stirred,
Stately and slow, she went away:
Sounds of farewell, the harbour heard;
Music on board began to play.

Old, homely airs were thine, great ship!
Breaking from laughter into tears:
And through them all good fellowship
Spoke of a trust beyond all fears.

Still, as the gray mists gathered round,
Embracing thee, concealing thine;
Still, faintly from the Outward Bound
Came melodies of *Auld Lang Syne*.

Oh, sad to part! Oh, brave to go
Between the Piers of Hercules,
And through the seas of fame, and so
Meet eastern sun on eastern seas!

O richly laden! swiftly bear,
And surely, thy two thousand men;
Till round them burn the Indian air:
And English lips will hail them then.

RUDYARD KIPLING

## Danny Deever

'What are the bugles blowin' for?' said Files-on-Parade.
'To turn you out, to turn you out,' the Colour-Sergeant said.
'What makes you look so white, so white?' said Files-on-Parade.
'I'm dreadin' what I've got to watch,' the Colour-Sergeant said.
  For they're hangin' Danny Deever, you can hear the Dead March play,
  The regiment's in 'ollow square—they're hangin' him to-day;
  They've taken of his buttons off an' cut his stripes away,
  An' they're hangin' Danny Deever in the mornin'.

'What makes the rear-rank breathe so 'ard?' said Files-on-Parade.
'It's bitter cold, it's bitter cold,' the Colour-Sergeant said.
'What makes that front-rank man fall down?' says Files-on-Parade,
'A touch o' sun, a touch o' sun,' the Colour-Sergeant said.
  They are hangin' Danny Deever, they are marchin' of 'im round,
  They 'ave 'alted Danny Deever by 'is coffin on the ground;
  An' 'e'll swing in 'arf a minute for a sneakin' shootin' hound—
  O they're hangin' Danny Deever in the mornin'!

' 'Is cot was right-'and cot to mine,' said Files-on-Parade.
' 'E's sleepin' out an' far to-night,' the Colour-Sergeant said.

'I've drunk 'is beer a score o' times,' said Files-on-Parade.
' 'E's drinkin' bitter beer alone,' the Colour-Sergeant said.
  They are hangin' Danny Deever, you must mark 'im to 'is place,
  For 'e shot a comrade sleepin'—you must look 'im in the face;
  Nine 'undred of 'is county an' the regiment's disgrace,
  While they're hangin' Danny Deever in the mornin'.

'What's that so black agin the sun?' said Files-on-Parade.
'It's Danny fightin' 'ard for life,' the Colour-Sergeant said.
'What's that that whimpers over'ead?' said Files-on-Parade.
'It's Danny's soul that's passin' now,' the Colour-Sergeant said.
  For they're done with Danny Deever, you can 'ear the quickstep play,
  The regiment's in column, an' they're marchin' us away;
  Ho! the young recruits are shakin', an' they'll want their beer to-day,
  After hangin' Danny Deever in the mornin'!

RUDYARD KIPLING

## Gunga Din

You may talk o' gin and beer
When you're quartered safe out 'ere,
An' you're sent to penny fights an' Aldershot it;
But when it comes to slaughter
You will do your work on water,
An' you'll lick the bloomin' boots of 'im that's got it.
Now in Injia's sunny clime,
Where I used to spend my time
A-servin' of 'Er Majesty the Queen,
Of all them blackfaced crew
The finest man I knew
Was our regimental bhisti, Gunga Din.
      He was 'Din! Din! Din!
  You limpin' lump o' brick-dust, Gunga Din!
      Hi! slippy *hitherao*!
      Water, get it! *Panee lao*!
  You squidgy-nosed old idol, Gunga Din.'

The uniform 'e wore
Was nothin' much before,
An' rather less than 'arf o' that be'ind,
For a piece o' twisty rag
An' a goatskin water-bag
Was all the field-equipment 'e could find.

When the sweatin' troop-train lay
In a sidin' through the day,
Where the 'eat would make your bloomin' eyebrows crawl,
We shouted 'Harry By!'
Till our throats were bricky-dry,
Then we wopped 'im 'cause 'e couldn't serve us all.
        It was 'Din! Din! Din!
   You 'eathen, where the mischief 'ave you been?
        You put some *juldee* in it
        Or I'll *marrow* you this minute
   If you don't fill up my helmet, Gunga Din!'

'E would dot an' carry one
Till the longest day was done;
An' 'e didn't seem to know the use o' fear.
If we charged or broke or cut,
You could bet your bloomin' nut,
'E'd be waitin' fifty paces right flank rear.
With 'is mussick on 'is back,
'E would skip with our attack,
An' watch us till the bugles made 'Retire',
An' for all 'is dirty 'ide
'E was white, clear white, inside
When 'e went to tend the wounded under fire!
        It was 'Din! Din! Din!'
   With the bullets kickin' dust-spots on the green.
        When the cartridges ran out,
        You could hear the front-files shout,
   'Hi! ammunition-mules an' Gunga Din!'

I sha'n't forgit the night
When I dropped be'ind the fight
With a bullet where my belt-plate should 'a' been.
I was chokin' mad with thirst,
An' the man that spied me first
Was our good old grinnin', gruntin' Gunga Din.
'E lifted up my 'ead,
An' he plugged me where I bled,
An' 'e guv me 'arf-a-pint o' water green.
It was crawlin' and it stunk,
But of all the drinks I've drunk,
I'm gratefullest to one from Gunga Din.
        It was 'Din! Din! Din!
   'Ere's a beggar with a bullet through 'is spleen;
        'E's chawin' up the ground,
        An' 'e's kickin' all around:
   For Gawd's sake git the water, Gunga Din!'

'E carried me away
To where a dooli lay,
An' a bullet come an' drilled the beggar clean.
'E put me safe inside,
An' just before 'e died,
'I 'ope you liked your drink,' sez Gunga Din.
So I'll meet 'im later on
At the place where 'e is gone—
Where it's always double drill and no canteen.
'E'll be squattin' on the coals
Givin' drink to poor damned souls,
An' I'll get a swig in hell from Gunga Din!
    Yes, Din! Din! Din!
  You Lazarushian-leather Gunga Din!
    Though I've belted you and flayed you,
    By the livin' Gawd that made you,
You're a better man than I am, Gunga Din.

JOHN DAVIDSON

## In a Music-Hall

Who is my neighbour? *Luke* x. 29.

### Prologue

In Glasgow, in 'Eighty-four,
I worked as a junior clerk;
My masters I never could please,
But they tried me a while at the desk.

From ten in the morning till six
I wrote memorandums and things.
I indexed the letter-books too,
When the office-boy wasn't about.

And nothing could please me at night—
No novels, no poems, no plays,
Hardly the talk of my friends,
Hardly my hopes, my ambition.

I did as my desk-fellows did;
With a pipe and a tankard of beer,
In a music-hall, rancid and hot,
I lost my soul night after night.

It is better to lose one's soul,
Than never to stake it at all.

Some 'artists' I met at the bar,
And others elsewhere; and, behold,
Here are the six I knew well.

### I  Mary-Jane Macpherson

He thinks I'm a governess still,
   But I'm sure that he'll pardon my choice;
I make more, and rest when I'm ill,
   And it's only the sale of my voice.

I doubt it is sinful to dream;
   The World's the true God-head, I fear;
Its wealth, power, iniquity seem
   The mightiest Trinity here.

And this on a leaf of its book,
   Which is life, and is ne'er out of date,
Is the passage I see when I look
   As in Virgil for tidings of fate:

'You must each undergo a new birth;
   You must die to the spirit, and be
A child of the lord of the earth,
   Of our Saviour, Society.

'Get wisdom of wordly things,
   And with all your getting, get gold;
Beware of the tempter who sings
   Of other delights than are sold.

'But of all things a poor girl should shun,
   It is the despising of pelf;
And another as notable one
   Is the loving a lad like herself.

'Because while she dreams day and night
   Of love, and good fortune, and bliss,
Oppression, disgrace, and despite,
   Glad fiends that are never remiss,

'The world's evil angels of wrath
   Pursue him she loves with their rods,
Till he falls overcome in the path;
   For the World's the most jealous of gods.'

Then I read in my heart, and I see
 The heresy taught by my dear;
Before he was parted from me,
 He whispered it into my ear:

'I go to make money, my sweet;
 I'll join the gold-worshipping crew,
And soon bring the world to my feet,
 For I'll worship and labour for you.

'Your work is to dream, dearest heart,
 Of the happiest, happiest life.'
I whispered, 'I'll manage my part;
 I'll dream day and night I'm your wife.'

But that is so long, long ago,
 Such daily eternities since;
And dreaming is sinful, I know,
 And age all my poor darling wins.

Time patiently weaves from his sands
 My life, a miraculous rope:
I would sever the cord in his hands
 And die; but I hope, and I hope.


## II Tom Jenks

A fur-collared coat and a stick and a ring,
 And a chimney-pot hat to the side—that's me!
I'm a music-hall singer that never could sing;
 I'm a sort of a fellow like that, do you see?

I go pretty high in my line, I believe,
 Which is comic, and commonplace, too, maybe.
I was once a job-lot, though, and didn't receive
 The lowest price paid in the biz., do you see?

For I never could get the right hang of the trade;
 So the managers wrote at my name, 'D. B.',
In the guide-books they keep of our business and grade,
 Which means—you'll allow me—*damned bad,* do you see?

But a sort of a kind of a pluck that's mine
 Despised any place save the top of the tree.
I needed some rubbing before I should shine,
 Some grinding, and pruning, and that, do you see?

So I practised my entrance—a kind of half-moon,
    With a flourishing stride and a bow to a T,
And the bark and the yelp at the end of the tune,
    The principal things in my biz., do you see?

Oh, it's business that does it, and blow all the rest!
    The singers ain't in it alongside of me;
They trust to their voices, but I know what's best—
    Smart business, like clockwork and all, do you see?

I'm jolly, and sober, and fond of my wife;
    And she and the kids, they're as happy as me.
I was once in a draper's; but this kind of life
    Gives a fellow more time to himself, do you see?

### III  Lily Dale

She's thirty, this feminine cove,
    And she looks it at hand, you'll allow.
I was once on the streets. By Jove,
    I was handsomer then than now;

Thin lips? Oh, you bet! and deep lines.
    So I powder and paint as you see;
And that belladonna that shines
    Where a dingier light ought to be.

But I'm plump, and my legs—do you doubt me?—
    You'll see when I go on the stage!
And there isn't a pad, sir, about me;
    I'm a proper good girl for my age!

I can't sing a bit, I can't shout;
    But I go through my songs with a birr;
And I always contrive to bring out
    The meaning that tickles you, sir.

They were written for me; they're the rage;
    They're the plainest, the wildest, the slyest;
For I find on the music-hall stage,
    That that kind of song goes the highest.

So I give it them hot, with a glance
    Like the crack of a whip—oh, it stings!
And a still, fiery smile, and a dance
    That indicates naughtiest things.

And I like it. It isn't the best:
    There are nurses, and nuns, and good wives;

But life's pretty much of a jest,
　And you can't very well lead two lives.

But sometimes wild eyes will grow tame,
　And a voice have a tone—ah, you men!—
And a beard please me—oh, there's my name!
　Well? I take a week's holiday then.


### IV　Stanley Trafford

This of me may well be said—
　Of a host as well as me:
'He held himself as great; he made
　His genius his own protégé.'

I loved the beauteous star-veiled truth,
　I strove and failed, and strove again.
I wrote some verses in my youth,
　And knew two noted poets then.

Now I wear a tinsel dress,
　Now I strum a gilt guitar;
For I made my first success
　As 'The Sentimental Star'.

I could be more glad than most,
　I was born for happiness.
Since despair began to boast,
　No one ever tasted less.

The sun, the stars, the moon, the sea—
　I say no word of these—a sign,
A little good sufficed for me,
　A rose's scent made heaven mine.

But most some old thing newly thought
　By some fresh thinker pleased my sense,
And strong, sweet words with rapture wrought,
　And tempered with intelligence.

I craved not wealth, I craved not fame,
　Not even a home; but only time
To dream the willing dreams that came,
　And keep their record in a rhyme.

Wherefore I starved, and hither fell,
　A star in this the nether heaven.
Without, I shine; within, is hell.
　What might have been had I still striven,

Had I not sold my soul for bread!
  But what is this? I'm dull to-night;
My heart has quite seduced my head;
  I'm talking poetry outright.

Ha, ha! I'll sing my famous song,
  I feel I can recall its tone;
The boy's dream suits the gas-lit throng!
  Mark—'Words and music all my own.'

And then, oh, then! Houp-la! Just so!
  Selene, Lily, Mary-Jane?
With which, I wonder, shall I go
  And drown it all in bad champagne?


### V  Selene Eden

My dearest lovers know me not;
  I hide my life and soul from sight;
I conquer all whose blood is hot;
  My mystery is my mail of might.

I had a troupe who danced with me:
  I veiled myself from head to foot;
My girls were nude as they dared be;
  They sang a chorus, I was mute.

But now I fill the widest stage
  Alone, unveiled, without a song;
And still with mystery I engage
  The aching senses of the throng.

A dark-blue vest with stars of gold,
  My only diamond in my hair,
An Indian scarf about me rolled:
  That is the dress I always wear.

And first the sensuous music whets
  The lustful crowd; the dim-lit room
Recalls delights, recalls regrets;
  And then I enter in the gloom.

I glide, I trip, I run, I spin,
  Lapped in the lime-light's aureole.
Hushed are the voices, hushed the din,
  I see men's eyes like glowing coal.

My loosened scarf in odours drenched
    Showers keener hints of sensual bliss;
The music swoons, the light is quenched,
    Into the dark I blow a kiss.

Then, like a long wave rolling home,
    The music gathers speed and sound;
I, dancing, am the music's foam,
    And wilder, fleeter, higher bound,

And fling my feet above my head;
    The light grows, none aside may glance;
Crimson and amber, green and red,
    In blinding baths of these I dance.

And soft, and sweet, and calm, my face
    Looks pure as unsunned chastity,
Even in the whirling triple pace:
    That is my conquering mystery.

## VI  Julian Aragon

Ha, ha, ha! ho, ho, ho! hee, hee, hique!
I'm the famous Californian Comique!
    I'm as supple as a willow,
    And as graceful as a billow,
I'm handsome, and I'm strong, and I've got cheek.

Cheek's nothing; no, by Jingo! I'm obscene!
My gestures, not my words, say what I mean,
    And the simple and the good,
    They would hiss me if they could,
But I conquer all volition where I'm seen.

I twist, contort, distort, and rage and rustle;
I constrain my every limb and every muscle.
    I'm limber, I'm Antaean,
    I chant the devil's paean,
I fill the stage with rich infernal bustle.

I spin, and whirl, and thunder on the board;
My heart is in my business, I'm encored;
    I'm as easy as a sprite,
    For I study day and night,
I dream, devise—I travail, by the lord!

'My nature's a perennial somersault,'
So you say, and so I think; but whose the fault?

If I don't know good from evil,
Is it wrong to be a devil?
You don't get lime-juice cordial out of malt.

But I'm plump, and soft, and strong, and tall, and sleek,
And I pocket twenty guineas every week;
I journey up and down,
I've sweethearts in each town,
I'm the famous Californian Comique.

### Epilogue

Under the earth are the dead,
Alive and asleep; overhead
Are the angels, asleep and dead.

Not even shadows are we,
But the visions these dreamers see.

These dreamers below and above—
The dream of their dreams is love.

But we never will count the cost;
As dreams go, lusty and stout,
We make us a heaven and hell.

There are six dreams I knew well;
When I had sung them out,
I recovered my soul that was lost.

ERNEST DOWSON

*Vitae summa brevis spem nos vetat incohare longam*

They are not long, the weeping and the laughter,
Love and desire and hate:
I think they have no portion in us after
We pass the gate.

They are not long, the days of wine and roses:
Out of a misty dream
Our path emerges for a while, then closes
Within a dream.

ERNEST DOWSON

## Non Sum Qualis Eram Bonae sub Regno Cynarae

Last night, ah, yesternight, betwixt her lips and mine
There fell thy shadow, Cynara! thy breath was shed
Upon my soul between the kisses and the wine;
And I was desolate and sick of an old passion,
    Yea, I was desolate and bowed my head:
I have been faithful to thee, Cynara! in my fashion.

All night upon mine heart I felt her warm heart beat,
Night-long within mine arms in love and sleep she lay;
Surely the kisses of her bought red mouth were sweet;
But I was desolate and sick of an old passion,
    When I awoke and found the dawn was gray:
I have been faithful to thee, Cynara! in my fashion.

I have forgot much, Cynara! gone with the wind
Flung roses, roses riotously with the throng,
Dancing, to put thy pale, lost lilies out of mind;
But I was desolate and sick of an old passion,
    Yea, all the time, because the dance was long:
I have been faithful to thee, Cynara! in my fashion.

I cried for madder music and for stronger wine,
But when the feast is finished and the lamps expire,
Then falls thy shadow, Cynara! the night is thine;
And I am desolate and sick of an old passion,
    Yea, hungry for the lips of my desire:
I have been faithful to thee, Cynara! in my fashion.

ERNEST DOWSON

## Autumnal

Pale amber sunlight falls across
    The reddening October trees,
    That hardly sway before a breeze
As soft as summer: summer's loss
    Seems little, dear! on days like these

Let misty autumn be our part!
  The twilight of the year is sweet:
  Where shadow and the darkness meet
Our love, a twilight of the heart
  Eludes a little time's deceit.

Are we not better and at home
  In dreamful Autumn, we who deem
  No harvest joy is worth a dream?
A little while and night shall come,
  A little while, then, let us dream.

Beyond the pearled horizons lie
  Winter and night: awaiting these
  We garner this poor hour of ease,
Until love turn from us and die
  Beneath the drear November trees.


JOHN DAVIDSON

## Christmas Eve

'A letter from my love to-day!
  Oh, unexpected, dear appeal!'
She struck a happy tear away
  And broke the crimson seal.

'My love, there is no help on earth,
  No help in heaven; the dead-man's bell
Must toll our wedding; our first hearth
  Must be the well-paved floor of hell.'

The colour died from out her face,
  Her eyes like ghostly candles shone;
She cast dread looks about the place,
  Then clenched her teeth, and read right on.

'I may not pass the prison door;
  Here must I rot from day to day,
Unless I wed whom I abhor,
  My cousin, Blanche of Valencay.

'At midnight with my dagger keen
  I'll take my life; it must be so.
Meet me in hell to-night, my queen,
  For weal and woe.'

She laughed although her face was wan,
  She girded on her golden belt,
She took her jewelled ivory fan,
  And at her glowing missal knelt.

Then rose, 'And am I mad?' she said.
  She broke her fan, her belt untied;
With leather girt herself instead,
  And stuck a dagger at her side.

She waited, shuddering in her room
  Till sleep had fallen on all the house.
She never flinched; she faced her doom:
  They two must sin to keep their vows.

Then out into the night she went;
  And stooping, crept by hedge and tree;
Her rose-bush flung a snare of scent,
  And caught a happy memory.

She fell, and lay a minute's space;
  She tore the sward in her distress;
The dewy grass refreshed her face;
  She rose and ran with lifted dress.

She started like a morn-caught ghost
  Once when the moon came out and stood
To watch; the naked road she crossed,
  And dived into the murmuring wood.

The branches snatched her streaming cloak;
  A live thing shrieked; she made no stay!
She hurried to the trysting-oak—
  Right well she knew the way.

Without a pause she bared her breast
  And drove her dagger home and fell,
And lay like one that takes her rest,
  And died and wakened up in hell.

She bathed her spirit in the flame,
  And near the centre took her post;
From all sides to her ears there came
  The dreary anguish of the lost.

The devil started at her side
  Comely, and tall, and black as jet.
'I am young Malespina's bride;
  Has he come hither yet?'

'My poppet, welcome to your bed.'
  'Is Malespina here?'
'Not he! To-morrow he must wed
  His cousin Blanche, my dear!'

'You lie; he died with me to-night.'
  'Not he! It was a plot.' 'You lie.'
'My dear, I never lie outright.'
  'We died at midnight, he and I.'

The devil went. Without a groan
  She, gathered up in one fierce prayer,
Took root in hell's midst all alone,
  And waited for him there.

She dared to make herself at home,
  Amidst the wail, the uneasy stir.
The blood-stained flame that filled the dome,
  Scentless and silent, shrouded her.

How long she stayed I cannot tell;
  But when she felt his perfidy,
She marched across the floor of hell;
  And all the damned stood up to see.

The devil stopped her at the brink:
  She shook him off; she cried, 'Away!'
'My dear, you have gone mad, I think.'
  'I was betrayed: I will not stay.'

Across the weltering deep she ran—
  A stranger thing was never seen:
The damned stood silent to a man;
  They saw the great gulf set between.

To her it seemed a meadow fair;
  And flowers sprang up about her feet;
She entered heaven; she climbed the stair;
  And knelt down at the mercy-seat.

Seraphs and saints with one great voice
  Welcomed that soul that knew not fear;
Amazed to find it could rejoice
  Hell raised a hoarse half-human cheer.

JOHN DAVIDSON

## *Thirty Bob a Week*

I couldn't touch a stop and turn a screw,
    And set the blooming world a-work for me,
Like such as cut their teeth—I hope, like you—
    On the handle of a skeleton gold key;
I cut mine on a leek, which I eat it every week:
    I'm a clerk at thirty bob as you can see.

But I don't allow it's luck and all a toss;
    There's no such thing as being starred and crossed;
It's just the power of some to be a boss,
    And the bally power of others to be bossed:
I face the music, sir; you bet I ain't a cur;
    Strike me lucky if I don't believe I'm lost!

For like a mole I journey in the dark,
    A-travelling along the underground
From my Pillared Halls and broad Suburbean Park,
    To come the daily dull official round;
And home again at night with my pipe all alight,
    A-scheming how to count ten bob a pound.

And it's often very cold and very wet,
    And my missis stitches towels for a hunks;
And the Pillared Halls is half of it to let—
    Three rooms about the size of travelling trunks.
And we cough, my wife and I, to dislocate a sigh,
    When the noisy little kids are in their bunks.

But you never hear her do a growl or whine,
    For she's made of flint and roses, very odd;
And I've got to cut my meaning rather fine,
    Or I'd blubber, for I'm made of greens and sod:
So p'r'aps we are in Hell for all that I can tell,
    And lost and damned and served up hot to God.

I ain't blaspheming, Mr Silver-tongue;
    I'm saying things a bit beyond your art:
Of all the rummy starts you ever sprung,
    Thirty bob a week's the rummiest start!
With your science and your books and your the'ries
        about spooks,
    Did you ever hear of looking in your heart?

I didn't mean your pocket, Mr, no:
   I mean that having children and a wife,
With thirty bob on which to come and go,
   Isn't dancing to the tabor and the fife:
When it doesn't make you drink, by Heaven! it makes
     you think,
   And notice curious items about life.

I step into my heart and there I meet
   A god-almighty devil singing small,
Who would like to shout and whistle in the street,
   And squelch the passers flat against the wall;
If the whole world was a cake he had the power to take,
   He would take it, ask for more, and eat it all.

And I meet a sort of simpleton beside,
   The kind that life is always giving beans;
With thirty bob a week to keep a bride
   He fell in love and married in his teens:
At thirty bob he stuck; but he knows it isn't luck:
   He knows the seas are deeper than tureens.

And the god-almighty devil and the fool
   That meet me in the High Street on the strike,
When I walk about my heart a-gathering wool,
   Are my good and evil angels if you like.
And both of them together in every kind of weather
   Ride me like a double-seated bike.

That's rough a bit and needs its meaning curled.
   But I have a high old hot un in my mind—
A most engrugious notion of the world,
   That leaves your lightning 'rithmetic behind:
I give it at a glance when I say 'There ain't no chance,
   Nor nothing of the lucky-lottery kind.'

And it's this way that I make it out to be:
   No fathers, mothers, countries, climates—none;
Not Adam was responsible for me,
   Nor society, nor systems, nary one:
A little sleeping seed, I woke—I did, indeed—
   A million years before the blooming sun.

I woke because I thought the time had come;
   Beyond my will there was no other cause;
And everywhere I found myself at home,
   Because I chose to be the thing I was;
And in whatever shape of mollusc or of ape
   I always went according to the laws.

I was the love that chose my mother out;
 I joined two lives and from the union burst;
My weakness and my strength without a doubt
 Are mine alone for ever from the first:
It's just the very same with a difference in the name
 As 'Thy will be done.' You say it if you durst!

They say it daily up and down the land
 As easy as you take a drink, it's true;
But the difficultest go to understand,
 And the difficultest job a man can do,
Is to come it brave and meek with thirty bob a week,
 And feel that that's the proper thing for you.

It's a naked child against a hungry wolf;
 It's playing bowls upon a splitting wreck;
It's walking on a string across a gulf
 With millstones fore-and-aft about your neck;
But the thing is daily done by many and many a one;
 And we fall, face forward, fighting, on the deck.


JOHN DAVIDSON

## Holiday at Hampton Court

Scales of pearly cloud inlay
 North and south the turquoise sky.
While the diamond lamp of day
 Quenchless burns, and time on high
A moment halts upon his way
 Bidding noon again good-bye.

Gaffers, gammers, huzzies, louts,
 Couples, gangs, and families
Sprawling, shake, with Babel-shouts
 Bluff King Hal's funereal trees:
And eddying groups of stare-abouts
 Quiz the sandstone Hercules.

When their tongues and tempers tire,
 Harry and his little lot
Condescendingly admire
 Lozenge-bed and crescent-plot,
Aglow with links of azure fire,
 Pansy and forget-me-not.

Where the emerald shadows rest
  In the lofty woodland aisle,
Chaffing lovers quaintly dressed
  Chase and double many a mile,
Indifferent exiles in the west
  Making love in cockney style.

Now the echoing palace fills;
  Men and women, girls and boys
Trample past the swords and frills,
  Kings and Queens and trulls and toys;
Or listening loll on window-sills,
  Happy amateurs of noise!

That for pictured rooms of state!
  Out they hurry, wench and knave,
Where beyond the palace-gate
  Dusty legions swarm and rave,
With laughter, shriek, inane debate,
  Kentish fire and comic stave.

Voices from the river call;
  Organs hammer tune on tune;
Larks triumphant over all
  Herald twilight coming soon,
For as the sun begins to fall
  Near the zenith gleams the moon.

JOHN DAVIDSON

## From *To the Street Piano*

### A Labourer's Wife
Tune: *Ta-ra-ra-boom-de-ay*

All the day I worked and played
When I was a little maid,
Soft and nimble as a mouse,
Living in my father's house.
If I lacked my liberty,
All my thoughts were free as free;
Though my hands were hacked all o'er,
Ah! my heart was never sore.

Oh! once I had my fling!
I romped at ging-go-ring;
I used to dance and sing,
And play at everything.
I never feared the light;
I shrank from no one's sight;
I saw the world was right;
I always slept at night.

What a simpleton was I
To go and marry on the sly!
Now I work and never play:
Three pale children all the day
Fight and whine; and Dick, my man,
Is drunk as often as he can.
Ah! my head and bones are sore,
And my heart is hacked all o'er.

Yet, once I had my fling;
I romped at ging-go-ring;
I used to dance and sing,
And play at everything.
Now I fear the light;
I shrink from every sight;
I see there's nothing right;
I hope to die to-night.

JOHN DAVIDSON

## In Romney Marsh

As I went down to Dymchurch Wall,
    I heard the South sing o'er the land;
I saw the yellow sunlight fall
    On knolls where Norman churches stand.

And ringing shrilly, taut and lithe,
    Within the wind a core of sound,
The wire from Romney town to Hythe
    Alone its airy journey wound.

A veil of purple vapour flowed
    And trailed its fringe along the Straits;
The upper air like sapphire glowed;
    And roses filled Heaven's central gates.

Masts in the offing wagged their tops;
　　The swinging waves pealed on the shore;
The saffron beach, all diamond drops
　　And beads of surge, prolonged the roar.

As I came up from Dymchurch Wall,
　　I saw above the Downs' low crest
The crimson brands of sunset fall,
　　Flicker and fade from out the west.

Night sank: like flakes of silver fire
　　The stars in one great shower came down;
Shrill blew the wind; and shrill the wire
　　Rang out from Hythe to Romney town.

The darkly shining salt sea drops
　　Streamed as the waves clashed on the shore;
The beach, with all its organ stops
　　Pealing again, prolonged the roar.


SIR HENRY NEWBOLT

## Moonset

Past seven o'clock: time to be gone;
Twelfth-night's over and dawn shivering up:
A hasty cut of the loaf, a steaming cup,
Down to the door, and there is Coachman John.

Ruddy of cheek is John, and bright of eye;
But John it appears has none of your grins and winks;
Civil enough, but short: perhaps he thinks:
Words come once in a mile, and always dry.

Has he a mind or not? I wonder; but soon
We turn through a leafless wood, and there to the right,
Like a sun bewitched in alien realms of night,
Mellow and yellow and rounded hangs the moon.

Strangely near she seems, and terribly great:
The world is dead: why are we travelling still?
Nightmare silence grips my struggling will;
We are driving for ever and ever to find a gate.

'When you come to consider the moon,' says John at last,
And stops, to feel his footing and take his stand;

'And then there's some will say there's never a hand
That made the world!'
                              A flick, and the gates are passed.

Out of the dim magical moonlit park,
Out to the workday road and wider skies:
There's a warm flush in the East where day's to rise,
And I'm feeling the better for Coachman John's remark.


W. E. HENLEY

## From a Window in Princes Street

Above the Crags that fade and gloom
Starts the bare knee of Arthur's Seat;
Ridged high against the evening bloom,
The Old Town rises, street on street;
With lamps bejewelled, straight ahead,
Like rampired walls the houses lean,
All spired and domed and turreted,
Sheer to the valley's darkling green;
Ranged in mysterious disarray,
The Castle, menacing and austere,
Looms through the lingering last of day;
And in the silver dusk you hear,
Reverberated from crag and scar,
Bold bugles blowing points of war.


W. B. YEATS

## Down by the Salley Gardens

Down by the salley gardens my love and I did meet;
She passed the salley gardens with little snow-white feet.
She bid me take love easy, as the leaves grow on the tree;
But I, being young and foolish, with her would not agree.

In a field by the river my love and I did stand,
And on my leaning shoulder she laid her snow-white hand.
She bid me take life easy, as the grass grows on the weirs;
But I was young and foolish, and now am full of tears.

W. B. YEATS

## *When You Are Old*

When you are old and grey and full of sleep,
And nodding by the fire, take down this book,
And slowly read, and dream of the soft look
Your eyes had once, and of their shadows deep;

How many loved your moments of glad grace,
And loved your beauty with love false or true,
But one man loved the pilgrim soul in you,
And loved the sorrows of your changing face;

And bending down beside the glowing bars,
Murmur, a little sadly, how Love fled
And paced upon the mountains overhead
And hid his face amid a crowd of stars.


J. K. STEPHEN

## *After the Golden Wedding*
### *(Three Soliloquies)*

### I  The Husband's

She's not a faultless woman; no!
   She's not an angel in disguise:
She has her rivals here below:
   She's not an unexampled prize:

She does not always see the point
   Of little jests her husband makes:
And, when the world is out of joint,
   She makes a hundred small mistakes:

She's not a miracle of tact:
   Her temper's not the best I know:
She's got her little faults in fact,
   Although I never tell her so.

But this, my wife, is why I hold you
   As good a wife as ever stepped,
And why I meant it when I told you
   How cordially our feast I kept:

You've lived with me these fifty years,
　　And all the time you loved me dearly:
I may have given you cause for tears:
　　I may have acted rather queerly.

I ceased to love you long ago:
　　I loved another for a season:
As time went on I came to know
　　Your worth, my wife: and saw the reason

Why such a wife as you have been
　　Is more than worth the world beside;
You loved me all the time, my Queen;
　　You couldn't help it if you tried.

You loved me as I once loved you,
　　As each loved each beside the altar:
And whatsoever I might do,
　　Your loyal heart could never falter.

And, if you sometimes fail me, sweetest,
　　And don't appreciate me, dear,
No matter: such defects are meetest
　　For poor humanity, I fear.

And all's forgiven, all's forgot,
　　On this our golden wedding day;
For, see! she loves me: does she not?
　　So let the world e'en go its way.

I'm old and nearly useless now,
　　Each day a greater weakling proves me:
There's compensation anyhow:
　　I still possess a wife that loves me.


### II  The Wife's

Dear worthy husband! good old man!
　　Fit hero of a golden marriage:
I'll show towards you, if I can,
　　An absolutely wifely carriage.

The months or years which your career
　　May still comprise before you perish,
Shall serve to prove that I, my dear,
　　Can honour, and obey, and cherish.

Till death us part, as soon he must,
　　(And you, my dear, should show the way)

I hope you'll always find me just
    The same as on our wedding day.

I never loved you, dearest: never!
    Let that be clearly understood:
I thought you good, and rather clever,
    And found you really rather good.

And, what was more, I loved another,
    But couldn't get him: well, but, then
You're just as bad, my erring brother,
    You most impeccable of men:—

Except for this: my love was married
    Some weeks before I married you:
While you, my amorous dawdler, tarried
    Till we'd been wed a year or two.

You loved me at our wedding: I
    Loved some one else: and after that
I never cast a loving eye
    On others: you—well, tit for tat!

But after all I made you cheerful:
    Your whims I've humoured: saw the point
Of all your jokes: grew duly tearful,
    When you were sad, yet chose the joint

You like the best of all for dinner,
    And soothed you in your hours of woe:
Although a miserable sinner,
    I *am* a good wife, as wives go.

I bore with you and took your side,
    And kept my temper all the time:
I never flirted; never cried,
    Nor ranked it as a heinous crime,

When you preferred another lady,
    Or used improper words to me,
Or told a story more than shady,
    Or snored and snorted after tea,

Or otherwise gave proofs of being
    A dull and rather vain old man:
I still succeeded in agreeing
    With all you said, (the safest plan),

Yet always strove my point to carry,
    And make you do as I desired:

I'm *glad* my people made me marry!
    They hit on just what I required.

Had love been wanted—well, I couldn't
    Have given what I'd not to give;
Or had a genius asked me! wouldn't
    The man have suffered? now, we live

Among our estimable neighbours
    A decent and decorous life:
I've earned by my protracted labours
    The title of a model wife.

But when beneath the turf you're sleeping,
    And I am sitting here in black,
Engaged, as they'll suppose, in weeping,
    I shall not wish to have you back.

### III    The Vicar's

A good old couple! kind and wise!
    And oh! what love for one another!
They've won, those two, life's highest prize,
    Oh! let us copy them, my brother.

SIR ARTHUR QUILLER-COUCH

## The Planted Heel

By Talland Church as I did go,
I passed my kindred all in a row;

Straight and silent there by the spade
Each in his narrow chamber laid.

While I passed, each kinsman's clay
Stole some virtue of mine away:

Till my shoes on the muddy road
Left not a print, so light they trod.

Back I went to the Bearer's Lane,
Begged the dead for my own again.

Answered the eldest one of my line—
'Thy heart was no one's heart but mine.'

The second claimed my working skill,
The third my wit, the fourth my will:

The fifth one said, 'Thy feet I gave;
But want no fleetness here in the grave.'

'For feet a man need have no care,
If they no weight of his own may bear.

'If I own naught by separate birth,
What binds my heel e'en now to the earth?'

The dead together answered back—
'Naught but the wealth in thy knapsack.'

'Nay, then,' said I, 'that's quick to unload':
And strewed my few pence out on the road.

'O kinsmen, now be quick, resume
Each rag of me to its rightful tomb!'

The dead were silent then for a space.
Still I stood upright in my place.

Said one, 'Some strength he will yet conceal.'
'Belike 'tis pride of a planted heel?'

'Man has but one perduring pride:
Of knowledge alone he is justified.

'Lie down, lie down by us in the sod:
Thou shalt be wise in the ways of God.'

'Nay, so I stand upright in the dust,
I'll take God's purposes all on trust.

'An inch of heel for a yard of spine,
So give me again the goods that are mine!'

I planted my heel by their headstones,
And wrestled an hour with my kinsmen's bones.

I shook their dust thrice into a sieve,
And gathered all that they had to give.

I winnowed knowledge out of the heap:
'Take it,' I said, 'to warm your sleep.'

I cast their knowledge back on the sod,
And went on my journey, praising God.

Of all their knowledge I thought me rid:
But one little grain in my pack had hid.

Now, as I go, myself I tell—
'On a planted heel man wrestles well.'

But that little grain keeps whispering me—
'Better, perhaps, on a planted knee.'


THOMAS HARDY

### Friends Beyond

William Dewy, Tranter Reuben, Farmer Ledlow late at plough,
    Robert's kin, and John's, and Ned's,
And the Squire, and Lady Susan, lie in Mellstock churchyard now!

'Gone,' I call them, gone for good, that group of local hearts and heads;
    Yet at mothy curfew-tide,
And at midnight when the noon-heat breathes it back from walls and leads,

They've a way of whispering to me— fellow-wight who yet abide—
    In the muted, measured note
Of a ripple under archways, or a lone cave's stillicide:

'We have triumphed: this achievement turns the bane to antidote,
    Unsuccesses to success,
Many thought-worn eves and morrows to a morrow free of thought.

'No more need we corn and clothing, feel of old terrestrial stress;
    Chill detraction stirs no sigh;
Fear of death has even bygone us: death gave all that we possess.'

*W. D.*—'Ye mid burn the old bass-viol that I set such value by.'
*Squire*—'You may hold the manse in fee,
    You may wed my spouse, may let my children's memory of me die.'

*Lady S.*—'You may have my rich brocades, my laces; take each household key;
    Ransack coffer, desk, bureau;
    Quiz the few poor treasures hid there, con the letters kept by me.'

*Far.*—'Ye mid zell my favourite heifer, ye mid let the charlock grow,
    Foul the grinterns, give up thrift.'
*Far. Wife*—'If ye break my best blue china, children, I shan't care or ho.'

*All*—'We've no wish to hear the tidings, how the people's fortunes shift;
    What your daily doings are;
  Who are wedded, born, divided; if your lives beat slow or swift.

'Curious not the least are we if our intents you make or mar,
    If you quire to our old tune,
  If the City stage still passes, if the weirs still roar afar.'

— Thus, with very gods' composure, freed those crosses late and soon
    Which, in life, the Trine allow
(Why, none witteth), and ignoring all that haps beneath the moon,

William Dewy, Tranter Reuben, Farmer Ledlow late at plough,
    Robert's kin, and John's, and Ned's,
And the Squire, and Lady Susan, murmur mildly to me now.

## SIR HENRY NEWBOLT

### Messmates

He gave us all a good-bye cheerily
    At the first dawn of day;
We dropped him down the side full drearily
    When the light died away.
It's a dead dark watch that he's a-keeping there,
And a long, long night that lags a-creeping there,
Where the Trades and the tides roll over him
    And the great ships go by.

He's there alone with green seas rocking him
    For a thousand miles round;
He's there alone with dumb things mocking him,
    And we're homeward bound.
It's a long, lone watch that he's a-keeping there,
And a dead cold night that lags a-creeping there,
While the months and the years roll over him
    And the great ships go by.

I wonder if the tramps come near enough
    As they thrash to and fro,
And the battle-ships' bells ring clear enough
    To be heard down below;
If through all the lone watch that he's a-keeping there,
And the long, cold night that lags a-creeping there,
The voices of the sailor-men shall comfort him
    When the great ships go by.

W. B. YEATS

## The Ballad of Father Gilligan

The old priest Peter Gilligan
Was weary night and day;
For half his flock were in their beds,
Or under green sods lay.

Once, while he nodded on a chair,
At the moth-hour of eve,
Another poor man sent for him,
And he began to grieve.

'I have no rest, nor joy, nor peace,
For people die and die';
And after cried he, 'God forgive!
My body spake, not I!'

He knelt, and leaning on the chair
He prayed and fell asleep;
And the moth-hour went from the fields,
And stars began to peep.

They slowly into millions grew,
And leaves shook in the wind;
And God covered the world with shade,
And whispered to mankind.

Upon the time of sparrow-chirp
When the moths came once more,
The old priest Peter Gilligan
Stood upright on the floor.

'Mavrone, mavrone! the man has died
While I slept on the chair';
He roused his horse out of its sleep,
And rode with little care.

He rode now as he never rode,
By rocky lane and fen;
The sick man's wife opened the door:
'Father! you come again!'

'And is the poor man dead?' he cried.
'He died an hour ago.'
The old priest Peter Gilligan
In grief swayed to and fro.

'When you were gone, he turned and died
As merry as a bird.'
The old priest Peter Gilligan
He knelt him at that word.

'He Who hath made the night of stars
For souls who tire and bleed,
Sent one of His great angels down
To help me in my need.

'He Who is wrapped in purple robes,
With planets in His care,
Had pity on the least of things
Asleep upon a chair.'


SIR ARTHUR QUILLER-COUCH

## Doom Ferry

Boatman, have they crossed? 'Not all:
   The inn, there, hath an upper chamber,
And a window in the wall
   Where the small white roses clamber.

'Many shelves run round the room;
   On a shelf, and no man near them,
Two are talking low i' the gloom—
   From the trellis' foot may'st hear them.'

Who are they? 'At dawn they came
   By the Passage, calling *Over!*
She the corpse of a comely dame,
   And the man, methinks, her lover.'

Boatman, land and climb the stair:
   By the scented window-boxes
Lower me that loving pair
   Here among the crimson phloxes.

Boatman, is this honey-dew
   Dripping from the window-boxes?
Nay, I cannot tell its hue
   Here against the crimson phloxes.

Take a guinea and a groat:
  One in ale shall keep thee merry;
Let the other fee the boat
  Tiding these across the ferry.

Take this purse: it shall persuade
  Him who digs i' th' acre yonder
Them to bed with a cunning spade
  Cheek by jowl, no turtles fonder.

Cheek by jowl, and heart by heart,
  But a thought in either buried,
That shall push them wide apart—
  Wide enough ere a third be ferried.

So, between, my body I'll thrust,
  Laughing, straightening out my knees there,
Either hand in a little dust
  Dabbling, at my cool dead ease there.


ALICE MEYNELL

## The Roaring Frost

A flock of wings came flying from the North,
Strong birds with fighting pinions driving forth
  With a resounding call:—

Where will they close their wings and cease their cries—
Between what warming seas and conquering skies—
  And fold, and fall?


W. B. YEATS

## The Fiddler of Dooney

When I play on my fiddle in Dooney,
Folk dance like a wave of the sea;
My cousin is priest in Kilvarnet,
My brother in Mocharabuiee.

I passed my brother and cousin:
They read in their books of prayer;
I read in my book of songs
I bought at the Sligo fair.

When we come at the end of time
To Peter sitting in state,
He will smile on the three old spirits,
But call me first through the gate;

For the good are always the merry,
Save by an evil chance,
And the merry love the fiddle,
And the merry love to dance:

And when the folk there spy me,
They will all come up to me,
With 'Here is the fiddler of Dooney!'
And dance like a wave of the sea.

A. E. HOUSMAN

## From *A Shropshire Lad*

### XXI   Bredon Hill

In summertime on Bredon
  The bells they sound so clear;
Round both the shires they ring them
  In steeples far and near,
    A happy noise to hear.

Here of a Sunday morning
  My love and I would lie,
And see the coloured counties,
  And hear the larks so high
    About us in the sky.

The bells would ring to call her
  In valleys miles away:
'Come all to church, good people;
  Good people, come and pray.'
    But here my love would stay.

And I would turn and answer
  Among the springing thyme,

'Oh, peal upon our wedding,
  And we will hear the chime,
  And come to church in time.'

But when the snows at Christmas
  On Bredon top were strown,
My love rose up so early
  And stole out unbeknown
  And went to church alone.

They tolled the one bell only,
  Groom there was none to see,
The mourners followed after,
  And so to church went she,
  And would not wait for me.

The bells they sound on Bredon,
  And still the steeples hum.
'Come all to church, good people,'—
  Oh, noisy bells, be dumb;
  I hear you, I will come.


### XXVII

'Is my team ploughing,
  That I was used to drive
And hear the harness jingle
  When I was man alive?'

Ay, the horses trample,
  The harness jingles now;
No change though you lie under
  The land you used to plough.

'Is football playing
  Along the river shore,
With lads to chase the leather,
  Now I stand up no more?'

Ay, the ball is flying,
  The lads play heart and soul;
The goal stands up, the keeper
  Stands up to keep the goal.

'Is my girl happy,
  That I thought hard to leave,
And has she tired of weeping
  As she lies down at eve?'

Ay, she lies down lightly,
    She lies not down to weep:
Your girl is well contented.
    Be still, my lad, and sleep.

'Is my friend hearty,
    Now I am thin and pine,
And has he found to sleep in
    A better bed than mine?'

Yes, lad, I lie easy,
    I lie as lads would choose;
I cheer a dead man's sweetheart,
    Never ask me whose.


FRANCIS THOMPSON

## At Lord's

It is little I repair to the matches of the Southron folk,
    Though my own red roses there may blow;
It is little I repair to the matches of the Southron folk,
    Though the red roses crest the caps, I know.
For the field is full of shades as I near the shadowy coast,
And a ghostly batsman plays to the bowling of a ghost,
And I look through my tears on a soundless-clapping host
    As the run-stealers flicker to and fro,
        To and fro:—
O my Hornby and my Barlow long ago!


A. C. BENSON

## The Ant-Heap

High in the woodland, on the mountain-side,
    I ponder, half a golden afternoon,
Storing deep strength to battle with the tide
    I must encounter soon.

Absorbed, inquisitive, alert, irate,
  The wiry wood-ants run beneath the pines,
And bustle if a careless footfall grate
  Among their travelled lines.

With prey unwieldy, slain in alien lands,
  When shadows fall aslant, laden they come,
Where, piled of red fir-needles, guarded stands
  Their dry and rustling dome.

They toil for what they know not; rest they shun;
  They nip the soft intruder; when they die
They grapple pain and fate, and ask from none
  The pity they deny.


SIR HENRY NEWBOLT

## He Fell among Thieves

'Ye have robbed,' said he, 'ye have slaughtered and made an end,
  Take your ill-got plunder, and bury the dead:
What will ye more of your guest and sometime friend?'
  'Blood for our blood,' they said.

He laughed: 'If one may settle the score for five,
  I am ready; but let the reckoning stand till day:
I have loved the sunlight as dearly as any alive.'
  'You shall die at dawn,' said they.

He flung his empty revolver down the slope,
  He climbed alone to the Eastward edge of the trees;
All night long in a dream untroubled of hope
  He brooded, clasping his knees.

He did not hear the monotonous roar that fills
  The ravine where the Yassin river sullenly flows;
He did not see the starlight on the Laspur hills,
  Or the far Afghan snows.

He saw the April noon on his books aglow,
  The wistaria trailing in at the window wide;
He heard his father's voice from the terrace below
  Calling him down to ride.

He saw the gray little church across the park,
  The mounds that hide the loved and honoured dead;
The Norman arch, the chancel softly dark,
  The brasses black and red.

He saw the School Close, sunny and green,
  The runner beside him, the stand by the parapet wall,
The distant tape, and the crowd roaring between
  His own name over all.

He saw the dark wainscot and timbered roof,
  The long tables, and the faces merry and keen;
The College Eight and their trainer dining aloof,
  The Dons on the daïs serene.

He watched the liner's stem ploughing the foam,
  He felt her trembling speed and the thrash of her screw;
He heard her passengers' voices talking of home,
  He saw the flag she flew.

And now it was dawn. He rose strong on his feet,
  And strode to his ruined camp below the wood;
He drank the breath of the morning cool and sweet;
  His murderers round him stood.

Light on the Laspur hills was broadening fast,
  The blood-red snow-peaks chilled to a dazzling white:
He turned, and saw the golden circle at last,
  Cut by the Eastern height.

'O glorious Life, Who dwellest in earth and sun,
  I have lived, I praise and adore Thee.'
                              A sword swept.
Over the pass the voices one by one
  Faded, and the hill slept.

OSCAR WILDE

# From *The Ballad of Reading Gaol*

IV

There is no chapel on the day
    On which they hang a man:
The Chaplain's heart is far too sick,
    Or his face is far too wan,
Or there is that written in his eyes
    Which none should look upon.

So they kept us close till nigh on noon,
    And then they rang the bell,
And the Warders with their jingling keys
    Opened each listening cell,
And down the iron stair we tramped,
    Each from his separate Hell.

Out into God's sweet air we went,
    But not in wonted way,
For this man's face was white with fear,
    And that man's face was grey,
And I never saw sad men who looked
    So wistfully at the day.

I never saw sad men who looked
    With such a wistful eye
Upon that little tent of blue
    We prisoners called the sky,
And at every careless cloud that passed
    In happy freedom by.

But there were those amongst us all
    Who walked with downcast head,
And knew that, had each got his due,
    They should have died instead:
He had but killed a thing that lived,
    Whilst they had killed the dead.

For he who sins a second time
    Wakes a dead soul to pain,
And draws it from its spotted shroud,
    And makes it bleed again,
And makes it bleed great gouts of blood,
    And makes it bleed in vain!

.    .    .    .    .

Like ape or clown, in monstrous garb
  With crooked arrows starred,
Silently we went round and round,
  The slippery asphalte yard;
Silently we went round and round
  And no man spoke a word.

Silently we went round and round,
  And through each hollow mind
The Memory of dreadful things
  Rushed like a dreadful wind,
And Horror stalked before each man,
  And Terror crept behind.

                .   .   .   .   .

The Warders strutted up and down,
  And kept their herd of brutes,
Their uniforms were spick and span,
  And they wore their Sunday suits,
But we knew the work they had been at,
  By the quicklime on their boots.

For where a grave had opened wide,
  There was no grave at all:
Only a stretch of mud and sand
  By the hideous prison-wall,
And a little heap of burning lime,
  That the man should have his pall.

For he has a pall, this wretched man,
  Such as few men can claim:
Deep down below a prison-yard,
  Naked for greater shame,
He lies, with fetters on each foot,
  Wrapt in a sheet of flame!

And all the while the burning lime
  Eats flesh and bone away,
It eats the brittle bone by night,
  And the soft flesh by day,
It eats the flesh and bone by turns,
  But it eats the heart alway.

                .   .   .   .   .

For three long years they will not sow
  Or root or seedling there:
For three long years the unblessed spot
  Will sterile be and bare,

And look upon the wondering sky
  With unreproachful stare.

They think a murderer's heart would taint
  Each simple seed they sow.
It is not true! God's kindly earth
  Is kindlier than men know,
And the red rose would but blow more red,
  The white rose whiter blow.

Out of his mouth a red, red rose!
  Out of his heart a white!
For who can say by what strange way,
  Christ brings His will to light,
Since the barren staff the pilgrim bore
  Bloomed in the great Pope's sight?

But neither milk-white rose nor red
  May bloom in prison air;
The shard, the pebble, and the flint,
  Are what they give us there:
For flowers have been known to heal
  A common man's despair.

So never will wine-red rose or white,
  Petal by petal, fall
On that stretch of mud and sand that lies
  By the hideous prison-wall,
To tell the men who tramp the yard
  That God's Son died for all.

·  ·  ·  ·  ·

Yet though the hideous prison-wall
  Still hems him round and round,
And a spirit may not walk by night
  That is with fetters bound,
And a spirit may but weep that lies
  In such unholy ground,

He is at peace—this wretched man—
  At peace, or will be soon:
There is no thing to make him mad,
  Nor does Terror walk at noon,
For the lampless Earth in which he lies
  Has neither Sun nor Moon.

They hanged him as a beast is hanged:
    They did not even toll
A requiem that might have brought
    Rest to his startled soul,
But hurriedly they took him out,
    And hid him in a hole.

They stripped him of his canvas clothes,
    And gave him to the flies:
They mocked the swollen purple throat,
    And the stark and staring eyes:
And with laughter loud they heaped the shroud
    In which their convict lies.

The Chaplain would not kneel to pray
    By his dishonoured grave:
Nor mark it with that blessed Cross
    That Christ for sinners gave,
Because the man was one of those
    Whom Christ came down to save.

Yet all is well; he has but passed
    To life's appointed bourne:
And alien tears will fill for him
    Pity's long-broken urn,
For his mourners will be outcast men,
    And outcasts always mourn.

THOMAS HARDY

## The Impercipient
### (At a Cathedral Service)

That with this bright believing band
    I have no claim to be,
That faiths by which my comrades stand
    Seem fantasies to me,
And mirage-mists their Shining Land,
    Is a strange destiny.

Why thus my soul should be consigned
    To infelicity,
Why always I must feel as blind
    To sights my brethren see,

Why joys they've found I cannot find,
   Abides a mystery.

Since heart of mine knows not that ease
   Which they know; since it be
That He who breathes All's Well to these
   Breathes no All's-Well to me,
My lack might move their sympathies
   And Christian charity!

I am like a gazer who should mark
   An inland company
Standing upfingered, with, 'Hark! hark!
   The glorious distant sea!'
And feel, 'Alas, 'tis but yon dark
   And wind-swept pine to me!'

Yet I would bear my shortcomings
   With meet tranquillity,
But for the charge that blessed things
   I'd liefer not have be.
O, doth a bird deprived of wings
   Go earth-bound wilfully!

     .  .  .  .

Enough. As yet disquiet clings
   About us. Rest shall we.


JOHN DAVIDSON

## The Price

Terrible is the price
   Of beginning anew, of birth;
For Death has loaded dice.

Men hurry and hide like mice;
   But they cannot evade the Earth,
And Life, Death's fancy price.

A blossom once or twice,
   Love lights on Summer's hearth;
But Winter loads the dice.

In jangling shackles of ice,
    Ragged and bleeding, Mirth
Pays the Piper's price.

The dance is done in a trice:
    Death belts his bony girth;
And struts, and rattles his dice.

Let Virtue play or Vice,
    Beside his sombre firth
Life is the lowest price
Death wins with loaded dice.

THOMAS HARDY

## Wessex Heights

There are some heights in Wessex, shaped as if by a kindly hand
For thinking, dreaming, dying on, and at crises when I stand,
Say, on Ingpen Beacon eastward, or on Wylls-Neck westwardly,
I seem where I was before my birth, and after death may be.

In the lowlands I have no comrade, not even the lone man's friend—
Her who suffereth long and is kind; accepts what he is too weak to mend:
Down there they are dubious and askance; there nobody thinks as I,
But mind-chains do not clank where one's next neighbour is the sky.

In the towns I am tracked by phantoms having weird detective ways—
Shadows of beings who fellowed with myself of earlier days:
They hang about at places, and they say harsh heavy things—
Men with a wintry sneer, and women with tart disparagings.

Down there I seem to be false to myself, my simple self that was,
And is not now, and I see him watching, wondering what crass cause
Can have merged him into such a strange continuator as this,
Who yet has something in common with himself, my chrysalis.

I cannot go to the great grey Plain; there's a figure against the moon,
Nobody sees it but I, and it makes my breast beat out of tune;
I cannot go to the tall-spired town, being barred by the forms now passed
For everybody but me, in whose long vision they stand there fast.

There's a ghost at Yell'ham Bottom chiding loud at the fall of the night,
There's a ghost in Froom-side Vale, thin-lipped and vague, in a shroud of
    white,

There is one in the railway-train whenever I do not want it near,
I see its profile against the pane, saying what I would not hear.

As for one rare fair woman, I am now but a thought of hers,
I enter her mind and another thought succeeds me that she prefers;
Yet my love for her in its fulness she herself even did not know;
Well, time cures hearts of tenderness, and now I can let her go.

So I am found on Ingpen Beacon, or on Wylls-Neck to the west,
Or else on homely Bulbarrow, or little Pilsdon Crest,
Where men have never cared to haunt, nor women have walked with me,
And ghosts then keep their distance; and I know some liberty.


W. E. HENLEY

## Ballade of Dead Actors

### I. M.
### Edward John Henley (1861–1898)

Where are the passions they essayed,
And where the tears they made to flow?
Where the wild humours they portrayed
For laughing worlds to see and know?
Othello's wrath and Juliet's woe?
Sir Peter's whims and Timon's gall?
And Millamant and Romeo?
Into the night go one and all.

Where are the braveries, fresh or frayed?
The plumes, the armours—friend and foe?
The cloth of gold, the rare brocade,
The mantles glittering to and fro?
The pomp, the pride, the royal show?
The cries of war and festival?
The youth, the grace, the charm, the glow?
Into the night go one and all.

The curtain falls, the play is played:
The Beggar packs beside the Beau;
The Monarch troops, and troops the Maid;
The Thunder huddles with the Snow.

Where are the revellers high and low?
The clashing swords? The lover's call?
The dancers gleaming row on row?
Into the night go one and all.


*Envoy*

Prince, in one common overthrow
The Hero tumbles with the Thrall:
As dust that drives, as straws that blow,
Into the night go one and all.


THOMAS HARDY

## The Darkling Thrush


I leant upon a coppice gate
    When Frost was spectre-gray,
And Winter's dregs made desolate
    The weakening eye of day.
The tangled bine-stems scored the sky
    Like strings of broken lyres,
And all mankind that haunted nigh
    Had sought their household fires.

The land's sharp features seemed to be
    The Century's corpse outleant,
His crypt the cloudy canopy,
    The wind his death-lament.
The ancient pulse of germ and birth
    Was shrunken hard and dry,
And every spirit upon earth
    Seemed fervourless as I.

At once a voice arose among
    The bleak twigs overhead
In a full-hearted evensong
    Of joy illimited;
An aged thrush, frail, gaunt, and small,
    In blast-beruffled plume,
Had chosen thus to fling his soul
    Upon the growing gloom.

So little cause for carolings
    Of such ecstatic sound
Was written on terrestrial things
    Afar or nigh around,
That I could think there trembled through
    His happy good-night air
Some blessed Hope, whereof he knew
    And I was unaware.

# Biographical and Explanatory Notes

GRANT ALLEN (1848–1899). Born in Canada, but educated in France and England (Merton College, Oxford). He was a scientist and writer, and most of his publications were in the field of evolutionary science.

MATTHEW ARNOLD (1822–1888). Son of Thomas Arnold, the great headmaster of Rugby School; educated at Rugby, and Balliol College, Oxford. He became an Inspector of Schools in 1851, and was Professor of Poetry at Oxford, 1857–67. His work includes poetry, literary criticism, social criticism (*Culture and Anarchy*, 1869), and religious criticism (*Literature and Dogma*, 1873).

'Marguerite' has been identified as Mary Claude, the daughter of a French family settled in Germany (see Park Honan, *Matthew Arnold*, London 1981).

'Stanzas from the Grande Chartreuse'. Arnold visited the Grande Chartreuse during his honeymoon with Frances Lucy Wightman in 1851. The rigorous teachers are Carlyle and Goethe, among others (see *Arnold, The Complete Poems*, ed. Kenneth Allott; 2nd Edn, ed. Miriam Allott, London 1979, p. 304).

'The Scholar-Gipsy'. Arnold took the story from Joseph Glanvill, *The Vanity of Dogmatizing*, 1661, although he modifies it to suit his own purposes. In Glanvill the student has to leave the university because of his poverty, and attaches himself to the gipsies; he then uses the opportunity to practise some early sociology.

THOMAS ASHE (1836–1889). Born at Stockport, the son of a clergyman, and educated at St John's College, Cambridge. He became a schoolmaster at Leamington and Ipswich, and later a man of letters in Paris and London. He edited an edition of the poems and prose works of Coleridge.

WILLIAM BARNES (1801–1886). Born at Sturminster Newton, Dorset, and educated in Dorchester. He became a country schoolmaster, and later a vicar at Winterbourne Came, near Dorchester. He was a remarkable scholar and innovator, whose poetry was influenced by Persian and Welsh metrical patterns, such as the Welsh *cynghanedd*. 'Be'mi'ster' is Beaminster in Dorset; the poems to his wife, Julia, celebrate the happiness of the marriage and his grief at her death in 1852.

A.C. BENSON (1862–1925). Arthur Christopher Benson was educated at Eton, and King's College, Cambridge. He was a master at Eton, 1885–1903, then Fellow and subsequently Master of Magdalene College, Cambridge.

ROBERT BRIDGES (1844–1930). Educated at Eton, Corpus Christi College, Oxford, and later at St Bartholomew's Hospital. Bridges was a hospital physician until 1882, when he retired to devote himself to writing. He was appointed Poet Laureate in 1913.

ANNE BRONTË (1820–1849). The youngest of the Brontë sisters, author of *The Tenant of Wildfell Hall* and *Agnes Grey*. Her poems have been edited by Edward Chitham (London, 1979), who dates the poems selected here between 1842 and 1846.

EMILY JANE BRONTË (1818–1848). The most strong-willed and imaginative of the Brontë sisters; her passion for the moors near Haworth is reflected in *Wuthering Heights*. 'R. Alcona to J. Brenzaida' is a Gondal poem, arising from the imagined world of Gondal created by the Brontë sisters in childhood. It is sometimes called 'Remembrance', its title when first published in *Poems* by Currer, Ellis and Acton Bell (1846), names concealing the sex and authorship of Charlotte, Emily and Anne. Emily's poems have been edited by C. W. Hatfield (New York, 1941); according to Charlotte, 'No coward soul is mine' was the last poem written by Emily before her death from consumption.

ROBERT BROUGH (1828–1860). Journalist, playwright, and poet. His *Songs of the Governing Classes* (1855), from which 'My Lord Tomnoddy' is taken, was a satirical attack upon vanity, wealth, and inherited power.

ELIZABETH BARRETT BROWNING (1806–1861). Throughout her lifetime Mrs Browning was a more famous poet than her husband. Her secret marriage to Robert Browning and her elopement with him to Italy rescued her from the life of an overprotected invalid in the care of her possessive father. The Brownings lived in Italy, mainly in Florence, until her death. 'The Cry of the Children' was inspired by reports of a Parliamentary Commission to inquire into the employment of children in factories; 'Sonnets from the Portuguese' was a set of love poems written to Robert Browning before the marriage.

ROBERT BROWNING (1812–1889). Born at Camberwell, London, the son of dissenting parents. He married Elizabeth Barrett in 1846, and they lived in Italy until her death in 1861. Thereafter he returned to England, and lived in London. His unusual and original manner delayed recognition by his contemporaries; he later became revered as a moral philosopher and ethical teacher. Of 'The Bishop Orders His Tomb at St Praxed's Church' Ruskin said, 'I know of no other piece of modern English, prose or poetry, in which there is so much told, as in these lines, of the Renaissance spirit.' There is a church of S. Prassede in Rome, but it has no tombs resembling those in the poem. Browning had a liking for imaginative reconstructions of history, especially if they were connected with minor, forgotten figures. Baldassare Galuppi, for instance, was a lesser Venetian composer (1706–85). Fra Filippo Lippi lived from 1412 to 1469. The details of his life are taken from one of Browning's favourite source books, Vasari's *Lives of the Painters*. Other references to painters in the poem include those to Fra Angelico ('Brother Angelico'), Lorenzo Monaco ('Brother Lorenzo') and Masaccio ('Guidi' or 'Hulking Tom'; he was actually born before Fra Filippo Lippi, in 1401). It is not difficult to see why Browning was attracted to Fra Filippo Lippi as a subject: the impish charm of his angels and child figures is unusual in the Renaissance.

WATHEN MARK WILKS CALL (1817–1890). Educated at Cambridge, he became a clergyman, resigning because of doubt in 1856.

C. S. CALVERLEY (1831–1884). After a brilliant career at Harrow, Oxford and Cambridge, Charles Stuart Calverley was called to the Bar in 1865; but in the winter of 1866–7 he had a skating accident, from which he never fully recovered. He published *Fly Leaves*, a collection of light verse and parodies, in 1872.

LEWIS CARROLL (1832–1898). The pen name of Charles Lutwidge Dodgson, educated at Rugby and Christ Church, Oxford, and lecturer in Mathematics in the University of Oxford, 1855–81. Author of children's books (*Alice's Adventures in Wonderland*, 1865; *Through the Looking Glass*, 1872) and mathematical works.

JOHN CLARE (1793–1864). Northamptonshire peasant-poet, born at Helpston, near Peterborough, and deeply attached to the local countryside. Much of his best poetry dates from before the Victorian period, including *The Village Minstrel* (1821), and *The Shepherd's Calendar* (1827), in which a countryman's experience of work and weather is combined with a marvellous sensitivity to nature. During the 1830s he became mentally ill, and after a period in an asylum in Essex he was sent to the hospital in Northampton. The poems in this volume date from the 1840s, and have an intensity which is remarkable, even unique. A 'clock-a-clay' is a ladybird.

ARTHUR HUGH CLOUGH (1819–1861). Educated at Rugby (where he was 'the best goal-keeper on record' and 'one of the first swimmers of his day') and Balliol College, Oxford. Became Fellow of Oriel College, resigning in 1848 because of doubts about the Thirty-nine Articles. After resigning he travelled to Italy, where he witnessed Garibaldi's defence of the Roman Republic; this gave rise to 'Say not the struggle' and 'Amours de Voyage'. The latter is a brilliant informal poem, with Claude and the Trevellyns as English tourists. Claude has Murray's *Handbook to Rome* as a guide; finding the Corso (the main street) and the Via Condotti (which crosses it) empty, he goes to the Pincian Hill for a spectator's view of the battle taking place on the other side of the city. In letter VII, the killing of the man in the street is effectively linked with the memories of the French Revolution, and contrasted with the 'quidnuncs' (gossips) at Monaldini's (a bookseller in the Piazza di Spagna, who had reading rooms for tourists to look at newspapers and exchange information).

EDWARD JAMES MORTIMER COLLINS (1827–1876). Born at Plymouth, he became a schoolmaster at Queen Elizabeth's College, Guernsey, and a professional writer in later years. He was a poet and essayist, but wore himself out by the writing of romantic novels to make a living.

HUGH CONWAY (1847–1885). The pen name of Frederick John Fargus, born in Bristol, novelist and auctioneer. As a young man he wanted to be a sailor, and ran away from home to serve in the school frigate *Conway*; parental pressure, and the subsequent claims of the family business, prevented him from becoming a seaman. Interest in Falkland was considerable during the 1870s, when there was a public appeal to raise the monument which now stands to him at Newbury, where he fell in 1643. Matthew Arnold wrote an essay on him in 1877, in which he said: 'If we are to find a martyr in the history of the Great Civil War, let it be Falkland . . .'

WILLIAM CORY (1823–1892). Born in Devon, educated at Eton and King's College, Cambridge; schoolmaster at Eton, 1847–71.

JOHN DAVIDSON (1857–1909). Born at Barrhead, near Glasgow; was a laboratory assistant, pupil-teacher and clerk in Greenock and Glasgow. 'In a Music Hall' refers to his time as a clerk in a thread firm, 1884–5. Lived in London from 1890, supporting himself by writing articles, many of them for the *Glasgow Herald*.

AUSTIN DOBSON (1840–1921). Born at Plymouth, and educated in England and on the Continent. He became a civil servant at the Board of Trade, and a writer of delicate society verse.

DIGBY MACKWORTH DOLBEN (1848–1867). Educated at Eton; became strongly influenced by Roman Catholicism; drowned in the River Welland, 1867.

EDWARD DOWDEN (1843–1913). Professor of English, University of Dublin; writer of many critical books, including *Shakespeare: His Mind and Art* (1875).

ERNEST DOWSON (1867–1900). Educated in England and on the Continent, he went up to Queen's College, Oxford, but did not take a degree. He lived an irregular and bohemian life in London, and was one of the founder members of the Rhymers' Club (together with Lionel Johnson and W. B. Yeats) which met at the Cheshire Cheese, a public house in the Strand in London.

GEORGE ELIOT (1819–1880). The pen name of Mary Ann Evans, daughter of the agent for the Arbury estate, near Nuneaton. She was greatly influenced by Evangelical Christianity as a child, reacting against it to become an agnostic. She became sub-editor of the *Westminster Review*, and lived with George Henry Lewes, a man of letters and writer on scientific subjects, from 1853 until his death in 1878. Her great novels include *Adam Bede*, *The Mill on the Floss* and *Middlemarch*.

JOHN ELLERTON (1826–1893). Hymn writer and translator, born in London and educated at Trinity College, Cambridge. Rector of Barnes, 1876, and of White Roding, Essex, 1886.

SEBASTIAN EVANS (1830–1909). Born at Market Bosworth, Leicestershire, and educated at Emmanuel College, Cambridge; designer of stained glass, poet, journalist (editor of the *Birmingham Daily Gazette*, 1867–70), and barrister.

EDWARD FITZGERALD (1809–1883). Born in Suffolk, educated at Trinity College, Cambridge, where he was a friend of Richard Monckton Milnes and of Thackeray; later a friend of Carlyle and Tennyson. FitzGerald was very interested in oriental poetry, encouraged by his Ipswich friend E. B. Cowell, who became Professor of Sanskrit at Cambridge and who introduced Fitz-

Gerald to the work of Omar Khayyám. Omar Khayyám lived at Naishápúr, *c*.1060–1120. His *Rubáiyát*, or quatrains, are 158 in number, from which FitzGerald selected and made his own arrangement.

RICHARD GARNETT (1835–1906). Born at Lichfield, and privately educated; entered the British Museum service as an assistant in 1851, and worked his way up to become Superintendent of the Reading Room, and Keeper of Printed Books.

WILLIAM SCHWENK GILBERT (1836–1911). Educated at London University. Clerk in the Privy Council office, and barrister; collaborated with Sir Arthur Sullivan in the famous series of comic operas performed 1875–96, after 1881 at the Savoy Theatre.

EDMUND GOSSE (1845–1928). Son of an eminent zoologist, and author of *Father and Son*. Poet and man of letters; Librarian of the House of Lords, 1904–14.

DAVID GRAY (1838–1861). Born near Glasgow, the son of a handloom weaver; educated at the local school and at Glasgow University. Went to London to try to become a man of letters, and was befriended by Richard Monckton Milnes; but he became ill, returned to Scotland, and died.

DORA GREENWELL (1812–1882). Born at Lanchester, County Durham, daughter of a magistrate and Deputy Lieutenant of the County. She lived in Durham, 1854–71, and later in London. Hymn-writer and poet, she also wrote essays on social and medical questions.

THOMAS HARDY (1840–1928). Born in Dorset, and studied under a local architect, John Hicks. After a period in London, 1862–67, he returned to Dorset, and was employed by Hicks on church restoration; during one of these commissions, in Cornwall, he met Emma Gifford, who became his wife. Hardy's great novels were written between 1870 and 1896, when *Jude the Obscure* was published; he was writing poetry at the same time, although the full flowering of his poetic genius came in 1912–13, with the poems written in remorse and recollection after Emma's death.

ROBERT STEPHEN HAWKER (1803–1875). Vicar of Morwenstow, in north-east Cornwall; known as 'the sailor's friend' because of his willingness to pay for the burial of drowned seamen. His poetry is often concerned with local feeling and legend ('And Shall Trelawny die?', 1824); he is credited with having invented the Harvest Festival. The setting and inspiration of 'The Quest of the Sangraal' is Tintagel ('Dundagel'), the ruined castle on the north coast of Cornwall reputed to have been the palace of King Arthur. The Holy Grail (the 'Sangraal') was the cup used at the Last Supper, supposedly brought to England by Joseph of Arimathea. King Arthur speaks of evil times which have come over England, quoting the words of Merlin: 'Anathema' (a place accursed). The poem contains some remote legends and symbols: Sarras was the city where the shield of the Knight of the Quest was kept; Igdrasil is the mystic tree, the ash of Celtic ritual; the Raun is the mountain ash, another magic tree; the points of the compass depend on traditional readings of the crucifixion and burial of Christ – he was crucified facing westward, which is therefore the region of the people, and he was buried with his head towards the west, so that his right hand gave symbolic greeting to the south and his left hand gave a fatal aspect to the north.

W. E. HENLEY (1849–1903). William Ernest Henley was born at Gloucester, educated at the Crypt Grammar School; a cripple from boyhood, he spent some time at Edinburgh under the care of Joseph Lister. He became a friend of Robert Louis Stevenson, and was later the editor of various magazines and newspapers, notably the *Scots Observer* (later the *National Observer*).

THOMAS HOOD (1799–1845). Born in London, and apprenticed to an engraver; became a sub-editor of the *London Magazine*, but was forced to flee to the Continent on the failure of a business venture. He hoped to free himself from debt there, but was dogged by ill-health. He returned to England in 1840, becoming editor of the *New Monthly Magazine* and of a magazine established by himself, but died not long after its foundation.

GERARD MANLEY HOPKINS (1844–1889). Born at Stratford, East London, educated at Highgate School and Balliol College, Oxford. In 1866 he was converted to Roman Catholicism, and in 1868 he became a Jesuit novice. He burned his poetry as an act of voluntary sacrifice and wrote no more until 1875, when he was encouraged by his Superior to write 'The Wreck of the Deutschland'. It was rejected by *The Month*, the Roman Catholic magazine to which Hopkins sent it, presumably because it was too original; and during his lifetime almost the only readers of Hopkins's poetry were Robert Bridges and R. W. Dixon, a Canon of Carlisle. Bridges printed the poems for the first time in 1918. Hopkins served as a priest in several parishes, and taught classics at Stonyhurst School; he was appointed Professor at University College, Dublin, where he died of typhoid in 1889.

A. E. HOUSMAN (1859–1936). Alfred Edward Housman was educated at Bromsgrove School and St John's College, Oxford. He was a clerk in the Patent Office, London, 1882–92, Professor of Latin, University College, London, 1892–1911, and Professor of Latin at Cambridge from 1911 onwards. *A Shropshire Lad*, written when Housman was living in lodgings in London, expresses a deep love for his native country of the Welsh marches, and a poignant sense of human frailty.

JEAN INGELOW (1820–1897). Born at Boston, Lincolnshire, and subsequently lived in Ipswich and London. She also wrote novels and children's stories.

LIONEL JOHNSON (1867–1902). Educated at Winchester and New College, Oxford, where he was influenced by Walter Pater. He became a Roman Catholic in 1891. He died from a fractured skull after a fall.

CHARLES KINGSLEY (1819–1875). Born in Devon, educated at various schools and Magdalene College, Cambridge. Became vicar of Eversley, Hampshire. He was greatly influenced by Carlyle and F. D. Maurice, the Christian Socialist; his novels *Yeast* and *Alton Locke* show a strong sympathy with the agricultural labourer and the poor artisan. He was a fine athlete, and *The Saturday Review* called his ideas 'muscular Christianity'; he had a strong enthusiasm for nature, and embraced Darwinism, believing it to be tenable alongside Christianity.

RUDYARD KIPLING (1865–1936). Born in Bombay; educated at United Services College, Westward Ho!, Devon. Returned to India, and became assistant editor, *Civil and Military Gazette*, Lahore. Kipling was a prolific writer of stories and poems about India, the army, and the empire. He settled in London in 1889, and later in Sussex. He was awarded the Nobel Prize for Literature in 1907. His son was killed in the Great War, and much of Kipling's later energy was given to the work of the Imperial War Graves Commission.

ANDREW LANG (1844–1912). Educated at Edinburgh Academy, St Andrews University, and Balliol College, Oxford: scholar, folklorist, poet, and man of letters. He was a prolific journalist, interested in a variety of subjects including history and anthropology, with a special love of Scotland and Sir Walter Scott.

EDWARD LEAR (1812–1888). Born in London; he was an artist, employed as a draughtsman in the Zoological Society gardens, with special interest in birds. After 1837 he lived in Rome, where he became a drawing master; he also travelled widely, visiting India and Albania to paint landscapes. He died in San Remo. His *Book of Nonsense* was written for the grandchildren of the Earl of Derby when Lear was in the service of the Earl at Knowsley.

ROBERT LEIGHTON (1822–1869). Born at Dundee, and educated there. His brother was a shipowner, and Leighton travelled round the world in 1842–3. He later worked at Preston for the London and North Western Railway, and then at Ayr for a Liverpool firm.

WILLIAM JAMES LINTON (1812–1888). Educated at Stratford, East London, and apprenticed to a wood-engraver. Linton was a minor William Morris, with a similar versatility and a radical commitment to Socialism. He was a republican, and a friend of the Italian patriot Mazzini; he founded a monthly journal, *The English Republican*, and also established a private press; and he continued to be in great demand as a wood-engraver for magazines such as the *Illustrated London News*.

HENRY FRANCIS LYTE (1793–1847). Born at Ednam in the Scottish Borders, the son of an army officer; educated in Ireland, at Portora Royal School and Trinity College, Dublin. He took Holy Orders in 1815, and in 1823 he was appointed Perpetual Curate of Lower Brixham, Devon. He wrote other well-known hymns, such as 'Praise my soul, the King of Heaven'.

EDWARD ROBERT BULWER LYTTON (1831–1892). Only son of the novelist, he was educated at Harrow, and abroad. He had a distinguished career in the Diplomatic Service, becoming Ambassador to Paris and Viceroy of India. Created Earl of Lytton, 1880.

GEORGE MACDONALD (1824–1905). Born Huntly, Aberdeenshire, educated at King's College, Aberdeen. He was a preacher and religious writer, author of *Phantastes* (1858).

CHARLES MACKAY (1814–1889). Born at Perth, and educated in London and abroad. He was assistant editor of the *Morning Chronicle*, 1835–44, and subsequently editor of the *Illustrated London News*. There were outbreaks of cholera in London in 1849 and again in 1854.

WILLIAM HURRELL MALLOCK (1849–1923). Born in Devon, educated privately and at Balliol College, Oxford. He is best known as the author of *The New Republic* (1877), a dialogue in the Socratic manner which satirizes English society and ideas.

PHILIP BOURKE MARSTON (1850–1887). Born in London, the only son of John Westland Marston, a dramatist and poet. At the age of three he went blind; he enjoyed the company and friendship of many poets, including James Thomson, Swinburne, and Rossetti.

GERALD MASSEY (1828–1907). Born near Tring in a hut, the son of a canal boatman. He was sent to work in a silk mill at the age of eight, and later became an errand-boy in London. He joined the Chartist movement, and also became associated with the Christian Socialists under F. D. Maurice; subsequently he became a poet and radical journalist. George Eliot is thought to have based some features of Felix Holt on Massey.

GEORGE MEREDITH (1828–1909). Born and educated in Portsmouth, the son of a tailor. Articled to a lawyer in London, he began writing as a poet and journalist, and later as a novelist. His failed marriage to Mary Ellen Nicholls, widowed daughter of Thomas Love Peacock, is chronicled in 'Modern Love', a series of sonnets; elsewhere in his verse and novels Meredith celebrates a union with nature which anticipates Richard Jefferies and D. H. Lawrence, as he does in 'Love in the Valley'.

ALICE MEYNELL (1847–1922). Born at Barnes; in 1877 she married Wilfred Meynell, editor and writer. They were friendly with many writers, and rescued Francis Thompson from poverty and neglect. Alice Meynell published essays, two books, and poems.

RICHARD MONCKTON MILNES (1809–1885). Educated at Trinity College, Cambridge, where he was a friend of Arthur Hallam and Alfred Tennyson. Member of Parliament and man of letters, editor of *The Life and Letters of John Keats* (1848); created Lord Houghton, 1863. In his *Life* of Scott, Lockhart observed that during his last journey to Italy in 1832, 'the only very lively curiosity' shown by Scott in Rome was for relics of Prince Charles Edward and his father, and for their tomb in St Peter's.

WILLIAM MORRIS (1834–1896). Born at Walthamstow, educated at Exeter College, Oxford, where he met Edward Burne-Jones; subsequently articled to the established architect G. E. Street, but left Street's office to become a painter. With Rossetti, Burne-Jones and others, decorated the walls of the Oxford Union Society's debating hall. Morris was a man of immense energy, talent and versatility: he was also writing poetry, and published *The Defence of Guenevere and other Poems* in 1857. In 1861 he established a firm of decorators and manufacturers, based on the principles of good design and proper craftsmanship, believing that industrialization had led to dehumanized life and art. He was an active Socialist, becoming leader of the Socialist League; he continued to write poetry (including the voluminous *The Earthly Paradise*, and translations from Scandinavian literature); and he started the Kelmscott Press, to revive the art of good printing and bookmaking.

ROBERT F. MURRAY (1863–1894). The son of a Scottish Unitarian minister, his childhood was spent in different places: he was educated at Crewkerne Grammar School and St Andrews University. He attempted to become a man of letters, but was hampered by his reluctance to leave St Andrews; he did some proof reading and journalism, but his health was never good, and he died young.

SIR HENRY NEWBOLT (1862–1938). Born at Bilston, Staffs, educated at Clifton and Corpus Christi College, Oxford; he was called to the Bar in 1887 and practised law for twelve years. Later he became a full-time writer, and edited the *Monthly Review*, 1900–4. He was an expert on naval matters, and wrote two volumes of the official *History of the Great War: Naval Operations*; his spirited poems of naval history ('Drake's Drum') and of school and army life ('Vitaï Lampada') are only a part of his many-sided work.

GEORGE OUTRAM (1805–1856). Born near Glasgow, but moved to Leith as a child, and educated at the University of Edinburgh. He was called to the Scottish Bar, and practised as a lawyer; he became editor of the *Glasgow Herald* in 1837.

FRANCIS TURNER PALGRAVE (1824–1897). Born at Great Yarmouth, educated at Charterhouse and Balliol College, Oxford. Examiner and Assistant Secretary, Ministry of Education; friend of Tennyson, Arnold, Clough, and others. His selection of lyric poetry, *The Golden Treasury*, appeared in 1861: it became the most celebrated anthology of its day. He was Professor of Poetry at Oxford, 1885–95.

COVENTRY PATMORE (1823–1896). Born at Woodford in Essex, the son of Peter George Patmore, a friend of Hazlitt and Lamb. He became an assistant in the printed book department of the British Museum, and during this period he was a friend of Ruskin, the Pre-Raphaelites, and Tennyson (Patmore rescued the 'butcher's book' containing the MS of *In Memoriam* when Tennyson left it behind in his old lodgings). In 1847 he married Emily Augusta Andrews, and the marriage was a very happy one: *The Angel in the House* celebrates the delights of married love, combining a sublime and mystical view of love with informal and intimate domesticity. After his wife's death in 1862, Patmore married again and settled in Sussex. He became a Roman Catholic in 1864, and a friend and correspondent of Gerard Manley Hopkins and Francis Thompson. He was an expert on the subject of metre and prosody.

HENRY CHOLMONDELEY PENNELL (1836–1915). Son of Sir Charles Henry Pennell, he became a civil servant, specializing in Egyptian affairs and later becoming an inspector of fisheries. He was a writer on angling topics, and editor of the *Fisherman's Magazine and Review*, 1864–5; he was a contributor to *Punch*, and a noted writer of light verse.

SIR ARTHUR QUILLER-COUCH (1863–1944). Born at Bodmin, Cornwall, and educated at Clifton and Trinity College, Oxford. He settled in London as a writer and journalist, moving to Fowey in 1892. He edited *The Oxford Book of English Verse* (1900), and was appointed King Edward VII Professor of English Literature at Cambridge in 1912.

CHRISTINA ROSSETTI (1830–1894). Daughter of Gabriele Rossetti, an Italian patriot who had been forced to leave Naples after rebellions in 1820 and 1821; he became a teacher of Italian in London, and subsequently Professor of Italian at King's College, London. Christina lived a devout and uneventful life, which was shaped in part by her Anglican religion: she rejected two suitors, one (James Collinson) because he was a Roman Catholic, the other (C. B. Cayley) because he was an agnostic.

DANTE GABRIEL ROSSETTI (1828–1882). Elder brother of Christina; he studied under several painters, including Ford Madox Brown, but lacked the patience and discipline to complete an adequate training; instead he founded the Pre-Raphaelite Brotherhood, together with Holman Hunt, Millais, and four others (1848). This movement was a revolt against the academic style of much Victorian painting, and it called (as such movements usually do) for a return to nature; in particular it preferred the simplicity of early Italian art to the high Renaissance style of Raphael and the Bolognese school. It was a literary as well as a pictorial movement, with a short-lived magazine entitled *The Germ* (1850). 'The Blessed Damozel' first appeared in it; the celebrated painting by Rossetti dates from much later. In 1850 Rossetti met Elizabeth Siddal, a beautiful girl who became a Pre-Raphaelite model and later Rossetti's wife. She died in 1862, and Rossetti, grief-stricken, placed his poems in her grave. They were disinterred in 1869, and formed part of the volume of poems which Rossetti published in 1870. *The House of Life* is a sonnet sequence which appeared in its final form in 1881, though parts had been published earlier.

J. K. STEPHEN (1859–1892). James Kenneth Stephen was born in London, and educated at Eton and King's College, Cambridge. He was called to the Bar in 1885, but also practised journalism, founding a weekly newspaper called *The Reflector*, which failed after seventeen issues. He returned to Cambridge in 1891 and set up as a tutor; but his health was not strong, and he died in the following year. He was a fine writer of light verse, with a notable skill at parody.

ROBERT LOUIS STEVENSON (1850–1894). Born at Edinburgh, and educated privately and at Edinburgh Academy between bouts of ill-health. He attended Edinburgh University, and was called to the Scottish Bar, but he never practised law. His health compelled him to spend winters outside Scotland, in Switzerland, France and America; he finally settled in Samoa, where he was known as 'Tusitala' (teller of tales). *Treasure Island* (1882), *Kidnapped* (1886), and *The Strange Case of Dr Jekyll and Mr Hyde* (1886) were three of the best known of his many novels and short stories; *A Child's Garden of Verses* was published in 1885.

JOSEPH SKIPSEY (1832–1903). Born near North Shields, the son of a miner; his father was shot by a special constable during a miners' strike. He was sent down the mine at Percy Main at the age of seven, but taught himself to read and write. Later, through the help of friends and patrons, he became an assistant in the library of the Literary and Philosophical Society of Newcastle-upon-Tyne, and the Curator of Shakespeare's Birthplace.

ALGERNON CHARLES SWINBURNE (1837–1909). Born in London, but brought up in the Isle of Wight, except for long visits to the ancestral home at Capheaton, Northumberland. Educated at Eton and Balliol College, Oxford. He lived in London from 1860, and became the friend of Rossetti and Meredith; his health deteriorated during the 1870s, and in 1879 his friend Watts-Dunton took him to live at The Pines, Putney, where he remained for the next thirty years.

LORD DE TABLEY (1835–1895). Before succeeding to the title, he was the Hon. John Byrne Leicester Warren, educated at Eton and Christ Church, Oxford; in 1852 he was called to the Bar, and he stood unsuccessfully as Liberal candidate for mid-Cheshire in 1868. Apart from this single political excursion, he had an uneventful life, becoming an expert in botany, bookplates, and Greek coins.

ALFRED TENNYSON (1809–1892). Born at Somersby, Lincolnshire, and educated at Louth Grammar School and privately; he was a precocious poet, writing *The Devil and the Lady* in imitation of Elizabethan drama in 1823–4, and publishing (with his brother Charles) *Poems by Two Brothers* in 1827. In the same year he went up to Trinity College, Cambridge; there, probably in 1829, he met the brilliant A. H. Hallam, who became engaged to Tennyson's sister Emily. Hallam's death in September 1833 was a terrible blow: it gave rise to poems such as 'Break, break, break' and 'Ulysses', and later to *In Memoriam*. The success of *In Memoriam* led to Tennyson's appointment as Poet Laureate in 1850, and to his position as the pre-eminent Victorian poet. He lived at Farringford in the Isle of Wight, 1853–68; during these years he published *Maud* (1855), *Idylls of the King* (1859 and 1862) and *Enoch Arden* (1864). Later he lived at Aldworth, near Haslemere, Surrey; he became Lord Tennyson in 1884.

I have not chosen some of Tennyson's best-known early poetry because it first appears in *Poems, Chiefly Lyrical* (1830) and in *Poems* (1832). Although poems such as 'The Lady of Shalott' and 'Mariana' were revised for *Poems* (1842), their original conception is pre-Victorian.

*In Memoriam A.H.H.* The sections were written at intervals between 1833 and 1850, with one section added later. Hallam died in Vienna on 15 September 1833; his body was brought by sea to England via Trieste (the 'Italian shore') and buried at Clevedon. The complete poem begins with the poet's grief and the arrangements for Hallam's burial, and ends with a marriage ode on the wedding of Tennyson's sister Cecilia to Edmund Lushington. As Tennyson said: 'It was meant to be a kind of *Divina Commedia*, ending with happiness'; between the opening despair and the concluding hope, there are opportunities for the poet to explore important questions of the meaning and purpose of life, and the nature and providence of God, seen in the light of new geological discoveries and the Higher Criticism of the Bible.

*Maud* was published in 1855, though it incorporates earlier material, including 'Go not, happy day', which was intended for *The Princess* (see Christopher Ricks, *The Poems of Tennyson*, London, 1969, p.1038). Against a background of oppression and snobbery the young man loves Maud; he kills her brother in a fight, and goes mad with guilt and with the loss of the loved one; at the end he seeks his fate in the Crimean War.

CHARLES TENNYSON-TURNER (1808–1879). The elder brother of Alfred Tennyson, co-author with him of *Poems by Two Brothers* (1827); educated at Trinity College, Cambridge; he changed his name to Turner on receipt of a legacy from his great-uncle. He became Vicar of Grasby, Lincolnshire: 'His verse is saturated with the sense of his duties and his position as a parish priest' (Alfred H. Miles, *The Poets and the Poetry of the Century*, V.47). His *Collected Sonnets* were published in 1880.

FRANCIS THOMPSON (1859–1907). Born at Preston; educated at Ushaw College, Durham, in preparation for the Roman Catholic priesthood, but he left there for Owens College, Manchester, where he intended to study medicine. He failed his examinations, on more than one occasion, and finally went to London, where he became destitute and addicted to opium. He was rescued through the agency of Wilfred and Alice Meynell, and later lived in North Wales and London. His Roman Catholicism was suited to his ascetic and mystical temperament, but he also enjoyed watching cricket in Lancashire and in London.

JAMES THOMSON ('B.V.') (1834–1882). Born at Port Glasgow, the son of a sailor; spent much of his childhood in an orphanage. He became an army schoolmaster, but subsequently led a precarious existence as a writer and secularist in London. He was friendly with Charles Bradlaugh and other notable secularists, and their fellowship was the chief comfort of his short life. He is known as 'B.V.' to distinguish him from James Thomson, author of *The Seasons*: the initials stand for Bysshe Vanolis, a tribute to Shelley and to Novalis; they were used as a pseudonym by Thomson.

OSCAR WILDE (1854–1900). Born in Ireland, the son of Sir William Wilde, an eminent surgeon; educated at Portora Royal School, Trinity College, Dublin, and Magdalen College, Oxford. At Oxford and subsequently he cultivated an aesthetic pose, which was often admired and often satirized (see Gilbert, 'The Aesthete', above). In the 1890s he became a great comic playwright, culminating in the brilliant *The Importance of Being Earnest* (1895). In 1895 he brought an unsuccessful lawsuit against the Marquis of Queensberry, who had accused him of sodomy; Wilde's failure led to his arrest and imprisonment in Reading Gaol. After two years, ruined financially and broken in spirit, he was released; he lived in France on a small annuity purchased by his friends until his death in Paris in 1900.

W. B. YEATS (1865–1939). William Butler Yeats was born in Dublin, the son of the painter Jack Butler Yeats; he was educated in Dublin and in London; as a young man he received friendship and encouragement from W. E. Henley and William Morris. His early poetry was influenced by the aesthetic interests of the age, and he also became interested in theosophy and spiritualism. He was a member, with Ernest Dowson, Lionel Johnson, and others, of the Rhymers' Club, bringing to it his own flavour of Irish myth and legend, of which he was proudly conscious. He became deeply involved in the revival of the Irish theatre from 1899 onwards, with the help of his friend Lady Gregory; while his love for Maud Gonne drew him into a concern for Irish nationalism and its effects on the individuals who espoused it as a cause. His later poetry continues to reflect upon Ireland, but often in a mature, reflective, and philosophical manner.

# Acknowledgments

ANNE BRONTË 'Lines Composed in a Wood on a Windy Day', 'The Captive Dove', 'Memory', 'The Arbour' reprinted by permission of Macmillan and Co., Inc. from *The Poems of Anne Brontë*, edited by Edward Chitham.

EMILY JANE BRONTË 'R. Alcona to J. Brenzaida', 'Love and Friendship', 'In summer's mellow midnight', 'Death that struck when I was most confiding', 'No coward soul is mine' reprinted by permission of Columbia University Press from *The Complete Poems of Emily Jane Brontë*, edited by C. W. Hatfield.

JOHN CLARE 'The Nightingale', 'I Am', 'A Vision', 'Clock-a-Clay' reprinted by permission of J. M. Dent and Sons Ltd from *Selected Poems* by John Clare, edited by J. W. and Anne Tibble (Everyman's Library series).

THOMAS HARDY 'When I set out for Lyonnesse', 'Hap', 'Neutral Tones', 'Thoughts of Phena', 'Friends Beyond', 'The Impercipient', 'Wessex Heights', 'The Darkling Thrush' reprinted by permission of Macmillan Publishing Co., Inc. from *Complete Poems* by Thomas Hardy, edited by James Gibson.

GERARD MANLEY HOPKINS 'God's Grandeur', 'Spring', 'The Windhover', 'Pied Beauty', 'Binsey Poplars', 'Felix Randal', 'As kingfishers catch fire', 'No worst, there is none', 'Thou art indeed just, Lord' reprinted by permission of the Oxford University Press from *The Poems of Gerard Manley Hopkins*, edited by W. H. Gardner and N. H. MacKenzie.

A. E. HOUSMAN 'Bredon Hill' and 'Is my team ploughing?' reprinted by permission of the Society of Authors as the literary representative of the Estate of A. E. Housman, and Jonathan Cape Ltd, publishers of A. E. Housman's *Collected Poems*; and of Holt, Rinehart and Winston, Publishers, from 'A Shropshire Lad' (Authorized Edition) from *The Collected Poems of A. E. Housman*. Copyright 1939, 1940, © 1965 by Holt, Rinehart and Winston. Copyright © 1967, 1968 by Robert E. Symons.

RUDYARD KIPLING 'Danny Deever' and 'Gunga Din' reprinted by permission of the National Trust and Eyre Methuen Ltd.

SIR HENRY NEWBOLT 'Moonset', 'Messmates', 'He Fell among Thieves' reprinted by permission of Peter Newbolt.

SIR ARTHUR QUILLER-COUCH 'The Planted Heel', 'Doom Ferry' reprinted by permission of Miss Foy Quiller-Couch.

W. B. YEATS 'Down by the Salley Gardens', 'When you are old and grey and full of sleep', 'The Ballad of Father Gilligan', 'The Fiddler of Dooney' reprinted by permission of M. B. Yeats, Anne Yeats and Macmillan London Ltd, and of Macmillan Publishing Co., Inc. from *Collected Poems* by W. B. Yeats.

# Index of Authors and Titles

# Index of First Lines